CLÓVIS DE BARROS FILHO
PEDRO CALABREZ

IN SEARCH OF OURSELVES

CLÓVIS DE BARROS FILHO
PEDRO CALABREZ

IN SEARCH OF OURSELVES

Dialogues on human beings and their place in the universe

In Search of Ourselves

The contents of this book are the sole responsibility of the authors and do not necessarily reflect the views of the publisher.

ISBN: 978-1-64095-668-1
Ebook ISBN: 978-1-64095-669-8

Editorial production and distribution:

contato@citadel.com.br
www.citadel.com.br

Distributed in English language by:

SOUND WISDOM

P.O. Box 310 • Shippensburg, PA 17257-0310 • 717-530-2122
info@soundwisdom.com

For our students.

Without you, this book wouldn't exist.

"Cervantes brought us, through Don Quixote, one of the best definitions of human nature: 'I know who I am and who I can be, if I wish'. This is the great human journey. The authors instrumentalize us in the search for self-awareness of who we are, as well as our potential and the strength needed to achieve it, backed by our desire.

Clóvis de Barros Filho and Pedro Calabrez broaden our vision and horizons about what to expect from ourselves. Life is a school that never closes or stops. Finding people who help us in the process of building our being is a great find. In Search of Ourselves is one of those books that has the ability to read us. And here we find ourselves."

Carlos Netto

Banco do Brasil strategy director

"Why do people believe certain things, even when the majority of people say it's not true? Why do many people continue to defend their beliefs, even in the face of concrete evidence of error? Why do authorities still impose their personal preferences on others as if they were universal truths?

Clóvis de Barros Filho and Pedro Calabrez, a professor and a neuroscientist, describe the evolution of the complex process of construction of reality by the human brain, emphasizing that everything is representation, since reality is always a subjective construction of each individual. In this sense, each person encounters a different world when they relate to the world.

The book could certainly be very useful to political authorities, executives and couples who need to free themselves from the phenomenon the authors call socially accepted delusion, when people act as if their interlocutors think or feel about the world exactly as they do."

Augusto Rodrigues

Founder of Café Filosófico and chairman of the board of trustees of the Padre Anchieta Foundation

Foreword

Who am I? Where did the world come from? What should I do to live better? Why am I so sad? What happens inside me when I'm in love?

These are common questions, asked by all of us on a daily basis. Despite being everyday, they are not frivolous or useless. They are profound questions, asked by humanity's greatest thinkers over the last three thousand years. Today, they are the subject of scientific research at the world's leading universities.

Often, those who want to understand the ideas of great thinkers or recent scientific research encounter a difficult obstacle: the language of the texts is complicated and very uninviting.

As teachers, our aim has always been to make knowledge accessible to as many people as possible, without ever losing philosophical and scientific rigor. We want to break down the barriers imposed by the walls of universities and laboratories. We believe that knowledge is the best way to lead a *truly human* life. Above all, knowledge enables us to search for and fight for better ways of living and living together. We owe everything we call "progress" in the personal and social spheres of humanity to it. Therefore, any obstacle between human beings and knowledge must be questioned.

At first glance, this book may seem like a dialog between very distant fields of knowledge. On the one hand, philosophy (and the ideas of giants like Aristotle, Plato and Spinoza). On the other, the sciences of the mind (psychology and neuroscience).

Our aim, however, is to show the reader just the opposite: the reflections that philosophy and science propose are, to a large extent, complementary. Philosophers and scientists from ancient times to the present day are on a great journey, a mission in search of ourselves.

In this book, the reader will find discussions on different topics from equally different perspectives. We will offer some answers to the questions posed at the beginning of this preface. We will provide answers to many other questions. They won't be unique and absolute answers, of course. But they will allow the reader to reflect and perhaps come to their own conclusions.

In addition, we will offer questions for which we have no answers. Some ideas will be easy to understand. Others not so much. Nevertheless, we guarantee that all these reflections have been and continue to be important for understanding the human being and our role in the universe.

At the end of the book, we have included a series of notes and reading recommendations for all the ideas, systems of thought and scientific studies we have mentioned. This way, readers can continue to deepen their knowledge of the topics that interest them most. However, those who wish to read only the main text, without resorting to the notes and recommendations, can do so without any problem.

Our language on the following pages will be relaxed and informal. It is a dialog, after all. But not just a dialog between different fields of knowledge. It's a dialog between two friends in search of ideas to help us understand who we are, human beings, in this vast and complex universe.

Our greatest wish was to bring you a pleasurable and thought-provoking read. Who knows, as much as it was for us to write this book that is in your hands.

Cheers and happy reading!

Clóvis de Barros Filho and Pedro Calabrez
São Paulo, February 2017

SUMMARY

Part 1

THE REALITY

1

What is the world?

Clóvis de Barros Filho: What is the world to us? Is it what we see? Is it what we hear? Is it what we experience? Is it what we feel or smell?

Everything we call the world is just a perception of our body. Something it produces itself. Look, for example, at what you hear: it's clear that what you hear is not the world, but a production of your body. Just pierce your eardrum and the world will show its silent claws. Likewise, what you smell is not the smell of the world, but a production of your sense of smell. What you see is just the light, the light that reflects in your eye. It's your eye that produces what you see, and if the light goes out, there's no more world to see.

So it's normal that, since our bodies are different, we end up seeing and feeling different worlds. The world for me is not the same world for you. Lucky for those of us who, like me, are short on aesthetic capital, there will be someone to see the beauty in us. But it's their problem, because there is no beautiful objectivity.

If the world is just a production of our bodies and everyone sees a different world, then who can guarantee that there is only one world for everyone? Could it be that the world isn't just a delusion? Isn't the world just a vision? Is there really something outside of us?

These are the questions posed by the philosopher George Berkeley. He himself says no. He says that there is only mind, there is only soul, there is only perception: the world is just a movie, when it ends, it's because you've died.

Keep that one, my friend...

PEDRO CALABREZ: The feeling we get when we wake up in the morning or read these pages is that our head is a kind of video camera merely capturing reality, absorbing the real world in its entirety. It makes sense; after all, the colors of the world seem so real to us, the smells so real, the shapes and textures so obvious...

This is a fine example of the fact that not everything that makes sense is right.

Looking at the horizon, it makes a lot of sense to believe that the Earth is flat. Well, take a ruler!

When looking at the sky, it is consistent to believe that the Earth is immobile and that the rest of the universe moves around us. For a long time, those who opposed this view were mocked and, in some cases, severely judged by the Holy Office.

It turns out that scientific evidence invalidates such claims. Not everything that makes sense is right.

I like the word "production" to define what the world is. There's an even better one: "construction". Far from being captured or simply absorbed, the brain carries out a complex process of constructing the reality it perceives. Not just in relation to the five senses, but to all the most intimate aspects of our lives.

When we look at people moving in the street, for example, we have the feeling that the world is a continuous, fluid movie. However, we know that this is an illusion produced by the brain. Certain brain lesions cause people to see the world as a sequence of images, a kind of frame-by-frame movie.

When we look at our mother, our child or our dog, we have the feeling that they are familiar. Again, a brain construction. There are bizarre cases of brain damage that make you look at your mother and say: "Doctor, that's not my mother, she's an imposter!".

The famous neurologist Oliver Sacks recounted the famous case of the man who, after a brain disorder, mistook his wife for a hat. I used to teach neuroscience for the visual arts course at a university in São Paulo. I had students who, when looking at a number, always saw it in color. For example: 1 was always blue, 5 was green, 7 was purple. I've also had students who, when they heard a sound, felt a taste: a higher pitch was bitter, a lower pitch was sour. One of them tastes objects when he sees them. One day, at the end of a lesson, he came up to me and said: "Professor, I feel flavors when I see things? The other day, I was walking along Avenida Paulista,

I looked at the Fiesp building and I felt a very strange taste in my mouth!".

The name is synesthesia, a condition that probably has genetic components, in which perceptual structures and functions apparently become "tangled" in the brain. It is much more common in families and people who pursue artistic careers.

What about your body? It's his temple. It's there, right now, holding this book, that's for sure, right?

Wrong.

The body is also a construction of the brain. If I magnetically stimulate certain regions of your brain, you can have the vivid sensation that you are outside your body, watching yourself from the ceiling. The amputation of an arm leaves many people with the vivid sensation that the arm is still there, a phenomenon known as "phantom limb". If before the amputation the arm was paralyzed in a painful position, the pain also remains, this is called phantom pain. There is even a phantom uterus: women who have had a hysterectomy (removal of the uterus) often report menstrual cramps, i.e. pain in a uterus that is no longer there.

I once met Inri Cristo. He believes he is Christ. Our conversation was very interesting.

He said: "It's a pleasure to meet such a young teacher!".

I replied: "Oh, Inri, I'm not that young.

To which he replied: "Of course he is! Compared to me, I'm over two thousand years old!".

I could only agree: "Yes, you won".

I took a photo with him and posted it on Facebook, otherwise no one would believe this story.

Inri Cristo believes he is Christ just as much as you believe you are reading these words. You can criticize him without realizing that we all do similar things every day. In other words, we believe in something - and even though many disagree with us, we continue to believe.

You believe that your favorite dish is the tastiest thing in the world. It's your preference. If I criticize your favorite dish, saying it's not tasty, you won't stop preferring it. After all, of course it's good! You feel it's good, and that feeling is the truth for you. At most, you can recognize that my truth is different from yours... But many people can't. How many of our readers have heard something like this: "How can you not like this? It's delicious! You don't know anything about cooking!".

Some people believe that their soccer team is the best in Brazil. Many don't agree - but in the mind of the believer, it's the truth. There is no one who can prove otherwise, even if they show concrete data, statistics and *rankings*. This leads to arguments, fights and often wars between fans.

Similar beliefs underpin political positions. You may know someone who firmly believes that candidate X is salvation and candidate Y is perdition. And there's no point in confronting these beliefs with data, with logic and rationality.

Let's take another example.

Parents believe that their children are more beautiful than they really are. A friend and professional colleague once asked me to meet her family. At the time, she introduced me to her two or three-year-old son. When I saw the boy, I almost gasped. The boy was very ugly. He looked like a goat inside out. Her friend said: "He's beautiful, isn't he?". Unsure of what to say, I replied: "He looks just like his father!".

Some of our readers are married or dating. Spouse, boyfriend or girlfriend - you probably believe that this person is more beautiful than they actually are.

Something similar occurs in the way we see ourselves. Studies show that human beings believe they are more beautiful, intelligent, honest and competent than they actually are. Trying to convince them otherwise is a great recipe for losing friendships. I'll return to this theme later, explaining its psychological roots.

Right now, the big question is: why? Why do people continue to believe certain things, even when most people tell them that it's not true? Why, even in the face of concrete evidence of error, do many continue to cling to their beliefs and preferences? Why, moreover, do many impose their beliefs and preferences on others, as if they were universal truths?

Because beliefs, preferences, this book, the body, the arm, the uterus, pain, sensations, colors, our "I" and everything else... Everything is represented in - and produced by - the brain. The brain doesn't absorb the world like a video camera. It constructs reality, and this construction seems to us to be the perfect representation of the world as it is. In other words, the perceptions that our brain produces of the world are interpreted by us as real - and this leads many people to believe that they are universal, i.e. that they apply to everyone else.

So far we can agree with Berkeley: there is only mind, there is only soul, there is only perception.

But what is the mind anyway?

We all have a subjective experience of the world. Subjective: that which is proper to the subject, relative to the individual, in other words, that which is individual and particular. You, reader, have a subjective experience of the world. Your own, particular, individual experience. It is made up of various elements: memories, feelings, emotions, plans, sensory perceptions and many others. Not all of them are conscious, but they make up your experience of the world. The set of these elements is what we call the mind.

But the mind doesn't exist in isolation. As the excellent Harvard professor Steven Pinker would say: "The mind is what the brain does". After all, I've just reported that brain changes cause serious mental changes. And the brain is part of the body, just like the thumb and the stomach. We can therefore conclude that the existence of the mind is closely associated with the existence of the body.

It's also important to realize that the mind sometimes produces delusions and hallucinations. In other words, distorted sensations and perceptions.

Let's imagine three cases.

Case one: a person who hallucinates an alien abduction. Case two: a person who believes they are Superman (we call this a delusion). Case three: a person who admires a blue-sky afternoon in spring, feeling joy.

In all three cases, people feel these experiences vividly. However, the first two are distortions. So it seems that not everything is sensation and perception, and not everything is mind. After all, if there are distorted sensations, it means that *there is something that is distorted*. In other words, the concept of distortion doesn't exist in isolation. Distortion is always a distortion of something. To distort means to misrepresent something that wasn't misrepresented before.

What could this be that wasn't distorted before? The answer is obvious: the world.

Therefore, not everything is mind, not everything is soul, not everything is perception.

Everything is a relationship between body, mind and world. Between brain and world. Reality is the result of this relationship.

CLÓVIS: What we feel is nothing more than an interpretation that our body offers to the transformations it undergoes when it comes to relating to the world. And the world doesn't get out of the way. To live is to relate to it. Let's invade this idea.

When you encounter something and enter into a relationship with it, your body changes, and then you feel. Now, what you feel depends on two things: firstly, on you. You feel what you feel because you are what you are, you have the body you have, the cells, the expectations, the ideas you have. The other thing that influenced what you felt was the world you encountered. So your feeling is the result of the encounter. It depends on both: you and the world. And what does that mean? It means that if we change the world, you'll feel something else. You've probably already realized that.

It's also obvious that when a body other than your own encounters the same thing as you do, that other body, because it's different from yours, feels something else. So, a mistake not to be made: imagining that others feel the same as you do when they encounter the same world. In fact, we feel exclusively, we are emotional islands. Nobody feels what we feel because nobody has the body we have.

Another mistake not to make: imagine when a person is the cause of your affections. You meet them and they make you happy. What's the *prime* mistake to avoid? Believing that this person has to be as happy as you are when you meet them.

And why *prime* error? Because you make two mistakes in one. Think about it: when you meet someone, you feel, and that someone is the cause. When they meet you, it's the other person who feels, and you are the cause. Now, if what we feel is the result of our encounter with the world, our body and the world, there is no coincidence in the love encounter. When you meet someone who makes you happy, it's your body that's happy, and that person is only the cause. When he meets you, in the same encounter, at the same moment, it's his body that will feel it, and you are the cause. There is nothing to justify expecting someone else to feel what you feel, which is why it is tyranny or ignorance to expect people to feel for us what we feel for them. Okay?

I hope you've realized the following: when someone makes a point of making you feel what they feel, you experience the inconvenience of it yourself because you don't feel what they feel. Then there are two things: either they accept emotional diversity and leave you free to feel what you feel, or they try to impose their own feelings. People like this are unbearable. A typical example is wine connoisseurs. In fact, all those whose tastes are considered noble and who, by virtue of social acclaim, believe that their tastes are more valuable than the tastes of others. And so they try to push the crap they like on us as being good in itself. They are disgusting tyrants, unbearable Nazis. If it weren't for morals, I'd have eliminated four or five of them by now.

Today, my horoscope said that the sea is rough and that I'm not doing well at all...

CALABREZ: *Marketing* professionals have known for decades that consumers behave in a very peculiar way when they don't know the brand of the products they are consuming. Let's start with the example of soft drinks.

So-called blind tests, in which products are presented without the consumer knowing the brand, have long shown that most people prefer Pepsi to Coke. Pepsi even used this information in an advertising campaign called "Pepsi Challenge".

But studies show that this preference only occurs when consumers don't know the brand they're drinking. When the same people drink the soft drinks knowing the brands, most of them declare that Coca-Cola is tastier than Pepsi.

For one scientist, this begs the question: what happens in these people's brains? Is there anything different, from the brain's point of view, when drinking a soft drink knowing its brand *versus* drinking the same soft drink without knowing the brand?

The example of wine is perfect for our reflection.

Let's start with wine connoisseurs. A study showed that when researchers put a fancy label on wine (*grand cru classé*), students at an oenology college (the "science" of wine) tended to believe that the wine was tastier than when they drank from a bottle with a not-so-fancy label (*vin du table*). However, *everyone was drinking the same wine*. The *grand cru classé* was rated as "pleasant, woody, complex and balanced", while the *vin du table* was called "weak, short, light and problematic".

If this happens to oenology students, imagine it happening to ordinary people. In a recent study, participants drank wine while their brains were mapped using functional magnetic resonance imaging, a technique that precisely measures blood flows in the brain, indicating the areas that are activated and inhibited. The participants always drank the same wine, but were led to believe that sometimes the wine cost $5 and other times it cost $90. As expected, the participants tended to rate the supposedly more expensive wine as tastier.

The reader might criticize: "But the difference between five and ninety is huge! Even I would think that!".

The researchers then carried out new tests, leading the participants to believe that one wine cost $35 and the other $45 (as before, the wine was the same). Lo and behold: the result was the same. People tended to rate the $45 wine as tastier.

What was most interesting, however, was what happened when the researchers looked at the brains of these participants. The structures associated with taste and smell showed no difference when drinking "expensive" and "cheap" wine.

However, when drinking the "expensive" wine, one brain structure showed significantly more activity than when drinking the "cheap" wine: the medial orbitofrontal cortex. This structure is usually associated with a kind of integration between higher cognitive functions (such as expectations and conscious perceptions of the world) and affective processes (emotions and feelings, such as pleasure and motivation). This has led researchers to suggest that the experience of pleasure with wine is not only sensory, i.e. it does not derive solely from taste and smell. It involves higher cognitive functions, especially the expectations we have about the quality of the wine we drink.

A similar study was carried out with Coca-Cola and Pepsi, mapping the brains of participants when they drank the soft drinks without knowing the brands and then knowing the brand. The results were very similar.

My favorite study of this type was almost a joke... The researchers put dog food in a food processor to obtain a paste-like texture. They then offered the participants the dog food alongside liver pâtés. After the participants had eaten, the researchers revealed that one of the patties was actually dog food and asked them to identify which was the fake patty.

Again, as expected, most of the participants couldn't tell the difference between dog food and pâté.

CLÓVIS: This reflection problematizes an argument: biology has never been so hot. The biological argument par excellence is that all sensations are a mechanical consequence of a certain physical-chemical composition. If you feel pain, this is due to a certain state of your cellular organization. If you feel pleasure, this too is merely a mechanical consequence of the physical-chemical composition of your body. Such a statement would force us to consider that, given a certain identical physical-chemical composition, given a certain state of the body's cellular structure, we are determined to feel the same thing. My friend, there are two difficulties here.

The first is when it comes to proving the objectivity of the physical-chemical structure. The objectivity of the stimulus received by the body, for example, is difficult to demonstrate in sensation, because how can we know the pain felt by the person who feels it? We are condemned to reports, but we have to accept that between what we feel and what we say about what we feel, there is a border of oceanic imprecision. We never feel what the other person feels. For us to be able to compare, the researcher would have to feel everyone's pain to be sure that it was the same pain given to the same cell structure. Well, that doesn't happen.

And the second difficulty: let's admit that what patients report is our limit, that we have to trust it. This is another major problem because, every time we compare sensations, we realize that, faced with the same stimulus, the same drill that cures cavities, people seem to feel very different things. Consult those who work with pain and you'll see that sensitivity to identical situations fluctuates impressively. Therefore, we believe that between a concrete bodily situation and the sensations we experience, there is an abyss that still guarantees us some originality, some specificity, our own style of feeling pain and our own style of feeling pleasure. Thus, we will continue to know that when our genitals are stimulated, what we feel is probably not shared by anyone else.

CALABREZ: I think the studies I mentioned earlier teach us a great lesson: the very experience of pleasure we feel will, to a large extent, be the result of our expectations. These, in turn, will depend on numerous complex factors, such as our culture, our past experiences and our worldview.

What we feel is undoubtedly the fruit of our body's encounter with the world. And every body includes a brain. This brain of mine today was built from the relationship between biological variables (such as the genes I was born with) and environmental variables (my experiences, culture, language, nutrition and so many other things). As such, no brain will be perfectly the same as another. This means that the world will affect each person in different ways. Each encounter with the world will be relatively unique.

I say *relatively* unprecedented because obviously there are certain similarities between the human experiences of different people. It is possible to extract objective criteria from subjective phenomena. A perfect example is ophthalmology. When you go to the ophthalmologist, he asks you: "Can you see the letters?". After adjusting the lenses, he asks again: "And now, do you see better or worse?".

The patient's perception of "better" or "worse" is highly subjective. There is no objectivity in saying "this is better" or "worse", after all, we don't have a ruler of perception in our brains. We say that things are better (or worse) according to our particular perceptions.

However, from this subjective phenomenon, the doctor obtains objective data: the degree, in numbers, of the spectacle lenses to be produced. In other words, the objective measure (numerical degrees) of ophthalmology is obtained by medicine from the subjective data derived from patients' reports.

Thanks to this, I'm able to see - after all, I've been wearing glasses since I was three years old. Before that age, I didn't know how to communicate very well. I kept tripping, falling and hitting my face on the wall. My mother thought I was a bit of an idiot. Nowadays, it's possible to find out what degree a person's eyes need without having to ask questions. This makes it possible to create glasses even for babies. In my day, there was no such technology. Despite this, many doctors still prefer to adopt the traditional method (asking and adjusting) with patients old enough to communicate well.

Scientific research into subjective phenomena such as happiness, satisfaction, pleasure, etc. is based on similar principles. After all, even though my brain is different from yours, both are quite similar. Otherwise, brain science - neuroscience - would be impossible.

In fact, if everyone's reality were completely different, we'd be living in chaos. Take emotions, for example. Fear is universal. It exists in every human being with a healthy brain, everywhere in the world. However, what is the cause of the fear? How intense is it? What is the resulting behavior? This will tend to vary between individuals, will have cultural influences, etc. But they will be physiological, psychological and behavioral variations of the same phenomenon that we collectively call fear. We have very similar brains, after all.

It turns out that "very similar" is not synonymous with "identical". And this small difference between the brains of each of us produces different realities, different affections, different experiences, even if they are similar.

The problem is that I'll never know what it's like to have a brain other than my own. Just as you will never know what it's like to have a brain other than your own. Perhaps in the future, with technological advances, it will be possible to connect two or more human brains, but today this is still impossible. So, if none of us is capable of knowing what it's like to have another body, another brain, we're all led into a kind of delirium. The delusion mentioned by Clóvis, that other people think and feel about the world exactly as we do.

It's curious how we tend to think of delusions only in terms of diseases, disorders and disorders, as in the examples I gave earlier. If someone believes they are Superman or Thor, if someone believes they have been abducted by aliens, we say they are delusional or hallucinating. But aren't there various "diluted" forms of delusion? In other words, socially accepted delusions, distortions of reality as delusional as believing that you are Batman?

Wouldn't the guy who imposes his individual taste on us, who makes fun of us because we don't have a "refined" palate, who believes with all his heart that his wine is better than someone else's wine, be delusional to some extent? Just like those who believe that their political party is better, that their soccer team is better, that their view of the world is better...

They are in fact tyrants. They are imposing their individual experiences as if others were obliged to live in the same reality as them. They are attributing a universal character to reality by believing that all human beings live in the same reality, when in fact, as we have seen, our realities are always different, because our bodies are different and therefore our encounters with the world are always different (albeit similar).

But this can lead people to think that anything is possible. Since individual realities are always different, I can construct my reality as I please... If reality is totally malleable, then we can experience the world however we want. You just have to want to!

That's a big mistake. Regardless of our will, our desires, our efforts, our different experiences of the world... Regardless of all that, the sun rises and sets, the leaves fall in the fall. The sky is sometimes blue. At other times, it's gray and cloudy...

2

The world, desires and pleasures

CLÓVIS: To live is to live in the world. Wherever I've been, I've realized that the world doesn't get out of the way. To live is to interact with it. We can move, we can open doors and break down walls. We can move to another country. But when we get off the plane, we realize that the world is still there, ready to interact with us. We can move around the world as much as we like, in all directions, even believing that we are free - the illusion of free will - but we can't get out of ourselves, we can't get out of the world. You can even run away, but never escape. That's why despair has no boundaries. We are only born to suffer and to die. If we are reincarnated, we are only reborn to suffer and die again. There is nothing but pain.

What about pleasure?

It's when the pain subsides. So there is only pleasure when, for example, we reduce the pain of hunger. If there were no hunger, there would be no pleasure in eating. There is only pleasure when we reduce the pain of thirst. If there were no thirst, there would be no pleasure in drinking. And the pleasure of rest depends on tiredness. Therefore, all pleasure depends on the pain that is circumstantially diminished. How could there be eternal, permanent and stable happiness if all pleasure presupposes the pain that it only reduces?

In this whirlwind of our vital forces, we relate to the world through desire. But in the logic of desire, we will always lack something. Satisfaction only indicates a new desire, a new lack. For these reasons and others, there is no salvation, no other world. The world is this one, with its desires and its pains. The world is just the world and nothing more. Heaven is empty, there is no blue in it, no gods, no angels. Salvation is this very emptiness. The understanding of illusion. The acceptance of despair.

CALABREZ: This despair, it seems to me, comes from the realization that, even though our realities are subjective, individual, particular, even though our experiences of the world vary greatly between each one of us, we are all condemned to encounter a constant. A constant over which we have virtually no control: the world.

And there is no manual on how to unravel the world. What makes us happy today may not tomorrow. The person who loves us today may fall in love with someone else the next day. Sometimes we don't even know if we're really happy or if something is really giving us pleasure... There are things that give pleasure at the same time as causing the pain of guilt and regret - everyone who has ever attacked a fatty dessert while dieting knows what I'm talking about.

A father comes up to his son and says: "You have everything you need to be happy!". As we've seen, the right thing to say would be: "You have everything that I think would make me happy if I were you. "

Dad doesn't say that out of spite. It's often out of love... But there's no shortage of people and institutions in the world who want to tell us what the legitimate pleasure of the moment is, what the right way to conduct our bodies is...

A very difficult question then arises: how to desire? What really causes pleasure, if today's pleasure may not be the same as tomorrow's? Is pleasure from cheap wine less legitimate than pleasure from more expensive wine? Is the pleasure of the guy who ate bread and sausage in college different from the pleasure he feels today, as a successful man, when he eats caviar?

CLÓVIS: Pleasure? Well, pleasure is a word, the name we give to the sensations we like to feel, good sensations. Sensations, in turn, are an interpretation that our body gives to the transformations it undergoes. And these transformations happen non-stop, so we also feel all the time. Some sensations we are more aware of than others. Pleasure is one type of sensation. Of course, it's not the only one; there's also pain, for example, which is when we don't really like feeling what we feel, when our body doesn't approve of the transformation it has undergone. If you break your little toe, you feel pain, and your body interprets this encounter with disapproval.

Well, pleasures are sensations of a different kind. Sensations that we fight for, transformations approved by the body. And pleasures are not superior or inferior. What differentiates them is intensity and longevity. What can vary in quality is the cause of the pleasure; thus, we can have pleasure determined by more or less noble causes. But let's think about it: if it brings us pleasure, if our body approves of the world that now relates to us, how could we judge the cause of what we call pleasure negatively?

The problem is that we are not alone in the world. Each body is a body that has had a trajectory in the world. The body that feels today is not the body that was born, it is now shaped and forged in the social relationships that it has lived through. So there are pleasures determined by noble causes when dominant individuals in society transform what is a cause of pleasure into something noble. In this way, it's not the same to feel pleasure listening to a symphony at the Sala São Paulo or going to a funk dance. In fact, the transformation of the body is inescapable, the cells vibrate in both places. The difference is that, at the Sala São Paulo, we are experiencing pleasure determined by a cause authorized by a certain social segment, while, at the baile funk, by another social segment.

The important thing is to always remember that the body you have today has been "orthopedized" by life in society, by belonging to a social class and a group of people who applaud certain causes of pleasure and boo others. You see, sometimes it's not enough to have pleasure. You have to take pleasure in what others authorize.

CALABREZ: Socially legitimized pleasure, therefore... But it's interesting to realize that, from the point of view of the brain, the person listening to the symphony at the Sala São Paulo will have a different brain activation when listening to funk. This social "orthopedization" of pleasure actually manifests itself in a peculiar and distinct neurophysiological activity. It is not, therefore, a mere freshness. People who drink expensive wine do indeed experience a greater sense of pleasure than if they drank cheap wine. But a person who listens to funk can also experience greater pleasure than if they listened to Mozart.

The mistake, it seems to me, lies in the deluded belief that what brings me pleasure will necessarily also bring pleasure to others.

Just think of the criticism that many people level at the artist Romero Britto, as if his art had less value because it was more commercially appealing. Those who appreciate Romero Britto's art (and there are many, otherwise he wouldn't be so famous) get real pleasure from it. Their brains and bodies produce greater motivation and pleasure. To say that these people are wrong is delusional. How can someone be "wrong" to feel pleasure? There is no wrong in this pleasure, even after moral reflection; after all, it is a pleasure that harms no one.

As a neuroscientist, I tend to view art from the perspective of the brain and mind of the individual contemplating a work of art. Perhaps you, Clóvis, from the point of view of philosophy, can complement this vision.

CLÓVIS: Art has always fascinated people, but often, especially nowadays, people ask themselves: "But is this really art?".

When I was a teenager, I went to a biennale and saw an old car full of French rolls and wondered if that was art.

The definition of art has changed very little over the years. Art is a great idea embodied in a piece of matter. Thus, all art has two elements: a great idea and a piece of matter in which this great idea is encoded, translated into symbols. For example, Greek art, which is the translation, in architecture and sculpture, of the idea of the cosmos, the idea of an ordered, organized, harmonious, symmetrical universe. Or medieval art, which is the translation, in large stained glass windows and large canvases, of divine splendor, of divine creation.

You might ask: "But what great idea is behind contemporary art?".

The idea of deconstruction, of the shattering of the subject, that we are not completely rational, of the unconscious that contaminates our decisions, that the shattered subject is much more emotion than reason, that we are at the mercy of vital flows and affections that we know little about. So it's normal for works of art to end up codifying this whole range of important ideas, and it's clear that this codification can be very creative.

Art always has two elements: a great idea of the spirit, of our intellect, and the sensitive, corporeal translation available to our sensibilities in a piece of matter. For there to be full delight, full enjoyment in front of a work of art, you have to know what the great idea is that gives it its foundation and what symbolization strategy that artist used to translate that idea into that piece of art that is there for you to contemplate.

CALABREZ: In this way, I can understand the art historian who sees less value in Romero Britto. After all, a historian is intellectually equipped with the great ideas behind works of art. Therefore, he understands these strategies of artistic symbolization.

However, this does not diminish the pleasure of someone who enjoys Romero Britto, funk or sertanejo universitário compared to someone who enjoys Pollock, Mozart or Pink Floyd. Pleasure, the neurophysiological activity associated with pleasure, is amoral, that is, it has no value in itself, it is not good or bad, greater or lesser.

Value is assigned by us, by society.

Many of our pleasures are merely social conventions. But we are still under the illusion that conventions are natural, that they have always been there. In other words, that conventionalized (i.e. socially constructed) pleasure is natural, universal, and that therefore everyone should enjoy what "feels good" or in that particular way "feels good".

Today, women (and increasingly men too) shave their bodies. For many, hairless bodies are a greater source of pleasure than hairy ones. A few decades ago, however, things weren't like this. There was no hair removal. So I make an obvious observation: in those hairy days, bodies were still desired!

There are those who say: "Women who don't shave are disgusting!".

In this sense, they attribute a moral universality (through the feeling of purity) to a socially conventional practice (hair removal). Not shaving is synonymous with being "disgusting".

You see, for many dermatologists, shaving puts health at greater risk than not shaving (because of the wounds on the skin, which open the door to infections). Of course, not all dermatologists agree, but their disagreement only highlights the social convention of hair removal as a sign of hygiene.

I don't mean that we shouldn't criticize desires or that socially conventionalized desires aren't important. Wanting to brush your teeth is better than not wanting to. Wanting to wash your hands after going to the toilet is better than not wanting to. Wanting to have sex with someone without their consent is an abomination that should be repudiated and makes us worse as human beings.

I just want to say that there is a certain illusion in believing that Romero Britto or the band Calypso are essentially good or bad. Such values are attributions made by human beings - to a large extent, socially agreed upon.

I don't deny that there are invariant, universal aesthetic standards. There are many examples. Here we can talk about symmetry. Symmetrical faces and bodies tend to be considered more beautiful than non-symmetrical ones, and this seems to have little variation between different cultures. However, Picasso's works are a great example of breaking this pattern - and are considered beautiful by many. Even if there are universal aesthetic standards, the space of influence of social and cultural conventions is too great for us to want to impose our preferences on others.

CLÓVIS: A work of art is not an illusion, but there is a lot of illusion in it. The works exist, they are as real as many other things. So real, so familiar and born of the hand of man. A painting is much less mysterious than a shell housing a mollusc.

But illusion is everywhere. Not in the real work, not necessarily in the artist, because he knows the work of his hands and knows the dream that guided him. Art is a job before it is a religion, a craft before it is a mystery. The artist measures his effort by his fatigue. Ten percent inspiration and ninety percent perspiration.

Genius becomes modest through work, but the idle spectator forgets this work, ignores it and the work-work becomes work-miracle. Illusion is born of lazy contemplation. It is born and then unfolds. The great illusion of the work of art is the objectivity of beauty. This work that I admire without understanding is of such beauty that it seems to impose itself on everyone. Beauty is experienced as truly universal, eternal, absolute and present in the work we love. To think that something is beautiful is not just to recognize the pleasure it brings me. It's claiming the objectivity and universality of that pleasure. When something is beautiful, we attribute the same satisfaction to others. We don't judge beauty only for ourselves, but for others, as if it were a property of the thing contemplated and had to be caught by anyone. Then something is beautiful. Always, for anyone. That's why the beauty of art is never just a matter of taste, because if it were, it would be nothing.

CALABREZ: This is when we need philosophy. After all, at this point we could say that desire and the search for pleasure, from a physiological point of view, are the same between dogs, chimpanzees and human beings. The brain structures associated with reward (motivation and pleasure) and sexuality, for example, are very similar between mice, monkeys and humans. After all, they evolved from common ancestors.

But there is a difference. Animals with more complex brains, especially humans, have social brains, brains that have developed within a culture, brains whose structures have developed from a constant dialog between genetics and environment, between biology and society. Thus, human desire cannot be considered in isolation, in its animality...

We have to consider that the human brain has neocortical structures, that is, structures that are more recent evolutionarily, which allow for greater intelligence, abstract reasoning, social cognition, culture, morality and so many other "higher functions" of the intellect. And there's no disassociating these structures from the more primitive ones that we share with all mammals and even reptiles. All of this works in an intimately interconnected way.

Perhaps then we should try to differentiate animalistic desire from properly human desire. Perhaps we need to give another name to this human desire that goes beyond the guts, viscera and primitive brain circuits that so many other species possess. That, I repeat, is why we need philosophy. So that we can be more human.

CLÓVIS: Plato says that love is very important for life. But not just any love. Imagine that, for Plato, love is Eros. In *The Banquet*, Socrates defines Eros as desire: to love is to desire. You love what you desire, you love the one you desire, you love with the intensity you desire.

You, reader, think of something you want right now. What you want is what you love. Of course, you may have thought of a new car, a cold beer or a pair of spectacular buttocks that you'd love to touch. Everything you desire is what you love, simply because, for Plato, love and desire are the same thing.

But what about desire? Desire is what we don't have, it's energy channeled into the search for what we need. We love what we don't have, we love what we aren't, we love what we can't achieve. The equation is complete: you love what you want and you want what you don't have. Either you love and want what you don't have, or you have it, but in that case you don't love it and don't want it anymore. This is an irritating situation. When you get married and have a woman for yourself, she becomes undesirable and impossible to love, so you start to desire and love your sister-in-law - always impossible, always desirable, always desirable in impossibility.

This logic of Eros is extremely interesting for the world of life. In fact, we see that the things we need end up deserving our incredible attention. We also see that those things that are very easy to get hold of, that offer themselves to us all the time, end up not deserving our attention or any value at all. It seems that all the time we are overvaluing what we don't have and depreciating what we have already achieved. This is a life divorced from reality, divorced from the world, a life only desired in fantasy, in chimera. An example of a bad life. The logic of Eros, Plato's thought.

And would there be a way out?

Plato proposes what he calls asceticism, elevation. The idea is that, when it comes to relating to things in the world, let's say there are some things that are worth more than others.

Let's imagine that a woman with impressive buttocks passes by on the other side of the street, and you say: "Wow, what a woman! What an ass!".

You have an appreciation for a particular buttock and are attracted to it. Let's say that this appreciation is worthy of a rather poor life, an inferior life in fact. A higher level of appreciation would be appreciation for the beauty of the female body. And then it would no longer be a specific butt, but a generic body, an idea of the female body.

But perhaps there is a greater appreciation than that of the generic beauty of the female body. It would be the appreciation of the beauty of anything: the female body, the landscape, a work of art, music, in other words, the appreciation of beauty wherever it is. Notice that we are moving upwards, starting with specific buttocks, passing through the generic female body and finally arriving at beauty sprinkled wherever it is, beauty itself, which is not particularized in one thing or in a specific body, but which can be anywhere.

Is there any greater appreciation than that?

Perhaps we could imagine an appreciation for something greater than beauty, which is an appreciation for being itself. Note that being is more generic than being beautiful. So we're going up: from the ass of the woman across the street to being, we're ascending step by step.

I hope you're beginning to understand the solution that Plato is proposing, because you'll agree with me that the being I'm referring to now is far removed from the woman across the street and much closer to your head, your ideas, your thinking soul, your intelligence. The more appreciation has an idea as its object, the more it is indicative of a life well lived, a life that is humanly worthy. The more appreciation is for the particular, for the physical captured by the senses and sensibilities, the closer we are to animality, the less dignified our life will be, the poorer our existence will be.

•••••

In his dialogues, Plato always spoke of two worlds: the first is that which is closest to us, a world of sensible things, of things we can see, find, touch, smell. The other is that which we reach through thought, through the use of reason, through intellectual activities.

Plato always had contempt for sensibility, for sensory perceptions. He considered that the result of these perceptions provided us with second-rate, error-prone knowledge.

He always defended the thesis that the senses deceive us and for this reason he gave enormous primacy, hierarchical superiority even, to those truths reached by reason, without the aid of the senses, without the participation of the body.

And why did Plato hate the senses so much? Why did he despise the findings of the senses so much?

To cut to the chase, what Plato is saying is that the senses make us believe in diversity, in the existence of different things, when in fact we are facing the same thing. The senses, therefore, convince us of the plural, when in fact we are facing the singular.

The classic example is water and ice. When you look at water, you notice certain characteristics, when you look at ice, you notice others. If you touch it, the difference increases; however, when you put your mind to it and do a scientific investigation, you discover that both liquid water and ice are H_2O, they are the same thing.

Thus, for Plato, our intelligence, our reason, leads us to only one thing: H_2O. But our senses force us to see diversity, plurality, the difference between water and ice.

Based on this type of argument, Plato is convinced that our senses lead us astray. For this reason, the invitation is to use reason, which will be all the more guaranteeing of reliable knowledge the less it depends on our sensory observations.

Many criticize Plato for this kind of conviction.

But if we trust our senses, we'll imagine that a coin could be the same size as the Sun, it all depends on the distance. Distance is already a matter of intelligence. When you simply look at it, the coin and the sun are identical in size. This is where all the importance is given to reason, to the articulation of ideas in search of what is unequivocally true.

Let's take beauty as an example. You could imagine that beauty is related to how your body feels when it looks at the world. If you were attracted to the world, it would be beautiful; if you were repulsed by it, it would be ugly. But in this case, beauty would depend on your body, it would depend on perception. If you had colic one day, you wouldn't find it so beautiful, and the beautiful would become ugly because of the colic. It can't be like that.

Beauty has to be unquestionable and can't depend on your cramps, perspective, distance or good mood. Beauty has nothing to do with whether you feel attracted or repulsed. It is an idea that you construct through your intelligence. And this idea is already in you, it has always been in your soul. It's up to you to try to quieten down the torch a bit - the cock or the pecker - and let your head do its job, to look for what is unquestionably beautiful. And if what is unquestionably beautiful doesn't please your body, try to educate it to like what is beautiful and hate what is rationally and unequivocally ugly.

• • • • •

If there is something that characterizes us as desirous, it brings us closer to everything that lives. Desire is our greatest trademark. It has objects that run through our heads, objects of desire. And so it can be defined by everything that is lacking. Desire is always for what we don't have, what we aren't and what we can't achieve. In this sense, desire is unlimited.

But desire isn't just the object that crosses our minds. It's also energy. Life energy that we make available to go after what we need, and then our desire is limited. After all, our energy has boundaries: the boundaries of finitude, of the body, of cells, of our specific matter. So desire really is ambivalent. Unlimited in its object and limited in the energy we make available to achieve it. Perhaps that's why there's so much frustration and anguish. To seek the unlimited, we only have what has limits.

Desire is energy plus object. Desire thus differs from appetite, because the latter is just energy without an object, without self-consciousness. Appetite is what brings us closer to the rest of the animals. After all, how can we know what's going on in a crab's head? But crabs have an appetite, you just have to watch them scurrying after their prey. Whether they think, cogitate or have a desire, we don't know. Maybe a crab can solve a second-degree equation faster than we can. Maybe you have to be a crab to know what goes on in a crab's head.

As for will, the problem is the same. Does the crab have moral criteria for conduct? Philosophy - much of it - says no. I have my cautions, after all, looking at a crab, I realize that there is only mystery there.

Will is not to be confused with appetite or desire. Will is energy, it is also the desired object, so it contains appetite and desire. But will is more than the two together, because it includes reflection, weighing up, judging the appropriateness of the desire, analyzing the relevance and value of the object of desire. That's why there's a huge difference between desire and will.

Desire is a cell thing, a neuron thing. Desire imposes itself on us. Will does not. Will shows our freedom. Our freedom from our desiring body, from our ability to desire, but not to act in search of what we want. After all, not everything we want is right to go and get, and not everything we want to do is right to do. And there are so many things we would like to do that we decide, in our will, not to do. All the time and at every moment, we are faced with impulses from our body which, for some reason, we don't translate into action. That's why appetite, desire and will are part of our lives.

CALABREZ: I've always found Plato's reflection on desire beautiful, as well as his criticism of the mistakes that immediate sensory perception can lead us to make. It's a tribute to human rationality, to our ability to appreciate the purity of ideas, to the marvelous complexity of the human intellect.

The distinction between will and desire, in turn, seems to me to be appropriate even from a neurophysiological and psychological perspective.

From the brain's point of view, the will has a strong negative aspect. In other words, the manifestations of the will often occur through the denial of desires - and not through the affirmation of new desires. To put it more simply: our brain has the freedom to say no to affective impulses (desires, emotions and feelings) - but it doesn't have the power to rationally and voluntarily create such impulses.

The freedom to deny the fatality of desire by choosing other paths, different from the one that desire would take us on, involves a series of brain circuits. One in particular is key to this process: the prefrontal cortex. Prefrontal activity is associated, among a number of other functions, with our ability to imagine the future consequences of something we are doing now. It is also associated with our ability to inhibit affective processes, in other words, to put the brakes on our feelings and emotions.

A perfect example of this is when we drink alcohol. Alcohol is a substance that inhibits neurons. In other words, neurons start firing at a lower frequency.

At this point, people get a flea behind their ear: "But, Pedro, the last thing I get when I drink is inhibited! On the contrary, I'm uninhibited!".

Well, this is because one of the effects of alcohol is to inhibit the prefrontal cortex. Since this structure is involved in curbing emotions, alcohol makes the brain's "reins" over emotions looser. That's why, when drunk, people fight much more easily. That's why drunks tend to be reckless, inconsequential. That's why people drink and call or text their ex-boyfriend on WhatsApp - and then regret it.

I have a friend who, with his prefrontal inhibited, made the stupidest decisions I've ever seen. Years ago, he had a girlfriend. At the girl's graduation, he drank a lot. Towards the end of the party, he had the brilliant idea of asking her to marry him (in front of her parents). She accepted, overjoyed.

It turns out that the prefrontal cortex is also involved in the formation of memories, especially short-term memories, which we call working memories - and its inhibition can also impair the conversion of short-term memories into long-term memories. To make matters worse, alcohol also interferes with glutamate receptors (a compound that carries signals between neurons) in a deeper structure of the brain called the hippocampus, which is essential for long-term memory. During this interference, alcohol prevents certain receptors from functioning normally, while activating others that shouldn't be activated. This causes the neuron to produce steroids that impair neuronal communication (between neurons), distorting a process known as "long-term potentiation". This process is necessary for learning and the formation of memories. It is believed that this is why alcohol causes anterograde amnesia, when we forget what happened the moment we get too drunk.

The next day, my friend couldn't remember that he had asked the girl to marry him. No way, he got his ass kicked. But he was a very peculiar friend. One day he drank too much, for a change, and disappeared. After a lot of searching, we found him lying in the middle of the kitchen floor... all wrapped up in aluminum foil. To this day, I wonder *how* he did it in the first place. He looked like a silver croquette. But what really puzzles me is: *why* on earth would someone wrap themselves in aluminum foil? I don't think I'll ever know.

But I digress. Let's go back to the relationship between will and desire.

A healthy prefrontal is capable of curbing desires and therefore allowing the will to be exercised. However, this capacity is limited. I want to make it clear here that today there is a consensus within the sciences of mind and behavior (neuroscience, psychology, behavioral economics) that human beings do have the capacity to think rationally, but that rationality is not the standard mode of operation of the human brain. In other words, in everyday life we tend to be much less rational than we would like to be.

When I talk about this, I always remember the great Scottish philosopher David Hume in his *Treatise of Human Nature*: "Reason is, and can only be, the slave of the passions". I believe this is the philosophical passage most often quoted by neuroscientists. This is because we have known for decades that human rationality, praised by so many thinkers, is closely linked to emotional processes.

We have known for about thirty years that brain damage to structures responsible for mediating affective processes (emotions and feelings) usually leads to serious deficits in planning and decision-making processes (in other words, they alter what is typically considered a rational aspect of the personality). To put it more simply, damage to the emotional circuits of the brain also destroys the rational faculties of human beings. David Hume couldn't have been more right.

It's as if the brain worked from two systems: a slower, colder one (capable of being rational) and a faster, warmer one (responsible for emotions and habits, for example). These terms, cold system and hot system, are used by the great psychologist Walter Mischel, one of the world's leading authorities on the study of self-control and willpower. Daniel Kahneman, winner of the Nobel Prize for Economics in 2002, uses different terms: system 1 (fast) and system 2 (slow).

Many neuroscientists prefer the term *top-down* to indicate slow, cold processes. And the term *bottom-up* to indicate fast, hot processes.* This terminology is found in hundreds of scientific articles and refers, in a way, to the fact that the structures located at the "top" of the brain are generally more evolutionarily recent, while the structures located at the "bottom" of the brain are more primitive.

Well then, many people believe that system 2 (cold, slow) is always rational. This is a misconception. System 2 can work in two ways: as a scientist or as a criminal lawyer.

How does a scientist come to a conclusion? They go out into the world with a hypothesis. He then collects and analyzes the available evidence regarding this hypothesis. After all this, he finally comes to a conclusion.

How does the criminal lawyer reach a conclusion? First of all, he comes to the conclusion ("my client is innocent"). Next, he goes out into the world to look for evidence to support the pre-established conclusion.

* Note from Pedro Calabrez: these binary terms are figures of speech. There are not two perfectly separate and defined discrete systems in the brain, responsible for cold and hot, slow and fast, bottom-up and top-down processes, etc. We only use this duality for didactic purposes.

In other words, often system 2, instead of being rational, only works by seeking apparently rational justifications for processes that were actually totally irrational and often affective, emotional.

It's interesting to see how people pursue, desire and even idealize socially legitimized objects or ways of living imposed by society. This happens under the belief that acquiring a certain object or conducting life in a certain way will be pleasurable and, ultimately, bring happiness. Apparently rational justifications are created to support these desires.

For example, society tells us that we should work eight hours a day. If we work longer, even better. We are conditioned to want to work - or at least to want the fruit of our labor, which is money. From this, justifications are created, which even culminate in popular sayings: "God helps the early riser", "work ennobles man" and so on. We believe that these are rational justifications, but they are certainly not. They are attempts to attribute rationality to a desire (for money, career growth, etc.). This motivation is an affect, an emotion and a feeling socially constructed in our heads. Reason is a slave to passion.

Who said we should get up early? Who says we have to work to be "noble"? What the hell does "noble" mean? Who said that we should invest half of our working hours in building a career or making money in order to find happiness?

Studies show that, from a certain level of monetary income, essentially from the moment we enter the so-called "middle class", the accumulation of more money no longer brings significant increases in our satisfaction with life.

How many great executives are out there who are totally dissatisfied with their lives? How many unhappy billionaire entrepreneurs?

The reader might think: "So working too much is bad!". Of course not. Working hard can be bad for some, while it can be synonymous with joy for others. The mistake is in attributing universality, saying that work ennobles all men, that God helps those who rise early and, therefore, everyone should rise early.

CLÓVIS: In this world of matter and energy in which we live, nothing comes from nothing, everything has a cause. Matter determines matter, energy determines energy.

So too are our speeches, what comes into our heads, what we think and sometimes enunciate. Our speeches don't come out of nowhere. From the moment we are born, we are bombarded by them and long before we start speaking we are already listening, immersed in a discursive polyphony. Little by little, we begin to speak too. We begin to participate in this powerful network of discourses that makes up our social fabric. What we say is not a copy of what we hear. We take something from here, something from there and formulate our own statements. We are creative. What we say is unprecedented, but the raw material comes from outside, it's given to us by society.

What we say about ourselves, the definition we give of ourselves, the attributes we use to define ourselves also come from outside. No one knows who you are at birth. Nobody tells you at birth that you are generous, contributive and proactive. We learn this by listening to others talk about us. Thus, even what we say about ourselves, apparently coming from the most intimate of intimacies, is nothing more than the result of learning in the world of life, in the world of encounters with other people. So much so that if you try to say things about yourself that society doesn't agree with, you'll pay a heavy price in ridicule and exclusion.

This is a concern I've always had: when it comes to explaining their own behavior, people change their criteria, they change their paradigm, depending on the success or failure of their initiatives. If man has succeeded in what he wanted to achieve, he usually explains his conduct by free choice, by the successful freedom to define the appropriate means to the desired ends. When man fails, he usually relates his conduct to variables outside himself, variables that he cannot control. Freedom disappears, the condition of choosing the best means to the best end disappears, and what is known as determinism comes into play. Given certain external variables, I could do nothing different. Thus, man blames the reasons why he acted badly on the weather, the climate, the behavior of others, the institutions, the system.

We could think of a footballer when he chooses the right side to dribble, beats his opponent, shoots properly, scores and leads his team to victory. He is a genius and will be praised for his choice. When the same player doesn't achieve any of these things, his failure is almost always attributed to the opposition's defensive system, to being chased around the pitch, to the referee not having seen all the fouls he received, to it not being a good day, to his teammates not supplying him with the necessary number of balls so that he could, faced with all this range of alternatives, at least at some point find a goal solution.

You see, freedom, free choice and the intelligent adaptation of similar means are the stuff of those who have done well, but attributing them to external factors that you can't control is the stuff of those who have done badly. And when you deny your own freedom, deny your own choice, deny the possibility of having done things differently. This is what we call bad faith, the artifice of losers.

CALABREZ: These convenient speeches are the work of our system 2. To be more specific, it's system 2 acting as a criminal lawyer, as I explained earlier.

This reflection brings me to one of the topics I find most interesting within the sciences of the mind: what we call cognitive consistency (or psychological consistency).

I always ask people: "Which is easier to change: a belief or a behavior?".

I'd like the reader to think about the question...

Most people answer: "A behavior". It seems that, in most people's view, beliefs are ingrained and difficult to change.

Following this answer, I ask: "So which is easier: for you to start the diet now, right now, or to firmly believe that you'll start the diet next week?".

At this point you realize that we change beliefs very easily. But why is that?

Imagine that our mind is like a computer, the kind we have at home.* Imagine that, like our computers, it has several folders and that each one holds the contents of a dimension of our life. For example, we have a folder called "work", another called "family", yet another called "leisure" and so on.

The principle here is this: the human mind will necessarily seek to make the contents of these folders consistent. In other words, it will try to avoid - at all costs - inconsistencies. Inconsistencies are nothing more than conflicting information within the folder, information that contradicts itself. Scientists have been calling these inconsistencies "cognitive dissonances" since the 1970s.

Let me give you an example.

My 18-year-old students often fall in love when they enter college. Infatuation, from the brain's point of view, resembles a hypermotivational state of temporary dementia

* Note from Pedro Calabrez: I want to make it clear that this is a metaphor. There is no supercomputer today that even comes close to what a human brain is capable of. There are researchers who believe that digital supercomputers (very powerful versions of computers similar to ours) will be able to simulate brain activity in the future, others claim that the brain is not a digital computer (the great Brazilian neuroscientist Miguel Nicolelis defends the thesis that the brain is an analog-digital computer - he sets out these ideas in his book The Relativistic Brain) and still others claim that the brain is not a computer, that is, it is not an information processing machine (an example of this thinking is the great American psychologist Robert Epstein).

lasting twelve to 24 months. I think our readers have already realized that when they fall in love, they become a little demented. Falling in love leads to prefrontal inhibition, which is similar to getting drunk, as I mentioned earlier. That's why people in love make stupid decisions. We'll talk a lot about infatuation in the third part of the book.

Well, my 18-year-old students fall in love. They start dating. Imagine a conversation between these lovers about three months into their relationship, in other words, at the peak, at the crest of the wave of dementia.

One turns to the other and says: "Baby, do you love me?".

The answer is obvious: "Of course!".

Then comes the fateful question: "Forever?".

At this point, they could be rational. Observing the situation coldly, system 2, scientist, *top-down*. Let's imagine the rational response:

"Do you love me?"

"Of course!"

"Forever?"

"Never. You see, love, based on calculating the simple arithmetic average of my previous relationships, I think we'll be together for another nine months or so, with a margin of error of one and a half. "

Imagine the "dating" folder, created three months ago in the couple's mind. It's probably full of mostly positive content (memories, plans, feelings, etc.).

Rationality and intellectual coldness will now add negative information to this folder ("one day our relationship will end"). Given that the previous contents of the folder are consistently positive, this negative information will cause a conflict, an inconsistency. In other words, this conflicting information will produce a dissonance.

A kind of psychological mechanism for maintaining consistency comes into play. Our mind will find a way to resolve the inconsistency, and the most common way in this case is to produce a belief: that it will last forever.

Notice that young people, when they say "I love you forever", genuinely believe in the idea. They are not lying or being deceitful. The belief in the eternity of the relationship maintains psychological consistency, eliminating the dissonance derived from the cold awareness that one day the relationship will end.

You see, our mind is equipped with a consistency maintenance mechanism. This mechanism will kick in whenever inconsistencies (dissonances) arise. I now want to highlight an additional feature of this mechanism: it will be all the more present the more difficult it has been to correct the inconsistency through action.

The reader may not have understood the idea at this point. It sounds complicated, so let's take an example to explain. The perfect example is the difference between a twenty-year-old single girl and a woman who has been married for fifteen years.

The young single woman in her twenties goes to the club. After having a few drinks and dancing on the dance floor, she sees a young man, a seemingly nice guy, definitely handsome. He approaches her and the two of them start chatting. "What a nice guy!" she thinks. After a few minutes of chatting, she decides to stay with him and just waits for the right moment.

It was at that moment that the young man, without interrupting the conversation, looked into the young woman's eyes and stuck his finger up his nose. Not satisfied, he keeps his finger there, almost poking his brain, digging around like a real oil miner. Then he pulls out a slime the size of an olive and, still looking into the girl's eyes, wipes his finger on his shirt.

The young woman feels disgusted.

Let's analyze the psychology of the situation: has there been an inconsistency?

Of course! Remember what I just said, about the mind as a computer.

The "party boy" folder had just been created. Until then, it had only positive content: handsome, nice, interesting guy, "I want to be with him". Then conflicting information entered the folder: he's disgusting. A dissonance arose.

How can we resolve this dissonance? Easy: by changing behavior, in other words, by taking action. The girl says: "I'm going to the bathroom and I'll be right back, okay?".

And it disappears.

This is a situation in which correcting inconsistency through action is easy, and it's probably what most young women would do.

Now for another example: a woman who has been married for fifteen years. Before getting married, she had been dating for four years. Nineteen years of relationship, then. Two children. The apartment is in both their names.

The couple are at home late on a Sunday afternoon. They're sitting at the dining table, eating the typical "afternoon snack": fruit, cheese rolls, orange juice, granola and strawberry-flavored Activia Zero yogurt.

Then the husband suddenly sticks his finger up his nose and digs around for a while... He pulls out a mess the size of an olive. Then he wipes it on his shirt.

What does the wife do? Does she get up, leave and never come back? "Honey, I'm going to buy a cigarette" - and disappear forever?

Of course not!

She says angrily: "Oh, love! That's disgusting! Don't touch the bread!".

And that's it, life goes on.

Again, let's analyze the psychology of the situation: has an inconsistency occurred?

Obviously! The beloved husband did something disgusting!

But realize that this situation is very different from the previous one at the club. Correcting this inconsistency through action is very difficult, because a marriage is a much more stable, solid and interdependent relationship than a flirtation at the club. Acting to change the situation here is much more difficult.

As I said earlier, the more difficult it is to correct inconsistency through action, the more present the psychological mechanism for maintaining consistency will be.

The wife, in the second example, has changed her beliefs about what is disgusting and acceptable in a relationship. Her current beliefs allow her to accept something that, at the beginning of the relationship, would have been unacceptable.

"Oh, he's disgusting, but he's my love!", "He's not that disgusting!", "He hardly ever does things like that". Ideas like these appear spontaneously in the wife's mind. Such ideas maintain psychological consistency, avoiding dissonance.

No wonder some people call this psychological mechanism "self-deception".

Imagine a person who has just been dumped. Shortly afterwards, ideas pop into their head like: "He/she didn't deserve me", "everything has a reason for happening", "I already knew it wouldn't work out", "now I can find a better person". These ideas appear spontaneously in the head of the person who has been dumped. It's an automatic, unconscious process. All because being dumped is something that usually produces psychological inconsistency. And our minds can't stand inconsistency.

Well, now I can answer the question raised by Clóvis.

Why do people use speeches of freedom when they succeed ("I went out there, I faced the difficulties and I was victorious!") and deterministic and fatalistic speeches when they fail ("there was nothing I could do, it's my boss's fault")?

First of all, we need to understand that we often have a distorted view of ourselves. Various studies have shown that human beings tend to believe that they are more intelligent, competent, honest and beautiful than they actually are. In this way, we adapt our worldviews to a distortedly positive image of ourselves.

Because of this, imagine the psychological impact of looking in the mirror and saying to yourself: "My failure is the result of my free choices". Or: "I am responsible for my failure".

It's easy to see that this would produce a huge inconsistency. Realize that the failure has already occurred, there's nothing to be done. In other words, there are no actions that can correct this inconsistency. That's why we produce a belief: the belief that it wasn't our fault, that we couldn't have done anything differently, that factors totally beyond our control were responsible for our failure.

I will return to this principle of maintaining consistency throughout our reflections, because it is very important and underlies a number of characteristics of human behavior.

But right now, my friend, since I've just been talking about romantic relationships, I'd like to raise a question. If, for Plato, desire is Eros, in other words, it only occurs in lack, so that when we get what we want, we no longer want it, how can we explain the expression "erotic", so often used nowadays especially to designate a type of pleasure, sexual pleasure? It seems to me that, during erotic sexual pleasure, we desire permanence, we want that pleasurable moment to last longer.

CLÓVIS: Let me talk about the expression "erotic pleasure". Apparently, it contains contradictory terms, after all, erotic comes from Eros, which means desire.

Desire, in turn, is always for what is missing, always for what we don't have, for what we aren't and would like to be, for what we don't do and would like to be able to do. Therefore, the object of desire is always in our imagination. The object of desire is always a conjecture of the intellect, never the world actually found.

Pleasure is the opposite of desire. Pleasure is in the presence, it is in the encounter, it is a sensation of the body in front of a world actually encountered. Pleasure is a kind of reaction of the body to a specific relationship with the world in front of it.

Erotic pleasure is a mixture of pleasure that needs to be present and desire that needs to be lacking. It doesn't seem to be a coherent expression, but it is possible to think of the pleasure of a world that has actually been encountered and that has already been desired in the past. Thus, desire indicates the lack of the past that materializes in the present encounter. Erotic pleasure therefore indicates a lack that is resolved in presence. The world desired in the past is found and determines the cause of pleasure. It's what you would like to find and have found. You would like to have and you did. You would like to do and you did.

There are pleasures that are not erotic, in other words, pleasures that were not desired in the past. This is when, for example, you suddenly meet someone or something that gives you pleasure, but which you had never wanted. On the other hand, there are pleasures that have been deeply desired for years and suddenly turn into a real and deeply pleasurable encounter. There is also Eros that never becomes pleasure. Desires that resist forever in absence and never become presence. This is why it is often said that pleasure is the suicide of desire. Desire that needs lack seeks the presence that annihilates it, that destroys it. That's why all desire is suicidal, and pleasure is the moment that culminates in the suicide of desire.

CALABREZ: From a scientific point of view, we can also make this distinction between the search for the object of pleasure and pleasure itself. The search for the object of pleasure is typically called motivation. A motivating stimulus is essentially one that produces in us an inclination to *do more of what we are doing*.

Let's take an example.

Imagine you're hungry. A portion of fries arrives at your table. You eat a fry. What happens to your body? What is your immediate inclination after eating a fry? To eat another and another, until you're satisfied. In other words, the inclination to do more of what you were doing. This can happen with all kinds of stimuli: a professional project, an interesting book, a thought-provoking conversation, sex, food and so on.

Pleasure, on the other hand, is the subjective sensation associated with the stimulus. In the case of potatoes, it's the delicious sensation, the positive taste experience.

Today there are interesting debates and studies about how motivation and pleasure are manifested in the brain.

Many researchers suggest that some of the brain circuits responsible for each of these functions are in fact different.

Motivation and pleasure are typically referred to simultaneously under the term "reward". Rewarding stimuli are those that promote motivation and pleasure.

There are two types of reward.

There are stimuli that are intrinsically rewarding or, to put it another way, intrinsically rewarding. This means that they are naturally rewarding. The most common examples are: water, food, sex, comfort and maternal/paternal affection. Obviously, there are social influences on which foods or which sexual practices, for example, will be more pleasurable or even authorized. However, the reward for these stimuli is usually born with us and with a number of non-human animals. Society will influence the details, refining our preferences.

On the other hand, there are extrinsically rewarding stimuli or, in other words, extrinsic rewards. In these cases, we are talking about stimuli that become rewarding through association and, therefore, through a learning process. A perfect example is money. Nowadays, earning money is highly rewarding. However, money is not an intrinsically rewarding stimulus. It becomes rewarding through associations we learn in society (associations between money and a greater number of sexual partners or money and happiness, for example). We could give other examples: consumer goods, diplomas and academic degrees, likes and followers on social networks and so on.

Part 2

THE COSMOS AND HUMAN LIFE

1

Homer's *Odyssey*

CALABREZ: Following on from these concerns and continuing our great theme - a reflection on what reality is, what the world is - we're now going to talk about some of the great worldviews. Visions of how the totality of things that we call the universe or cosmos works. Since the origins of Western thought, we have had fantastic contributions, extremely thought-provoking and beautiful views on the nature of reality in general and of human beings in particular. Nowadays, we find some of the greatest scientists on the planet dedicating their lives to understanding the cosmos. In the midst of this vast and complex universe, we human beings find ourselves. We will then take a journey through the cosmos and human life within the cosmos - from antiquity to the present day.

CLÓVIS: A very present idea in Greek thought is that the world is ordered. In this sense, it could be compared to a machine made up of parts. And these parts are not found in the machine by chance. Each one has its purpose, its function. In this way, the things of nature fulfill their role: the wind cools, the tide fertilizes, the frog swallows flies, the knee bends, the intestine "peristals". It is essential that each part fulfills its function so that the universe as a whole works well.

Within this orderly conception of the universe, which the Greeks called the cosmos, man occupies a particular position; after all, he is also essential for the proper functioning of the cosmos. Thus, the good life implies the harmony of each person who lives with the whole, with the cosmos. Just as the wind blows in harmony and thereby collaborates with the cosmos, each of us must also, by living a specific life, collaborate with what the cosmos expects of our lives. The difference is that the wind blows, there is no other alternative for it. But in our case, there are many alternatives. We can live a life in harmony with the cosmos, just as we can opt for many others that would be disharmonious and therefore out of step with the cosmic order.

In the first case, our lives would be good and there would be happiness. In the second case, we would suffer and suffer, as well as jeopardizing the universal order. Therefore, one of the great problems of Greek thought is: what should each person's life be like in order to guarantee harmony with the cosmos and, therefore, happiness? Which life would I have to choose in order to fulfill the role that the cosmos expects of me?

The resolution of this problem has always intrigued Greek thinkers, ever since mythology.

• • • • •

It was Zeus who made the cosmos orderly and organized and distributed each piece to each of his co-workers. And the cosmos put each thing in its place, each thing with its specific activity. Happiness is harmony with the cosmos, and you achieve this harmony in the full blossoming of your own nature.

But this idea of cosmos was already present before philosophy arose, in mythological accounts. It was already to be found, for example, in Homer's *Odyssey*, which is an account of the journey from chaos to cosmos.

The *Odyssey* is the story of Ulysses wanting to return home. He went to the Trojan War, ended up becoming a hero, but had difficulties returning home. The *Odyssey* tells of this return. Ulysses was from the island of Ithaca, he lived with Penelope, in other words, he was in the right place, in his place. If you take the idea of the cosmos, where everyone has their own place, Ulysses was in Ithaca, which was a kind of right-back position for Cafu or an attacking command position for Romário. Ulysses was forced to go off to war, since he was king in Ithaca. Once the war was over, he desperately tried to return home, but ran into many difficulties. And what does all this symbolize? That while Ulysses was away from Ithaca, he was out of harmony with the cosmos. But when he finally returns to Ithaca, he regains harmony with the cosmos, and life becomes good again, worthwhile again.

Of course, the chaos prior to Ulysses' return to Ithaca is complex. It is an absolutely sophisticated chaos, explained in an unmissable and fantastic narrative that shows how out of place Ulysses was, how he didn't want to be where he was. Ulysses' effort to return to Ithaca was an effort to get back, to retake his place in this ordered, cosmic space.

The chaos that Ulysses gets himself into begins at the wedding of Thetis and Peleus. She, a goddess, and he, a human. Marriages between humans and gods were not uncommon in mythology. Zeus, god of the gods, threw a party on Olympus and "forgot" to invite Eris, who was a bag, goddess of discord, like those people who like to poke, prod and annoy. An intriguer. Eris didn't like it and went to the wedding anyway - as befits every intriguer - leaving a beautiful golden apple on the table with the dedication: "To the most beautiful". Then the chaos began, a terrible discord started. Eris got what she wanted.

• • • • •

In the Trojan War, Ulysses ended up piercing the eye of the Cyclops Polyphemus - a very bad thing, since a Cyclops only has one eye. He blinded Polyphemus, son of Poseidon, god of the seas. Poseidon felt obliged to avenge his son - even though Polyphemus was a prick - and decided to make it difficult for Ulysses to return to Ithaca. This is the *Odyssey*, the "Ulisseia", the adventure - or misadventure - of Ulysses trying to return home. There is a new situation of chaos in contrast to the cosmic harmony that is Ulysses' definitive return to Ithaca. The first situation is the discord proposed by Eris. The second is the Trojan War itself and its atrocities.

And the third is the *Odyssey,* in which Ulysses tries but fails to return home.

All the obstacles that Poseidon placed in the way of Ulysses were linked to forgetfulness and the loss of the meaning of life. If the meaning of Ulysses' life was in Ithaca, with Penelope, the forgetfulness of the way back and all the difficulties he faced symbolize chaos and oppose the cosmic order that is the definitive return.

There's no doubt that the most interesting part of this return is Ulysses' time on the island of Calypso. So much so that of the ten years it takes him to return home, seven are spent on the island. These years are the symbol of a failed life, in chaos.

However, there is a contrast that needs to be made clear: not all the difficulties that Ulysses had in returning home were painful. One example is that there was a lot of pleasure in Calypso. But mythology and this specific story contrast a life of fortuitous pleasures with eudaimonic happiness, which is the adjustment to the cosmic whole.

Ulysses arrived on Calypso's island to refuel his boat, but when Calypso saw him, she fell madly in love and decided to hide him. In fact, Calypso comes from the Greek *kalýptein,* which means "to hide". And so Ulysses became her prisoner.

The island was paradisiacal, and Homer is absolutely accurate in saying that Calypso's role was to try to make Ulysses forget Penelope, forget Ithaca, forget the place where life would be in harmony with the cosmos.

Calypso adored Ulysses. And she was a wonderful deity, a spectacular, enchanting goddess. She had the charm of Juliana Paes mixed with the elegance of Deborah Secco and the magnitude of all the imposing actresses who enchant us. Make up Calypso however you like, mythology allows it.

What a strange punishment imposed on Ulysses by Poseidon! An island paradise, a *resort* with nymphs, a wonderful woman in love and absolutely crazy about sex? Some would mistake that for paradise itself!

And the truth is that Ulysses cried every night in the hope of returning home, to Penelope's arms, to the island of Ithaca, his natural place.

At one point, the news arrived that Zeus had ordered the release of Ulysses. Athena took pity and sent Hermes - a sort of DHL or Sedex 10 god, the god of communication - to tell him to let him go. When Calypso is forced to release him, she tries one last trick. She wants him to be on his own and offers him eternity and youth. But he refuses. When Ulysses refuses the offer to become a god, refuses the offer of eternity and youth on Calypso's island, there is a noble moment in the history of thought: Greek thought is teaching us that a mortal, finite life, a human life in the right place and in harmony with the cosmos, is preferable to an eternal life, but out of place, in disharmony and at odds with the cosmic order. If Ulysses accepted, he would become a god, would cease to be human, would therefore cease to be who he was and would live in a place far from his own.

I think you get the idea. Ulysses, in opting for Penelope, for Ithaca, opts to fit into the cosmic order, for the good, finite life, for mortality and for humanity. The truth is that Ulysses chose to be a man when he could have become a god.

This story points out some lessons that will be at the heart of Greek philosophical wisdom. The first of these is undoubtedly the victory over fear. We all know the fears that plague us. We know that fear has to do with a particular kind of drop in power, in vital energy, which is caused by something bad that goes through our heads. Obviously, the fear of fears is that of death. The death we're talking about is precisely this imagined death, the death that takes on various kinds of ghosts and imaginary forms in us, and which produces immense discomfort. The fear of death is certainly not exactly the fear of a coming event. It's the fear of things that cross our minds, it's the fear of the death of loved ones, it's the fear of the perishing of everything that makes us happy.

When Ulysses opts for finitude, he shows a boldness, a courage to face the fear of perishing. And of course this is a trait of wisdom, after all, our life is finite and if we are immobilized by fear, it obviously won't be as good as if we let it flow without thinking about it.

Realize how much the fear of death terrifies us. Our condominiums are absolutely surrounded by walls and private security guards, our vehicles are armored and marked by an immense boundary between the inside and the threatening outside. Fear closes us off from the world, closes us off from others and, to a large extent, prevents us from being able to encounter the world in joyful experiences. Therefore, victory over fear is the condition for the good life, the first lesson of Ulysses' choice of Ithaca and Penelope.

A second lesson from The *Odyssey* has to do with the time it took him to return home: twenty years. Ten fighting in Troy and another ten facing the obstacles that Poseidon imposed on him. During those twenty years, what Ulysses wanted most was to be in Ithaca. He remembers the times in Ithaca when, in Penelope's arms, everything was good. Notice that during these twenty years of living out of place, of living a failed life and a bad life, Ulysses' spirit is crossed by the memory of the times he had lived in Ithaca and the hope of one day returning home.

For the Greeks, these are two of the worst evils that can befall us. Instead of living life in life, enjoying the present moment and the best the world has to offer, we take refuge and our spirit wanders into the past. When the past was good, we regret that it's over, we live in nostalgia, in longing. When the past was bad, it's even worse; we live full of remorse, regret and guilt. These are the sad passions that plague us. The memory of a bad past massacres us, and when we finally free ourselves from what has already happened, our spirit wanders towards the future, towards what has not yet presented itself, towards the world that has not yet been found. Then, of course, we wish and have the illusion that everything will be better when something happens. These are thoughts like "when I change my wife", "when I change my house", "when I change my job", "when I change my car", and so we have the illusion that when the world is different from what it is, our lives will be better.

When Ulysses opts for Ithaca, he is opting for reconciliation with the world, reconciliation with the present, life in life, the richness of the instant, the beauty of the instant lived.

So give up nostalgia, give up hope. When life is good, every moment is worthwhile in itself. Memories and memories, projections and anticipations are no longer needed. We only escape when the threatening instant terrifies and haunts us.

Nietzsche called this reconciliation with reality and the world amor *fati*. The certainty that life will only be good if we manage to love reality as it is, without escaping into the past or the future, in other words, without nostalgia or hope.

• • • • •

Ulysses' return to Ithaca symbolizes the re-establishment of cosmic order. Ulysses begins to collaborate with the cosmos at home, ruling over his subjects in his own place, where everything suits him. You see, in the same way that the rice paddy suits the floodplain, the cactus the dry land, Ulysses suits Ithaca. Ulysses in Ithaca starts to do better, to live better, to have a eudaimonic existence and thus to collaborate with the cosmos.

You may have already thought about the question of eternity. What is eternity for us post-Christians? It is to continue living somewhere else after you die - perhaps with a body, perhaps without a body - forever. You live again and you don't die again, you keep your identity and you can still meet your loved ones. That's eternity. But the eternity suggested by Homer and taken up by Greek philosophy is a little different.

When you restore the cosmic order, you participate in the cosmos and become a fragment of eternity, because the cosmos is eternal. To participate in the cosmos is to participate in something eternal. Eternity belongs to the whole, and it is only possible because its parts are finite, deteriorate and disappear. How curious: in order for the cosmos to survive eternally, its parts have to die. So you participate in something eternal by dying. Finitude is the condition for the eternity of the whole, and you offer your life to the cosmic order, you die knowing that it is precisely in this condition that the cosmos will continue to exist. The matter that constitutes it will reorganize itself, nothing disappears, and what constitutes it today will reorganize itself into other beings, into other forms of being, and will give the cosmos survival.

My friend, between the eternity we believe in and the one suggested by Homer, let's agree that no one will lose the fear of dying with words like these as consolation. Don't be sad. Part of you will become a wild boar's testicles, another part will become a door handle and, who knows, another part will become a mangrove swamp. It would be better if we lived with our identity in eternity. But that's me talking. Homer and the *Odyssey* point to a different eternity.

• • • • •

The story of Ulysses gives us one last conclusion: the certainty that, for the Greeks who will use The *Odyssey* to reflect, ethics and happiness are two sides of the same coin. It's impossible to talk about one without talking about the other.

We already know that life in harmony with the cosmic whole is successful and worth living. When our body comes into harmony with the cosmic order, the moments of life are glorious and of great happiness. When this doesn't happen and we live out of place, then life is dull, sluggish and mediocre. And in every moment like that, we hope it will end soon.

If adjusting to the cosmic order is the condition for eudaimonia, the condition for happiness, it is also our greatest duty, because the universe is the reference point for our life. Our great obligation is to make the cosmos work, and we have a kind of life program to fulfill in this regard. If we don't fulfill it, we'll be compromising the functioning of the cosmos, we'll be living out of place, in disharmony. This is exactly what the Greeks called *hýbris*, a situation in which, by living out of place, you not only compromise your own life, but also the harmony of everything else.

For these reasons and others, your greatest duty is to investigate what life the cosmos expects you to live. That way you'll be fulfilling your duty to make the cosmos work and living in happiness. Duty and happiness are the same thing, they imply the same conduct.

For the Greeks, how could there be a duty that would lead us to an unhappy life? Our obligation is to live well, because our good life also allows the whole to live well.

This reflection is fascinating: ethics and happiness go hand in hand, with no possible fissure. To imagine duties that lead to sadness would, in fact, be very stupid.

But not everyone has thought or thinks that ethics and happiness are two sides of the same coin. Closer to us, in modern thinking, we'll find ethical thoughts that don't coincide with the way we see this relationship with happiness. I'll highlight two that I'm sure we'll talk about again.

We'll start with the utilitarian thinking of the English. Basically, they think that good conduct is that which results in the happiness of the majority; therefore, good conduct depends on its consequence. A conduct will be good when it leads to the happiness of the greatest number and bad when it leads to the sadness of the greatest number.

You might think that this is the correspondence between ethics and happiness. Not so, my friend, because the happiness of the greatest number may not coincide with the happiness of those who act. And this happens all the time. You have to choose between one path or the other: one will be more pleasurable, more convenient, but will ruin the lives of half the world; the other will be less pleasurable, perhaps even painful, but will bring joy to many people. According to utilitarianism, you, the agent, must opt for your own sadness in the name of the joy of the majority. You see that this correspondence between doing good and being happy is broken.

A second modern ethical theory, by Kant, would say that the true foundation of a good decision lies in the reasons why you decided to act the way you did - which he called maxims and which we can call principles, values. There are good reasons for you to act the way you do, such as the fact that anyone could do what you're doing at that moment, anyone could want everyone to do it that way, a kind of possible universalization of conduct.

Now, let's face it, this may or may not have something to do with our happiness. Often our pleasure, our well-being, implies conduct that we wouldn't want others to have with us and which, therefore, would be excluded from the list of good conducts.

I hope you have understood that what the Greeks said about acting well, living well, living in accordance with the cosmos and then feeling happy, this correspondence between the happiness of the agent and acting well, throughout the history of thought, has not always been sustained.

2

Plato and the search for truth

CLÓVIS: In The *Odyssey*, Ulysses emerges from chaos, from the disharmony of being out of place, and finally arrives in Ithaca, where cosmic order is re-established. This allegory that teaches us so much about the Greek way of thinking is present in the first philosophy.

A great name, perhaps the greatest of all time, is Plato. He wrote the *Dialogues* - apparently 35 of reliable authorship - in which he presents themes such as virtue, beauty, friendship, courage, justice, among others. Plato begins the dialogues by presenting the dominant opinions on these topics at the time. Therefore, he presents the state of the art, shows what the most influential people thought about that subject at that time. Once these various politically strong opinions, which he called *doxa,* had been presented, Plato would gradually set the ideas against each other, as if he wanted to rub them up against each other, to check and test their consistency. The aim was always to find some kind of satisfactory argument.

All Plato's dialogues are driven by a kind of desire for truth, a desire to find some kind of definition, an idea that would satisfy the initial curiosity about the proposed theme. Notice that, in the same way that Ulysses leaves the area of the Trojan War in search of Ithaca, of chaos in search of cosmic harmony, Plato, dialogue by dialogue, leaves the turbulence of *doxa*, the turbulence of the dominant opinions circulating in the city, and seeks a consistent truth, a truth that would be reassuring and that would correspond to the harmony of Ulysses in Ithaca. Notice that, in the same way that, for Homer, Ulysses leaves chaos for the cosmos, Plato invites us to leave the appearances of truth, or apparent truths, in search of something rationally consistent that can hover over the multiple impressions of circumstance.

For Plato, we are made up of body and soul. Our body is the one you know, the one you see. It has a certain duration, is finite, desires and has senses that allow it to have some contact with the world. The soul, among other functions, is responsible for thought, intelligence and ideas.

In fact, Plato believed that our souls already had contact with the truth of things before birth, that is, that we had already known this truth when the soul was still without a body, this soul that is eternal, that doesn't die along with the body. There is a moment in the soul's life when it is accompanied by the body, which Plato calls imprisonment. Imagine this: the soul is there, alone, in contact with truths. Then, for some strange reason, this soul ends up encapsulated, imprisoned by some body - like yours, for example - and has to live with this body until it deteriorates, which is when the soul will finally regain its freedom, that is, a life without a body, a life of solo career.

But if the soul was already in contact with true ideas, then when we were born we already knew everything.

In fact, the souls that make us up are very familiar with the truth, but at birth they go through a kind of oblivion. And what are we supposed to do during our lives? Try to remember what we've always known. The search for truth is not a completely dark and virginal adventure. It's a return to contact, the remembrance of things that our soul has always known very well. That's why, when our life allows our soul to regain contact with these ideas, it rejoices, because this is its beach, this is what is familiar to it. So our life is good because our soul smiles. What a great idea.

3

Hesiod's *Theogony*

CLÓVIS: Let's talk again about the way out of chaos into the cosmos. Ulysses leaving the Trojan War and returning to Ithaca.

I'm going to tell you about a well-known poem that is very difficult to read. While the *Odyssey* is pleasant and easy to read - there's even a children's version - Hesiod's *Theogony* is a really hermetic poem. Let's go.

She's talking about the first god. And do you have any idea who or what the first god of Greek mythology is? Well, that god is Chaos, and he couldn't be any other. Chaos is a god who doesn't yet have a human face. Other gods have a human face, like Zeus, for example, who is personified. But not Chaos. So how can we imagine a god who doesn't yet have a human face?

If you want to imagine Chaos according to Hesiod, imagine the dark, with dew, that strange drizzle, a damp climate. Imagine a bit of smoke, like at a party. Add the smoke, the humidity and the dark. Then imagine a precipice, a free fall.

And what's even cooler: an endless free fall that never ends. And Chaos finds a second god, or rather goddess: Gaia.

Gaia is the firm ground, it's the solid, it's the Earth, it's where the precipice ends, it's where you fall after the free fall. Gaia is the end of Chaos. It's when free-falling Chaos becomes ground to stand on. Gaia is where you're standing now, it's the solid that supports us, it's the missing reference. So, we already have a pair: Chaos, free-falling in the dark, and Gaia, where you step.

A third god will emerge from Gaia: Uranus. Heaven. Uranus, whom Gaia took out of herself and who was born without fertilization, was spontaneously generated. Uranus, despite being Gaia's son, did not leave her. He covered Gaia - in the sense of a blanket and in the sense of a lover. Uranus was voracious, he wouldn't stop having sex - and, let's face it, anyone who can have sex with the whole Earth must be a guy with interesting proportions and a reasonable grip. Uranus fertilized Gaia several times and in successive waves.

Uranus copulates with Gaia, he is obsessed with her. And from this intrepid and torrid love, several generations of children are born. The first are the Titans, the first gods with a human face. Six men and six women with unconscionable strength, great beauty, very close chronologically to Chaos; therefore, very violent. Gods of war, of the Earth. In addition to the Titans, the love of Uranus and Gaia gave rise to the Cyclops. As we already know, Cyclops have only one eye. And they will be part of the rest of our history, remember them, they will come back. They are Brontes, which means thunder, Steropes, the lightning, and Arges, which is lightning.

The third wave of gods is even more astonishing. They are stronger, more violent than the Titans, more monstrous. They are called hecatons, a name which in Greek means "a hundred arms". In addition to a hundred arms, they have fifty heads. They are of extraordinary strength. Hesiod, the author of this whole narrative, even says that it would be better not to mention their names, as it could be so dangerous. However, he does mention them, and the three hecatons are Coto, Briareu and Giges. They are the children of the mad love of Uranus and Gaia.

Uranus wouldn't leave Gaia, so she couldn't give birth to her children. They were uncomfortable in her womb. Gaia wanted to see their faces, she wanted to give birth to them, so she turned to her own children for help. She sends out a message saying that the children's father is a tyrant who won't allow them to give birth, so something has to be done. Cronos, the youngest of the titans, is the one who offers to help her. He uses the resources he has, the metals he has, makes a sharp instrument, holds the father's penis with his left hand and amputates it with his right. Uranus, overcome with pain, retreats, gets off Gaia and ends up in the sky.

Between Gaia and Uranus, between the Earth and the sky, there is time and space where Gaia's children can finally occupy their positions, where the generations will succeed each other, the space that will finally allow some order to be established in it one day. Kronos throws his father's penis into the sea. The blood of Uranus in contact with the Earth will give rise to the Erynias, the goddesses of vengeance, but at the same time, the mists of the sea in contact with the penile fluids of Uranus will give rise to Aphrodite, the goddess of love. From the same gesture by Kronos, two very different results: the emergence of the goddesses of vengeance and the goddess of beauty and love.

Look at the sophistication, complexity and subtlety of the possible interpretation. Kronos' behavior can be evaluated from a moral point of view under the aegis of salvation from his mother's torments, but also under the aegis of the cruelty of his father's amputation. Behavior of complex value that also had complex consequences in the world.

Kronos takes power from his father and reigns supreme. But he fears his children. Nothing could be more understandable for someone who had his father's penis amputated. Kronos adopts a curious strategy to prevent any threat to his sovereignty: he swallows his children as soon as they are born. You have to consider that, since the gods are immortal - and Kronos' children are gods - they remained alive in his womb. Kronos had six children, he swallowed five. The sixth had a different fate.

Kronos' wife, Rhea, a titan, was outraged by her husband's behavior and decided to protect their sixth son from his father's devouring lust. She hid him in Gaia's groves with her acquiescence. Kronos is tricked into eating stones instead of the child.

The last child to grow up protected will become a sublime god, of stunning beauty and extraordinary intelligence. He is the key to our story, to the transformation of chaos into cosmos. I'm talking about Zeus, god of gods, the greatest of them all. At some point in his career, Zeus - who was suckled by the goat Amalthea, from whose horn gushed ambrosia, the food of the gods, of unparalleled flavor and nourishing capacity - began to wonder why he was isolated, lonely, hiding and what was out there. After being quickly enlightened by Rhea, Zeus begins to realize that, in order to live normally, he has no choice but to show his face, explain to Kronos what has happened and confront his tyrannical father.

My friend, it is at this moment, when Zeus confronts Kronos, that the most spectacular event in our history begins: the war of the gods. The war between Kronos and his brothers, the Titans, against Zeus. Zeus frees his brothers from the womb of Kronos, and a fierce and grandiose struggle takes place between the first generation of gods, the Titans, and the second generation of gods, who, because they gather on Olympus, are called Olympians.

The war of the gods. Now the narrative heats up.

It's worth noting that since gods don't die, when one of them is swallowed, it's still alive and well. It's not a question of being chewed up like in the movie *Jaws*. The moment a god is regurgitated, it is returned in more or less the same state in which it was swallowed.

Kronos swallowed Zeus' brothers, and Zeus' first move, with the help of Gaia, was to make Kronos vomit them up, releasing the second generation of gods onto Earth. Zeus' next move was to get the Cyclops and the Hecatonchi out of the prison imposed by Kronos.

Kronos, you remember, was a titan. From the copulation between Uranus and Gaia came the titans and also the three Cyclops, Lightning, Thunder and the Hecatonchi, with a hundred arms and fifty heads. When Kronos took power, he locked both the Cyclops and the Hecatonchi in Tartarus. But Zeus freed them. At this point, there were already two teams assembled for the confrontation: on the one hand, the twelve titans, a practically invincible army; on the other, the brancaleones, the group of Zeus's brothers, the Cyclops, the Hecatonians and Zeus himself. There were all the conditions for an interesting confrontation.

You have to understand something in this story: as the gods appear, they take on an increasingly human face, they become personified, and this deserves interpretation. In other words, it is with the participation of a personified god - an intelligent god, and therefore a god who is distancing himself from the simple forces of nature, such as Chaos, Gaia and Uranus - that the cosmos can come into being. In other words, mythology indicates that, even among the gods, in the theogony, in the emergence of the gods, the path towards the cosmos passes through a personification and, therefore, a gain in intelligence, discernment and deliberative capacity. It's essential to realize this.

Back to the confrontation. We now have the teams set up. And what happens is the great war of the gods, described by many people. The way Hesiod tells it and the way others tell it is very cool, because it's purely the fruit of the human imagination, but of infinite richness as a production of that imagination. Even Max Weber, at the turn of the 19th to the 20th century, spoke of the great war of the gods. So I have the distinct impression that you realize that the emergence of the cosmos involves this confrontation between Zeus and his friends and the titans commanded by Kronos.

•••••

Zeus counts on the vomit of Kronos, who returns his brothers Hades, Poseidon, Demeter, Hestia and Hera. They had every reason to hate Kronos. Zeus also frees his uncles, the three Cyclops brothers of the Titans, born from the copulation of Uranus and Gaia, gaining three incredible allies: Lightning, Thunder and Lightning. He also frees the dreaded hecatons, also his uncles.

At this point, someone might think that all this is war strategy, strengthening the team, gathering war resources to face the titans, an invincible and super-fearless force. But there is actually an interpretation that interests us more, which is more subtle and more philosophical. It's the fact that, on Gaia's advice, Zeus puts everyone out to play. This means that, on the path from chaos to cosmos, no one will be left out, everyone will be understood and will have their fair share.

When Zeus makes Kronos vomit up his brothers - and in fact Kronos vomits more because of Gaia and Rhea's cunning than Zeus' - and also frees his uncles, the Cyclops and the

Hecatonchi, everyone who had already appeared comes back into play. The cast of the novel is all profiled to make it clear that, when it comes to building the cosmos, no one will be left with nothing. The cosmos is a universal organization that forgets no one and understands everyone. This interpretation is fundamental.

Zeus triumphs over the Titans and, defeating them, locks up his father and uncles for good. Of course, they don't die. They just keep going. When there's a *tsunami* in Japan or Indonesia, that's a titan who's had enough of staying at the bottom of the Earth and wants to take his place on it again.

The victory of Zeus is the point in mythology that begins our philosophical adventure. With Zeus, the cosmos will be possible, the victory over chaos is sacrosanct and now Zeus will distribute the universe among his co-religionists. And he will do this under the inspiration of two of his wives.

Zeus takes power. So we already have Uranus, Kronos and Zeus, the third holder of power, in this lineage. Zeus, instead of centralizing the exercise of power, distributes pieces of the world among his coreligionists. This distribution is seen as the ground zero of justice. Zeus - who would have swallowed his second wife, Themis, the goddess of justice - shares the universe, and this division is at the origin of the cosmos. You see, to attack the cosmos is to attack a decision and an action understood as symbols of justice. In the end, everyone was included. And Zeus was able to show clearly that everything in the cosmos is part of it and relevant to its functioning. Therefore, in the idea of the cosmos, there is no exclusion of any kind.

The fact is that all the myths - and there are so many - all the allegories, all the stories that Greek mythology teaches us can be reduced to two main types. The first is the attempt to disrupt the cosmos. These are myths that tell of the actions of gods or humans who, intending to gain some kind of personal advantage, act to disharmonize the cosmos, whether they are aware of it or not. Remember King Midas, who wanted to turn everything he touched into gold. Realize that this action, which enriches him, is directly linked to his pretensions, ambitions and desires and undermines the cosmic order, because Midas could destroy the universe by touching one thing after another.

The other type of myth are the stories about the protection of the cosmos, the initiatives to protect the cosmic order and prevent its destruction. These are stories that tell of the victory of harmony over disharmony. *The twelve labors of Hercules* are an excellent example.

Well, we now know where the idea of cosmos comes from, and this will make it much easier when it comes to finding the foundation of the good life, the foundation of ethics, of politics, the foundation of everything that is good in the life of man according to the view of classical philosophy. You understand that everything that is good is good because it fits into the cosmos. It's harmony within harmony. And everything bad is bad because it doesn't find a place in the cosmos and hinders its proper functioning.

4

The ship of Theseus

CLÓVIS: Mythology is full of stories. Little drawers, lots of little drawers, all fitted together.

Theseus was a young Athenian who ended up having to face the Minotaur. And Theseus was victorious. He returned home and his ship became the symbol of his heroism. And that ship was exhibited by everyone who told the story of Theseus with emotion and pride.

Little by little, the ship deteriorated and some of its pieces were replaced by new ones. But the story of Theseus' victories continued to be told. Time went by and there was nothing left, not a single slat of the original ship. Everything had been replaced. So the question arose: was the ship that was still there, being exhibited while Theseus' exploits were told, still his ship? There was no piece of the original wood there. It was all new. It was a completely different ship. What links the present ship to Theseus' ship? The answer is obvious: the narrative, the stories, the imagery, the discourse. And all this is in people's heads.

I hope you've understood what I'm getting at. Do you know why? Because there isn't much difference between Theseus' ship and your body. Cells are dying, others are emerging, and there's not much left today from the days of yore. If you look around, everything about you is different. Everything is new.

What is it that gives you unity? What is it that allows you to keep saying that you are you? Well, just like in Theseus' ship, what gives us unity is the narrative, the story, the discourse. It's the fact that we keep talking about ourselves and proudly pointing to our bodies. What's left of us is a narrative, even while we're still alive. I think it becomes even clearer after we die.

5

The Aristotelian cosmos

CLÓVIS: Aristotle was a great sage. He lived around 350 B.C. He talked about a bit of everything. For him, the essence of a thing, what a thing is, is not what it's made of, it's not its atoms or its cells. In fact, the essence of all things is the activities they typically carry out. They are the ends they pursue. Thus, the essence of each thing is its function. And function, in Greek, Aristotle called it *érgon*. If an organ is a heart, it's because its function is to pump blood. In essence, the heart is what pumps the blood. If it's a kidney, it's because its function is to clean the blood. The kidney is what cleanses the blood. When we know the function of a thing, we have a standard by which to evaluate it. A thing is good when it performs its function well.

If you want to know the value of everything in the world, there is a protocol to follow: check the quality of the function. For example: the function of a knife is to cut, so a good knife is one that cuts well. Virtue or excellence is the capacity that allows a thing to perform its function well; thus, the virtue of a knife is its sharpness, since being sharp is the condition for cutting well.

Aristotle takes these ideas about the function of artifacts and organs and applies them to human beings. We would all have a function. Aristotle argues that human beings have a characteristic function beyond the singular and particular functions of each one. There is a function that unites us all: the activity of the soul according to reasons, that is, you can be whoever you are, have whatever particularity you have, have whatever specificity you have, but we all have a common function. This is how he defines the soul's activity according to reasons. We'll simply call it rationality, remembering that it has practical aspects, oriented towards action, towards discerning what is best to do, and theoretical aspects, oriented towards the abstract evaluation of how the world works.

Well then, Aristotle concludes that happiness for each of us is rationality in accordance with virtue. This means that, in order to be happy in the specificity and singularity of our lives, we have to be virtuous in reason. In other words, we have to think well. Anyone who does not think well will not achieve the happiness that is common to us all. Aristotle also admits that this happiness does not depend on us alone, but on external factors that may favor a path that leads us to think better or not. So, you who are reading this book were lucky enough to pick it up, and I'm helping you to think better. You might not have picked it up and your rationality would have been diminished by not reading these reflections. Don't take it seriously, it's just a little joke.

Aristotle's claim that rationality is the human function common to all is controversial. Many believe that human beings are too complex to have a single characteristic function common to all. Others doubt that this function is rationality.

Now, we have to remember that Aristotle lived in his time, in his moment, within a way of thinking typical of the Greeks of his time. His lesson is very interesting because, for him, the happiness common to all of us depends on the blossoming of our soul. Think well, think better, and life has a better chance of being happy.

Whether you agree or not.

• • • • •

Now, I want to show the reader how the cosmos presented by mythology will influence Aristotle's philosophy and, more specifically, Aristotle's physics. This is important, since Aristotle's physics will remain unchanged until the beginning of modern times. This is described by a philosopher and historian of ideas called Alexandre Koyré. He wrote a book entitled *From the Closed World to the Infinite Universe*. And this is the first characteristic of Aristotle's cosmos: it is finite, it has a beginning, a middle and an end. It therefore differs completely from the understanding of the universe that we have come to have since modern times. And what consequences does this have for us?

When the world is finite, closed, with a beginning, middle and end, it is an absolute reference for us. In a closed world, there is inside and outside, north and south, left and right, and these references are the same for everyone, they are absolute. It's as if my position in the cosmos was between the jaboticaba tree and the fern. And that goes for anyone. When the universe comes to be understood as infinite, there is no inside and outside, no north and south, no left and right. From then on, all reference must be an understanding between us, a combination between us. Like, for example, Cartesian coordinates: a vertical axis and a horizontal axis around the zero point. And because of this understanding, we can locate a point P.

In Aristotle's cosmos, there was no need for this. Being finite and ordered, all things were in their place, and to position any point, any being, it was enough to have the references absolutely defined by the universe itself.

These differences between Greek and modern thought have ethical and political consequences. The good life, for the Greeks, is related to information that is absolutely valid for anyone: it is a good position in the cosmos. The good life, for us, has to result from an understanding, because the cosmos no longer provides us with anything.

• • • • •

Finitude allows the cosmos to be a reference for all its parts, like everything that is finite. If you imagine that your apartment has a beginning, middle and end, finitude allows each piece to have a position. From the edges of the apartment you can locate every centimeter of it.

You could also imagine the cosmos as a large movie theater, and your place in it would be seat 3-C. You can find it easily because there is a first row and the columns are divided alphabetically. The condition for finding seat 3-C is that there is 1-A. If there's no row 1 and no column A, you can't find 3-C. In other words, you can find your seat from a starting point.

Imagine now - after the year 1600 - the infinite universe. You'd think that theoretically there's a lot more room for you in the world. It's true. There's so much room for you, so many places, that there's no end. But what changes is that, although there's more room than if the universe were finite, there's no way of finding a position.

Why not?

My friend, again imagine a movie theater and your seat 3-C. You go back to number 1, but that's not the first seat. And then you see infinite rows and infinite columns. There's no beginning, there's no seat 1-A. If you don't have 1-A, you won't have 3-C either. Paradoxically, in the infinite universe, although there are infinite places for you, they are all undifferentiated. You have no position, you're adrift. So are we in the infinite universe: although there are infinite places, we are nowhere.

If in the cosmos you were a meter away from the door and you could situate yourself in the cosmic machine, now, in the infinite universe, you can no longer situate yourself. Unless you combine artificial references with everyone else in order to locate yourself. That's what Descartes did when he invented Cartesian coordinates.

That message is very crazy, very crazy. And we'll go from here to worse.

•••••

The second great characteristic of Aristotle's cosmos, also a legacy of mythology, is harmony. The cosmos is a harmonious space and what gives it harmony is the complementarity between functions. Thus, the wind blows and, by blowing, fulfills its role. The rain pours, the tide goes out, the frog croaks. If there is harmony, there is no conflict.

That's why Zeus distributed and gave everyone their due, counting on everyone's applause. But in this cosmos there is man, and, you know, man wants, is desirous, ambitious. And if it's enough for the wind to blow, it's never enough for man. He always wants more, and this desire seems to have no limits.

And isn't there an imminent conflict between men? After all, the world is scarce, there's no end to desire, and men therefore tend to bump into one another, one ambition into another. In that case, there would be conflict, which is the opposite of harmony.

That's why cosmic ethics dictates that people live fulfilling their roles. So, just as the wind won't fight with the rain, if each person fulfills their role and these roles are compatible with each other, there will be no conflict. This ethic, this sort of principle of life and conduct on Earth, allows people to live without having to fight each other over unreasonable and incompatible desires. You see, this harmonious cosmos between its parts is a reference for man's life, how he should act, how he should live. That's why cosmic physics is the reference for cosmic ethics, a reflection on how man's life should be.

•••••

The Aristotelian cosmos is a legacy of mythology, of Zeus' initiative to distribute the world among his co-religionists, giving each their due. Each one, with justice, receives what is theirs. This world is harmonious, the parts are in agreement with each other. There are no problems in a harmonious world, where conflict disappears in the name of justice.

As well as a reference for how we should live and how we should act - an ethical reference, therefore - this world also guarantees man a reference for beauty. Each thing that man encounters in the world will be beautiful to the exact extent that it is properly positioned in the cosmos. This leads us to conclude that this beauty could not be evaluated in isolation, in its isolated singularity, but rather in its integration with the rest, in such a way that we could think of the beauty of Sugarloaf Mountain in Rio de Janeiro, Table Mountain in Cape Town or any landscape that crosses your mind. This beauty is guaranteed if and only if we see a cosmic space there, in other words, something that is properly inserted into the whole. This also allows us, since the cosmos is a reference point for beauty, a criterion for evaluating works of art, i.e. the beauty of what man produces.

A work of art has always been and will always be the embodiment of a great idea in a piece of matter. For the Greeks, this great idea was the cosmic order. Therefore, any work of art will be beautiful to the extent that it represents this great idea of the cosmos when it presents itself as a microcosm. A kind of small translation of the great whole, ordered and organized.

We could go the other way and try to investigate, from the Greek works of art, which ones they really considered legitimate and what characteristics they had. In this way, we would also identify the characteristics of the cosmos in the imagination of the thinkers of that time.

The cosmos as an ethical reference, a life in harmony, the cosmos as a reference for beauty, the work of art as a microcosm, a small representation of the great universal order. These are the characteristics, for now, of the Aristotelian cosmos. It is finite, with a beginning, middle and end, and harmonious, a reference for ethics, a reference for beauty.

• • • • •

The third characteristic of Aristotle's cosmos is the hierarchical perspective.

In order to understand the extent to which the cosmos is made up of parts that are superior to each other and therefore respect a hierarchy of value and importance, we need to realize that this hierarchy of value is symbolized by a position occupied in the universe. Thus, some things were made to be at the top; others, at the bottom; some, on the left; others, on the right. Since the universe is finite, positions are easy to find. And this is exactly the central idea of Aristotle's physics. Each part of the cosmos tends to look for its natural place.

Smoke, for example. Aristotle would say that it rises because its natural place is at the top, in other words, smoke is endowed with characteristics that force it to occupy a place at the top. Stone, on the other hand, has characteristics that force it to the ground. It would be as if the smoke and the stone were endowed with a will. This is what we call animism. The parts of the cosmos are endowed with an inclination to go to their proper place. So, if the place of the smoke is at the top, it's as if it were deliberately heading for the top.

In this way, Aristotle explains movement as a natural tendency of the will of the parts of the cosmos to go each to its own corner. All movement would be a search for harmony with the cosmos and, therefore, a pursuit of the place where this harmony is most likely to occur.

Now you understand Aristotelian physics, which is bizarre because we know that smoke rises, but not because it wants to. From an early age, we learned about the law of gravity and the reasons why today's science explains the movement of bodies.

And you, faced with this richly imaginary explanation of the thinking of an era, must be wondering where man is in all this. Could it be that man's movement in the universe also obeys the logic of seeking his place above or below? Could it be that each man's nature already indicates his place? Could it be that there are smoke-men, who are naturally gifted at staying up high, and stone-men, who are naturally gifted at staying down low?

Man has a nature that should lead him to a certain place. Or not. He can decide to go against his nature. A man who should naturally go up can decide to go down. The man who should naturally stay down can stubbornly stay up. Just wait and see the difference: while in nature everything works out in the end, among us it may not. Finding our natural place, going in the right direction, respecting our nature is one of infinite possible options. Therefore, only we can live wrongly, only we can live against the cosmos, in disharmony, in sadness. While it's easy for the wind to blow, in our case, the path of nature and the full blossoming of our own essence are a possibility discovered by reason in relation to the many other possibilities that cross our minds all the time.

What about you? Are you smoke that rises or stone that falls? Do you respect your nature, resources and talents? Or are you a stubborn person who rows against the tide and ends up trying to live out of place? Aristotle's classic question for you to answer.

•••••

To make it easier for the reader to understand, let's use some allegories. Let's imagine the game of tug-of-war, in which two groups of people pull a rope, one on each side. Everyone pulling the rope on the same side is doing the same thing. They are all pushing the rope to their side. There is a difference in value between the team members, which is simply a comparison between the force exerted on the rope by each of them. In this example, it's easy to make the comparison: the goal is to pull the rope, and whoever can move it to their side most effectively is the best.

Another more sophisticated example is the game of soccer. On the pitch, the eleven players have one goal, which is to score, to win. However, each one plays a different role. In this case, the comparison is less straightforward. It's a bit different from tug-of-war, in which everyone does the same thing. In a soccer team, there are those who prevent the other from playing, prevent the other from scoring. There are those responsible for bringing the ball forward, for making runs down the side of the pitch, for playing the ball into the goal. It becomes much more complicated to make a comparison as to which one is worth more. How can I compare a striker who is responsible for scoring and a defender who is responsible for not letting the other play? Surely we can also propose that some players are more decisive than others for the team to win, and therefore better than others. Although I can't compare Romário's role, for example, with that of an average defensive player who works to prevent the other from playing, it's undeniable that Romário is more fundamental to getting the ball in the net. We can establish a hierarchy of value according to the group's overall purpose.

That's more or less what happens in the universe. Everyone has their own role and their own nature, which facilitates the performance of their function. But some roles, some competencies, are more decisive for the cosmos to function than others. That's why those people, or those parts of the cosmos with those resources, are superior to the others. So, just like in a tug-of-war, a cow that gives more milk than the other is superior. Both give milk, but one gives more milk.

There is also the possibility of evaluating different resources. We could ask ourselves, between an individual who thinks well and another capable of doing wonders with a ball at his feet, which one will contribute more decisively to the cosmic order? The answer in Aristotelian thought is clear: the great talent, the great natural resource of man is thought. Those who think better are superior to the others, they are more decisive in ensuring that there is a goal, that man fulfills his role.

• • • • •

The cosmos is finite, harmonious and hierarchical. One last characteristic remains: it is a space governed by functions.

Let's say you think about the function of eye drops, and I challenge you to answer this question without using the word "eyes". Without the eyes, we don't have the purpose of the eye drops. Thus, the eye drops find their full function in the eyes; therefore, outside of themselves.

Thinking that the purpose of something is always outside of itself, we can think in terms of a final cause. In this way, the cause of a thing would be in its finality, in other words, outside of itself. Thus, the wind is windy, and the cause of the wind's windiness is in its finality, which is the refreshment of that which is not itself. Therefore, eye drops are for the eyes just as everything that the wind refreshes is for the wind. Aristotle believed that the purpose of things is their main cause, that is, things move in the universe to achieve those purposes, as if they were endowed with a personal project, duly orchestrated with all the other parts of the cosmos, for their perfect functioning.

We now know that the causes are efficient and that if the wind blows in the direction it does, it's not to fulfill its purpose, but because something material causes the air to move from one point to another. In this case, the material thing is a difference in atmospheric pressure.

Notice that the transition from Greek Aristotelian thought to modern thought implies giving up a belief in final causality and accepting efficient causality. Perhaps the same perspective can be applied to our lives. If someone says that I teach to fulfill my mission, they are nostalgically resurrecting Aristotelian thought. If someone says that, given my material conditions, given the possibilities of professional practice, all very material causes, what I have left is just that, to be a teacher, they will be citing an efficient cause, matter determining matter in strict inexorability.

For Aristotle, the universe is a space of purposes. Everything moves to fulfill its role, and this implies the existence of an ordered whole, preferably ordered from outside, a transcendent instance that has established the place, role and purpose of each one so that everything can rotate harmoniously.

This transcendent body is Zeus, who, after defeating the first generation of gods, put the house in order. Thanks to him, everything has its place, its function, so to blaspheme against its purpose is to attack the cosmos and confront the will of Zeus.

• • • • •

If you were to ask people in the street what a just city is today, they would most likely remember that in a city some exercise power and others submit to it. Quickly, some would ask why it is some who exercise power and not others, where the basis of the exercise of power lies, why we have to accept that some deliberate, while others only submit to that deliberation. Most likely the answer would be: "Look, our scheme here is as follows: there is a will of the majority, and for that we hold elections. Whoever gets the most votes wins, and the person elected is certainly the one who had the support of the majority. So it's only fair that he should rule and exercise power."

Such an obvious conversation would be very strange to Aristotle. The foundation of the exercise of power in the city, for this Greek thinker, is a foundation of nature. A just city is not one whose decisions are taken by the majority, but one that imitates the cosmic order in the best possible way. You remember that in the cosmic order there are those who by nature must be at the top, like smoke, and others who by nature must be at the bottom, like stone. Among us, too, there are those who by nature are gifted and others who by nature lack resources. In this sense, it is normal for the gifted to exercise power, and to do so because they occupy a hierarchically superior position to the others.

Every time we think about it, we think about slavery. Aristotle was completely in favor of slavery. For Aristotle, there is the slave by nature, naturally inferior. Being naturally inferior, he doesn't have the full intellectual capacity to know what is best for him. Therefore, it's good for him to be a slave, it's good for his life to be decided by someone else. Crazy, isn't it?

There is also the war slave, and Aristotle thinks that in this case slavery may not necessarily be just. But slavery by nature is, because someone who lacks intellectual excellence is not in a position to rule himself or a city. Not only will he bring his life to ruin, but also the lives of others. It's good for everyone that there are slaves - slavery as a consequence of a distribution of natural resources and a legitimate exercise of power, legitimized by nature.

The story of slavery in the previous reflection aroused expressions of indignation, which is why I think it's worth returning to it; after all, my project is to take you by the hand. So let's give the floor to Aristotle. He says: "Reason shows as well as facts teach, after all, to command and to be commanded is part not only of indispensable things, but also of advantageous things, and it is from birth that a distinction has been made in many. Some are made to command, others to be commanded. Thus, some must command, and others must be commanded".

Now, my friend, if you loved Aristotle and thought he was one of the three greatest thinkers in history, keep on loving him and keep on being convinced, because he is! But we have to admit that the intellectual scenario he shared, the paradigm that was his, the way he thought about things no longer coincides with the way we think today.

Aristotle would have disliked the idea of human rights, for example. The passage is very clear: "It is immediately after birth that everything is determined, everything is decided. There are those who are gifted and well-born, and there are those who are gifted and ill-born, and this is probably even a little before birth". It is therefore a gift of principle. It doesn't have to do with dedication, drive or determination. It's something that comes with the person. Perhaps today we could call it a genetic endowment. Why not? This is the heart of the aristocratic principle. There are superiors, noble by nature, and there are inferiors, slaves by the same nature.

If you want me to go further, look at what Aristotle says next: "We find the same relationship between man and animals. There are wild animals and domestic animals. For domestic animals, it is better that there is someone to provide for them, decide for them and guide their lives."

I think it's no longer possible to deny that Aristotle's view of man was somewhat hierarchical and marked by inequality. Even the domestic animal served as a comparison.

• • • • •

Aristotle made comparisons, and those who compare don't say that it's the same thing. So we could say that, by nature, man is superior to woman. Aristotle's thought. In the same way, some men are superior to others, also by nature. Still Aristotle's thought. And men are superior to animals, also by nature. It is precisely this nature that legitimizes power relations. The city will be just when it is governed by its superiors, and this government by the superiors will be carried out in the interests of all. It is to the advantage of the inferior not to have the prerogative of governing themselves, let alone governing others.

Therefore, some inferences are essential. When a father exercises power over his son, the basis of that power lies in nature, it refers to his old age. We can also say that throughout the history of thought, this nature that legitimizes the exercise of power has given way to another basis of legitimacy, which is understanding, the contract. Instead of man exercising power because of his natural gifts, he exercises it because of a common understanding. In this way, relations between men and women have also moved towards equality, even if they remain as different as they were. Even relations between father and son, which were once governed by a foundation of nature, are now largely the result of an understanding. Thus, the superiority of the father's nature does not authorize physical violence, verbal aggression or humiliation.

In Brazil today, we have the Statute of the Child and Adolescent (ECA), a kind of common understanding. What it says, in short, is very simple: adults and children, parents and children are still as different in nature as they were two thousand years ago. But this difference in nature does not authorize everything today as it once did. Until recently, in fact.

If you want to fly through the history of thought, you should know that nature once legitimized and founded all power, but little by little this foundation was replaced by a contract, an agreement between everyone.

•••••

We talked about cosmogony in mythological thought and showed that many of the characteristics of this cosmos from mythology were used in philosophy. The characteristics of Aristotle's cosmos are largely inspired by mythological thought. But one caveat must be made: Aristotle didn't exactly believe that a transcendent god had put everything in order. It's a bit more subtle than that. Although the characteristics are the same, the mythological explanation is not exactly the one that Aristotle employs.

The truth is that Aristotle rejects the idea of a divine craftsman or artisan. But, of course, this doesn't mean that things don't have an order and that the parts of the world don't have a purpose. Aristotle treats the relationship between the part and the whole in the structures of animals, for example, as something essentially finalist. Animals have the parts they have so that they are able to perform the functions for which they were intended.

At times, Aristotle's recourse to the finalistic character of nature insinuates the conclusion that nature has its goals in mind very consciously. Just look at what he says: "Nature, like an intelligent human being, always assigns each organ to something that is capable of using it. The most intelligent will be able to efficiently use the greatest number of tools, and the hand seems to be not just a single tool, but a tool of tools. So nature has given the tool that is most widely useful to the hand, to the creature that is capable of acquiring the greatest number of skills, to the intelligent creature."

It's amazing how, although Aristotle didn't designate a god to put each thing in its place, he did believe that there is an intelligence embedded in nature that makes each part naturally go after its space, its place, and perform its most proper, most essential activity in an excellent way.

• • • • •

You remember that Aristotle's universe is finite and therefore a reference for whatever is inside it. It is harmonious, and, if it functions correctly, there is no conflict. It is hierarchical, because the things within it are not of equal importance. And finally, you remember that it is full of purposes. Now let's think about some of the consequences of this.

I think it's worth clarifying the question of the internal coherence of Aristotle's philosophy and the intimate relationship between physics and ethics. For Aristotle, the things within the universe move according to their own nature, which seeks to position them in their right place in the cosmos, in their natural place. Thus, things are endowed with a kind of soul that leads them towards a good life. Movements, therefore, are the result of each thing's desire to go to its right place.

Aristotle also says that some movements in the universe are the result of an external constraint. This means that you can pick something up and throw it away, or you can see something moving and stop it from continuing. In this way, we can classify movements into two types: natural ones, in which things look for their right place, and constrained ones, determined by external forces. These constrained movements can be disruptive to cosmic harmony and order, because they can direct things to a place other than their rightful place. We could thus establish a kind of duality or even confrontation.

The movements of good versus the movements of evil. The movements of good are those determined by our own nature. The movements of evil are those determined by external factors that attack our nature. If it's like that in physics, it's the same in our lives. In such a way that, if we let our nature speak, we will set ourselves in motion in the right direction, in the direction of happiness, of the life that satisfies us, completes us and puts us in harmony with everything else. But just like anything else in the universe, we can also fall victim to external forces that cause us to move in the opposite direction. In us too, therefore, there are movements of good and movements of evil.

Let's remember Ulysses. He wanted to return to Ithaca, but Poseidon's traps prevented him. Ulysses was fine in Ithaca, but the need to fight in the Trojan War made him move away from where he was supposed to stay. So I invite you to look at your own life and try to identify the relevance of Aristotle's reflections in your own path. In your good and evil movements. Of course, every time you have a dream that makes your eyes shine, it seems like a good direction for the movement of good. And every time someone tells you that a certain job doesn't make money and that you have to adapt to the needs of the market and the shortcomings of society, this seems to go against nature and is therefore profoundly evil.

6

Stoicism

Clóvis: Now let's talk about the Stoics. Theory in Greek means "contemplation of the divine", and for the Stoics, it is the knowledge of the world itself. And the world, for them, is comparable to a living organism. Two issues stand out here. The first is that every living organism is made up of parts, and these parts act together to make up the whole. The second is that each part is made in the best possible way to fulfill its function. So there is nothing better suited to seeing than the eye, nothing better suited to digesting than the stomach and intestines, nothing more perfect for breathing than the lungs, and for irrigating the blood and circulating it through the body, the heart.

There is, therefore, an idea very dear to the Stoics: that nature is a form of perfection of being with a view to a certain purpose. And this purpose is that of each part that makes up the whole. The whole is the divine itself. Therefore, the contemplation of the divine is the contemplation of the whole in its marvelous perfection.

It's clear that this perspective is very close to what mythology had already bequeathed us and what Aristotle had already taught us; after all, it is crossed by purposes, by parts that make up the whole and, in a way, by a whole that is also finite, harmonious and ordered. We are therefore faced with a kind of Aristotelian inheritance in Stoic thought.

Insisting on this is fundamental, because the Stoics had a very original conception of ethics and the good life. When you think of stoicism, when someone uses the word "stoic" or "stoically", it almost always refers to a behavior of resignation in the face of the pain of enduring great sacrifices, great suffering, with a view, of course, to a greater good. This common sense idea of the word "stoic" has a lot to do with what the Stoics recommended as the good life and philosophized in terms of an excellent existence, which we'll see in the next few reflections.

For now, it's enough to point out that the god of the Stoics, the divine for the Stoics, is in the wonder of the world itself. And do you know why? Because, in a way, man recognizes that living organisms, the things of nature, are wonderful. He didn't make them, and so they reflect the dimension of the divine that is impregnated in nature.

The first properly philosophical idea of the Stoic school is the radical determinism of all occurrences. What does this mean? Simply this: everything that happens has causes that determine it. This means that things can only happen the way they do. It also means that there is no room for luck, chance, chance or contingency.

In fact, the Stoics believed that every time you think about luck, misfortune or what could be different from what is, it's the result of ignorance of the causes that affect an event. If you really know the causes, you'll know the effects in advance. Believe it or not, but this radical determinism of the Stoics leads them to a philosophy of fate, of prediction, of anticipation.

Why?

That's crazy. It seems contradictory, because talking about determinism, about knowing the causes, means that you believe in reason as competent to explain everything that happens in the world. It's an exaggerated rationalism.

Wow, fate exists and we can know the future. That sounds like the stuff of pickpockets and charlatans.

But this contradiction is only apparent, because it works just as well. The truth is that this cartomantic ability to predict the future among Stoics is a kind of hyper-rationalism, an absurd trust in reason, because the causes of the future are spinning around here. If we know how to diagnose and interpret them, we can know their effects in advance. That's why a truly wise person is not only one who isn't surprised by the world when it happens, but one who is able to anticipate what is going to happen, diagnosing the causal relationships that will determine what is to come.

• • • • •

One of the great Stoics is Marcus Aurelius, a prominent figure in the Roman Empire. He was a great ruler and also a philosopher.

Marco Aurelio observes that if we look at the world too closely, we will have small fragments of the world that may seem ugly, disgusting. But he teaches us that the world will only seem ugly to us because of our cut-out, our fragmented perspective, our inability to contemplate the whole. He assures us that if we look at the world from a little further away, we'll realize that anything is wonderful. Everything you can see is wonderful precisely because it is inscribed in a world that is itself wonderful.

Marco Aurélio's example is wild boar drool. If you look closely, the slime is disgusting, gooey, even hideous. But if you take a step back and start to understand the function of the boar's drool, how the boar uses its drool to relate to other boars, you'll realize that this drool isn't so ugly. On the contrary. There's nothing that beats the boar's slobber when it comes to helping you shag another boar. The beauty of the world has to be understood from the whole, as a function of the whole. Then, because of the whole and its presence in the whole, each thing will find its own beauty.

Of course, this is a lesson in wisdom that teaches us something that, for the Stoics, was very obvious: either you understand yourself as belonging to a harmonious, beautiful, just, adjusted order, in which you are a piece and a part, and the parts only have beauty as parts because they are part of a greater whole, or you will continue to have fragmented perspectives of the world, and the world will never seem beautiful, just, harmonious or good to you. And then, of course, it makes all the difference whether you believe you live in a world that is closed, round, harmonious and beautiful, or whether you believe you live in a world that is a mess, chaotic, conflicted, ugly, hideous, slobbering, stinking, disgusting.

You see, the wisdom of the Stoics starts from the understanding that the universe is wonderful. That's the theory.

Realize that science will only be good if it allows us to understand how the whole works. Of course science will study the parts, it will study the small, it will study the fragmented. But it will only be good if, from this study, it helps us to understand the whole of the universe, the cosmic order that is the terrain on which we play this strange game of life.

•••••

Marco Aurelio's idea leaves some puzzled. The story of the boar's drool arouses intellectual curiosity. Since some are perplexed, let's take another example.

If you have a photo of Gisele Bündchen lying around, take her face and cut out just the nose. You'll see that her nose alone, isolated from the rest, is strange. But if you step back a little and put the nose back on the face, it won't be strange any more. If you step back a little more and join her face to her body, everything will be wonderful. You realize that if her nose wasn't the way it is, she wouldn't be as beautiful as she is. I think you've understood that the beauty of the part is not captured as an isolated part of the whole, but as part of a greater whole.

And what's so funny and important about this reflection? Very simply: the whole does not allow itself to be captured by the senses. The whole world, the cosmos, can only be understood by reason. What we are trying to say is that you will only understand and find the boar's drool beautiful if you place it in a whole that only exists for you in reason, intelligence, imagination and never in sensory perception. The world, however finite it may be, with a beginning, middle and end, cannot be apprehended by someone's senses. So, if the beauty of things depends on their position in the world, because they participate in a whole that is beautiful, just and harmonious, beauty is only definitively captured when it is inserted into a reality that is thought, cogitated, imagined and, therefore, something of reason.

What I'm trying to say is that if you don't have the development of intelligence and reason to understand the world as cosmic, integrated and harmonious, you won't be able to perceive the beauty of the things that are part of it, because this beauty can only be understood when it is situated in a whole that is itself thought, cogitated and imagined.

Let's imagine that at some point you meet me. When you look at me, what do you see? A bald, pudgy, slightly awkward, hunchbacked guy. And if you just look at me, you'll be disgusted. But Marco Aurelio helps me by telling you to put me in the cosmic context you've imagined. Then the world is beautiful, I'm part of the world, without me the world doesn't exist, so try to think I'm beautiful. I'm not worth it on my own, but I am worth it as part of a universal beauty.

Now we're going to bring another great philosopher from the Roman phase of the Stoics to talk to us: Epictetus. A contemporary of Jesus, he was a slave, he couldn't write, and what you read as a book by Epictetus wasn't written by him. He taught classes and there were big people who knew how to write, who attended his classes and wrote down what he said, which gave rise to the book called the *Manual*.

Look how cool: Marcus Aurelius, emperor. Epictetus, slave. That's the team of Roman Stoics.

And what is Epictetus' most curious, important and well-known idea?

There are two types of situation in your life, very different from each other: what depends on you and what doesn't depend on you. And it's very important to know how to distinguish between what depends on you and what doesn't. Do you know why? Because when it comes to what depends on you, you have to give everything, do your best, work hard and spend all your energy. But when it comes to what doesn't depend on you, there's no point in spending a penny because it doesn't really depend on you.

Let's imagine you're at one of those strange airports with uncertain weather conditions. Well, you know, planes only take off if the weather conditions are good, otherwise there's no way, the plane won't take off. What happens is simple: it has to be sunny and clear. You're distressed, you have an appointment, the flight has to leave on time, but it's clearly not up to you.

On the other hand, it's up to you to arrive on time for your flight, to make sure you can anticipate any setbacks. Drawing up a plan B in case the plane doesn't take off is up to you. So you quickly realize that some things are in your hands and others are not. The weather is not in your hands. But plan B is.

Epictetus says that some things depend on you. Like - what a funny thing - desire, for example. It's funny because the part of desire that depends on you is the part of its object, because desire is made up of vital energy, a kind of inclination towards the world, plus something that goes through your head, which is what you desire. Well then, the object of desire depends on you.

Another thing that depends on you is the quality of your judgments, your evaluations and judgments. Also the ability to find out about things, to be aware of things in the world. I don't know if you're starting to realize it, but the things that depend on you have a lot to do with your head, your intelligence and your reason.

Now, what is it that doesn't depend on you? Firstly, the things in the world that you don't control. Secondly, the things in your body that you don't control either. It's obvious that the affective part related to joys and sorrows largely happens without you being able to control it.

The lesson has been learned: knowing how to identify what depends on you and what doesn't is to put energy into what you can control and not waste energy, time and investment on what you can't control.

• • • • •

We've already said that, for the Stoics, everything is tied up in everything, everything is necessarily the way it is, nothing in the world is different from the way it should be.

The curious thing is that, for the Stoics, this thing of being attracted to the world or rejecting it, liking it or disliking it, is all a choice. Well, that's up to the Stoics. Let you draw your own conclusions. I personally can't even understand what this means. Dislikes and attractions are a choice. Well, in my view, anything but. But it doesn't matter. What matters here is what they said.

So what goes through our heads is the result of the freedom of the activity of thinking. But, interestingly enough, if everything in the world is necessarily the way it is, then, in our case, we have the freedom to judge, to think, to discern and to assign value. But let's be clear: since everything in the world is necessary, the Stoics say that this freedom is strictly internal and has no consequences in the practical world, in the world outside of us. So we think freely, but we act as we could only act in order to be part of the causal chain that is the world of nature.

My friend, that's a hard pill to swallow. After all, if everything in the world is necessarily the way it is - the wind blows, the tide goes out, the cat gates - why wouldn't our mind, our intelligence, work like that too? Why wouldn't our intelligence think the only thing it could think? Why should only our thoughts be different and subject to this inner freedom? Do we not call our ignorance of the conditions of our thinking, the material conditions of the production of our judgments, freedom to think? Is it not our ignorance that makes us believe in this freedom?

Suck on that sleeve, my friend. We're only free to think. When it comes to being in the world, we are also rigorously determined by the material causalities that make us be and exist as only we can be and exist.

• • • • •

For the Stoics, the beautiful is also necessarily the just and the good. Thus, justice, goodness and beauty are three perspectives of the same thing. There is no possibility of justice in ugliness or beauty in injustice. And why is that? Because, at the end of the day, the reference point for beauty, goodness and justice is the same. It's the cosmos. If something is just, it is because it is in accordance with the cosmos. If it is beautiful, it is because it is in accordance with the cosmos. Therefore, the cosmos could not confer goodness and ugliness at the same time.

So what is beauty? It would be an attribute of something in the world that is in harmony with the cosmos. If you are part of a beautiful whole and are in harmony with it, you can only be beautiful too.

And what would be fair? The same thing. Something adjusted to the cosmos. Of course, the just is another attribute, different from the beautiful. But what is beautiful is necessarily just and what is just is necessarily beautiful because both presuppose harmony with the universal whole.

Thinking along these lines, it makes perfect sense. But, between you and me, does this affirmation of the correspondence between beauty, goodness and justice coincide with our experience?

Normally, Hollywood heroes, the kind-hearted, vigilante, generous guys who restore the harmony of things, are also very handsome. This is our experience of television and film fiction. However, we have to recognize that, off the screen, it's not quite like that. How many beautiful people there are who use their beauty to deceive, to enslave, to terrorize their partners and suitors with emotional dependencies. How many fair people, of infinite goodness, who are aesthetically endowed with extreme ugliness. People who look smelly, ragged, shabby, but are capable of a gesture of great kindness and generosity. The same fiction gives us the beautiful and the beast. The hideous, monstrous beast is one of infinite moral beauty and immense generosity.

And in the world of life, outside of fiction? There we can find a total mismatch, a radical misalignment between what we call beautiful and attractive with what is just and good. For these reasons and others, we have to admit that this cosmic reference of the Stoics no longer makes any sense to us. But, since it's their word here, it was important to make it clear that, in their conception, beauty, justice and goodness are three corresponding perspectives of the same thing. The immense reference of the finite, ordered and harmonious universal whole.

7

Our role in the cosmos

CLÓVIS: As we've seen, theory is the contemplation of the divine. For the Stoics, the divine is the wonder of the universe, the fact that everything is tied up in everything, the fact that every piece of the universe has its incredible function and is wonderfully adjusted to it. Man is perplexed by the perfection of the adjustments and fittings. He knows he didn't do it, so he calls it divine.

Stop and think. In addition to theory, there is morality, which is our adaptation to this universe. And if everything is just right - the eye is just right for man to see, the knee is just right for man to squat, the cherry tree is just right for producing cherries and the wind is just right for cooling - then we are obliged to deduce that we too have in our nature the best way to fulfill our role.

Therefore, we need to investigate two things in order to think like a Stoic thinker: firstly, what our role is and, secondly, what the attributes of our nature are. There must be an extraordinary link between the two. If I have an enormous talent for drawing, it's because my role in the universe must have something to do with it. And what's most incredible: my talent is the best it can be to fulfill my purpose, which is to draw. There's nothing silly outside of us or inside us. And our resources are essential and the best possible to fulfill our function within the cosmic machine.

It's a great thought, because if your knee is perfect for bending, you must be perfect for something too.

• • • • •

Morality has always had to do with our choices about how we are going to act, because, in our case, life always gives us alternatives, and our conduct can always be one or the other, or also the other. There are always 360 degrees of paths to take, and our deliberate conduct will make us throw away so many others that we could have chosen, but which, for some reason, we decided not to choose, not to act that way, not to live that way.

So the Stoics also had their morals. Here's what Cicero says about this: "We can't have any kind of judgment about what is good and what is bad without knowing the whole system of nature".

Put this way, it seems enigmatic, almost incomprehensible. Why is it that, when it comes to deciding what I'm going to do with my life, in order to make the right decision and not make a mistake, I have to know the whole system of nature? Doesn't that seem too complicated to live life? After all, knowing the entire system of nature is a huge prerequisite. But what we're trying to explain is that, for the Stoics, every decision about one's conduct has to be related to the cosmos because right conduct is adjusted to it.

And how do I adjust to the cosmos?

You have to know it. I need to understand how it works, its mechanisms. Only then will I be able to see what my proper participation in this universal whole is and would be.

Imagine, for example, that when it came to deciding which university to go to, the Stoics had nature as their reference point. What would be the best course to take? The one that allows their nature to play its part. And when does nature fulfill its role? Precisely when it fits into the cosmic machine, making it work properly. And when does that happen? When you play your game, discover what your beach is, understand what your business is, because you are, as we've already said, the best possible way to fulfill your role.

Of course, someone will say that you should study law because there are plenty of job opportunities, public exams, and you'll lead a stable life in a country town. Of course, those who say this succumb to the temptation of a comfort offered by society and don't give a damn about your talent.

And when you say: "But what I really wanted, what makes my eyes shine, is to be a teacher" - wow! They'll throw up in front of you. Because our society disdains this choice and considers it paltry, ridiculous, unworthy, just like a teacher's salary.

But you will know what to do. For the Stoics, your nature and your natural resources tell you the answer, they show you the way. Because you are the best possible way to fulfill your role in the universe.

• • • • •

For the Stoics, nature is the reference. Justice is the fitting of your nature into the whole of nature, like a jigsaw puzzle. And by seeking excellence in yourself, you are thus fitting into the cosmic order. The fit is not static, it is dynamic. The fit is not one of standing still, but of action, of movement. And the search for your own nature in self-improvement is already the right fit in the cosmic whole.

The Stoics gave lessons that were a little different from what we have today as a philosophy class. Today, to do a degree in philosophy, you listen to professors, read texts by classical thinkers, eventually propose a text, write answers to exams, and the course takes place in a scheme of listening to speeches, reading speeches and producing speeches.

It wasn't quite like that at the Stoic school. It offered practical courses, so philosophy was translated into behavior. You were made to act as if you were in a laboratory and you learned the things taught by the Stoics by doing them. Just like in an art course or science laboratory.

And what could get in the way of the search for a good life? What could confront nature as a reference point, offering a misguided solution to life?

The Stoics certainly believed that society as it was at the time - the social convictions, habits, rules, distributions of prestige and notoriety, everything that existed in society at the time and still exists today - could be profoundly disruptive to a proper choice for one's life. Therefore, the Stoics taught how to face social pressure - or social repression - and subject themselves to situations of ridicule in order to be mocked, attacked, warned and harassed, and thus create a kind of armor that would make them armored against social pressures.

Zeno, the great thinker and founder of the Stoic school, was a student of the Cynic philosophers and learned a lot from them. It is said that Zeno used to pull a dead fish with a string, as if it were a dog, in order to make fun of society and even be ridiculed. In this way, he would learn how to protect himself and not be overwhelmed by social pressure, by malice.

It reminds me a lot of my social life. I was never taken for someone very conventional and I remember that when I was forced to do swimming training, I often went to the pool in my socks. The first few times I did this, I was thoroughly mocked by everyone. But after a while, they got tired of it and I realized that I had gained something: I wasn't bothered by what they said about me anymore. This is incredibly good when it comes to living, because if you have convictions and end up letting yourself be beaten down by the mockery, malice and ridicule that society imposes on you, you'll end up weakening your convictions and acting like a robot of social logic.

• • • • •

We know how nice it is when we get pats on the back, when everyone tells us we're great, when everyone applauds us. But sometimes all this recognition and glory comes with an expensive price to pay, which is to turn your back on yourself, your own talents, your own essence, your own nature and, therefore, your own good life.

The Stoics were convinced that if there is a clash between society and nature, we should opt for the latter and throw all those who want to lead us astray to their faces.

But there is a noble possibility in this story that is rarely mentioned: it is precisely when society applauds the full blossoming of our nature. It's when society reveres and recognizes everyone's natural talent. This tends to happen with some artists - a few, to be sure - and there is a kind of magical combination between living up to one's talents and receiving the glories that society knows how to bestow on us when it suits its interests. In this case, the combination - which rarely depends on our strength and intelligence, but on variables we can't control - seems very nice, and I think it's a condition for an irrepressibly happy life.

I could tell you that, many times in this life I've led, touring our country and giving talks in every corner, I feel that, as a speaker, I act within what is most favorable to me in terms of nature, because I understand that, in the midst of the immense weaknesses of my nature, facing large audiences is perhaps one of my strengths. It's clear, then, that by speaking I'm respecting, I suppose, what nature has given me in terms of strength. And society seems to applaud. At that moment, this combination is a showstopper for me, because both stoics and anyone else must recognize that the moment is magical. I don't have to face anything. I just have to do what my body tells me, and then the applause usually comes.

I hope you find the same path, have the same luck, work with what makes your eyes light up - and hope that this is perceived by society as worthy of applause. Then there's no way life won't be cool.

• • • • •

The Stoics were convinced that the universe is wonderful and that we are part of it. If we are in tune, life is good, when we are out of place, life is bad.

So what were sadness and boredom for the Stoics? What would anguish and all these sad passions be? They would be a kind of symptom, an indication that we are living wrong, in the wrong place, playing the wrong game, not making the most of what we have, blaspheming our own nature and out of tune with the cosmic order.

Crates, Zeno's master, had a wife who was a business from another world. Hipparchia. One of the most beautiful women in the history of philosophy. Which doesn't guarantee much, because philosophy isn't overrun with beauties, but it seems that Hipparchia was spectacular. And they liked having sex. They were one of those couples who were in tune with each other, liked each other, knew how to give pleasure, had no qualms when it came to having sex, and enjoyed everything. Hipparchia screamed when she had sex with Crates, she wasn't that little thing, belittled by the neighborhood, coerced by good manners. Hipparchia screamed because Crates knew how to poke in the right place. And when Crates was having sex with Hipparchia, he opened doors, windows and curtains so that the sex could be seen and witnessed by everyone. It was his way of making it clear that he understood that legal sex, intense sex, should be watched because it was a tribute to nature, to the cosmic order, a tribute to the pleasure that nature invites us to have, by giving us the tools it gives us. And those who didn't like it should go back to their resentful insignificance, because Crates and Hipparchia weren't hiding anything.

I wish I could be like Crates, either to be competent and give a woman so much pleasure, or to have the courage to shout out my pleasurable and happy nature with the door open.

• • • • •

One of the biggest problems the Stoics saw in making life good was how we approach the question of death itself.

In 2017, I'll be 52. I think that anyone who is turning fifty - those people who were born in the middle of the 1960s, like me - and doesn't think about dying at least once a day is a complete idiot. I think that, after a certain point in life, the imminence of death makes thinking about it almost obligatory. And since we all want to live - or at least the vast majority of us do - the certainty that we will die is a problem. When you think that you will cease to exist, that agency of matter and soul, that set of ideas, sensations, body and identity that is you is definitively over. This is perhaps the strangest thing that can exist for life to be good. At the beginning of life, it's far away, we have our whole lives ahead of us. But when you're 50, there isn't much left.

The Stoics knew this, they knew that things can get messy if you think about dying and get upset about it. And I'll go further: when you think about dying, it's not just that you cease to exist. What about the people who love you? What about the people you care about? What about those who depend on you, whether affectively, economically or socially? All of this is an obstacle to a good life.

What did the Stoics have to offer to counter this? They believed that it was worth betting on this story of fitting into the cosmos, of seeking excellence in oneself. Do you know why? Because they believed in an infinite and eternal cosmos. If the cosmos is eternal and you are part of it, then you are eternal too. You are a fragment of eternity, a piece of something eternal.

Realize that it's not an individual, singular eternal life, just you. That doesn't work. It's you as part of an eternal whole that becomes eternal to the extent that you participate in that whole. But participation in this eternal whole is strange, because it implies your death. This means that you will cease to be animated matter and will become something else, you will participate in other agencies. For example, when I die, part of me could become fertilizer or fuel, perhaps a bull's horn, and another part could become a doorknob or rain. Why not? In these crazy combinations of matter, I could be out there, spinning. Half torn apart, half reduced to an area, but I'll be out there. The cosmos is eternal, I'm part of it, so I'm eternal too.

8

The transition between Antiquity and the Middle Ages

CALABREZ: I'll start with a chronology so that the reader can situate the ideas in the timeline of our dialog. Both Hesiod's *Theogony* and Homer's *Odyssey* are believed to have been composed around the 8th century BC (between 700-800 BC). Plato lived between the 5th and 4th centuries BC (he was born in 428/427 and died in 348/347 BC). Aristotle lived in the 4th century BC (384-322 BC). All of them produced their main ideas and works in Greece.

The Stoic philosophers lived during the 3rd century BC, when the Stoic school was founded in Athens by Zeno of Scythia (334-262 BC). Other notable Stoics were Seneca (1 BC-65 AD), Epictetus (50-135 AD) and the emperor Marcus Aurelius (121-180 AD). The history of Stoicism therefore runs through both ancient Greece and Rome.

Around the time of Marcus Aurelius' death, Stoic thought began to give way to Christian thought. The last Stoic schools were closed down in the 6th century, in 529, by order of the Roman emperor Justinian I (who ordered the closure of all pagan, i.e. non-Christian, philosophical schools). The decline of Stoicism accompanied the decline of the Greco-Roman polytheistic religions.

The period between the composition of the *Odyssey* and the fall of the Roman Empire (5th century, year 476) is known as Classical Antiquity. The transitional period, which begins with the decline of the Roman Empire from the 3rd century onwards, culminating in its fall, is known as Late Antiquity. The end of Antiquity is marked by the beginning of the Middle Ages, which includes the period between the 5th and 6th centuries and the fall of the Eastern Roman Empire (the fall of Constantinople in 1453).

Ancient philosophy is dominated by worldviews in which the central element is order. The ancient world was largely based on the idea of an ordered cosmos. The reflections and descriptions that ancient thinkers made of reality are of impressive sophistication and beauty. Considering the limited resources they had to observe the universe - essentially, the senses of the body (looking at the sky with the naked eye, for example) and the ability to think and reflect - it is jaw-dropping, to say the least, how far they went, how much they captured the nuances and sensitivities of nature in general and human nature in specific.

Although the ancients spoke of gods and goddesses, mythological beings and the like, their thinking was guided by the search for an order, a reason, a rational logic (λόγος, or *logos* in Greek) behind natural phenomena. Western philosophy proper is considered to have begun with the work of the pre-Socratic thinkers, including Thales of Miletus (624-546 BC), Anaximander (610-546 BC), Pythagoras (570-495 BC), Heraclitus (535-475 BC) and Democritus (460-370 BC), among others.

The famous phrase "all things are full of gods" comes from Thales. The careless eye might see in this statement a vision of spiritual or even religious faith. However, Thales argued that all things had a physical, material principle behind them (ἀρχή, or *arché,* in Greek). He believed that this material substance that made up all things was water. This is an important principle in pre-Socratic philosophy, adopted by several other thinkers. Thales also argued that all matter is endowed with life, in other words, that there is animation in all the matter that makes up the universe - a principle that, as Clovis has shown us, is even held by Aristotle.

Anaximander of Miletus, a disciple of Thales, deserves a mention. He was the first to describe the celestial cosmos mechanically, without any mention of the gods. For Anaximander, the Sun, the Moon and the other planets were fire emanating from the hole in wheels that ran through the heavens. For this reason, he is considered by some historians to be the "father of scientific philosophy".

Everything flows, everything is transformed, nothing remains. This is the central idea of the thought of Heraclitus of Ephesus, "the Obscure One", according to Diogenes Laertius. Things change, and change is an alternation between opposites: hot things cool down, cold things warm up. For him, reality occurred in the harmony derived from this constant alternation - and its physical principle (*arché*) was fire, which always changes and is never the same.

Democritus, for his part, was the first to propose the "atomic theory". According to him, all things are made up of small particles - tiny, invisible stones, the atoms. As their name implies, Democritus' atoms are eternal and indivisible - atom comes from the Greek ἄτομον, or *atomon,* which means indivisible, that which cannot be cut.

Today, curiously, we know that everything is made up of atoms which, despite being divisible (into electrons, protons and neutrons - and the latter two into even smaller particles), are always in motion.

Pre-Socratic ideas, at first glance, can be banal.

Is everything water? Everything is fire? What nonsense!

That's why it's important to situate these ideas in the historical moment in which they emerged.

For its time, pre-Socratic thought was highly sophisticated. For the first time (on record), the Western world sought to understand reality (the world, nature, living beings and everything else) through reason and no longer with strictly religious explanations. This became even more evident with the emergence of Socrates (470/469-399 BC) and his main disciple, the young Aristocles, whom everyone knows by the nickname Plato - from the Greek Πλάτων, or *Plátōn,* meaning "the broad", because Plato had broad shoulders. Socrates and Plato influenced literally all subsequent thinkers. And they continue to do so today.

Ancient philosophy, then, is based on the principle that the search for truth takes place through the use of reason (and not faith). Furthermore, within the main worldviews proposed by the greatest thinkers of antiquity (these worldviews are called "philosophical systems"), the exercise of reason revealed that the universe is ordered and cohesive.

With the decline of Stoic thought and the other classical schools of philosophy, concomitant with the rise of Christianity in the Western world, the principle of using reason to search for truth was progressively replaced by the principle of faith.

In Stoic thought, the cosmic order (*logos*) is represented by the orderly and marvelous composition of all things. Clovis showed us that this harmonious composition is the divine, is god. It is very important to realize that the Stoic god is not a personal god, concerned with human beings and their ills. He is not kind or mean, pious or cruel. He has no intentions, wills or plans for human beings - he has no personality. The Stoic god is absolutely impersonal and, precisely for this reason, indifferent. He is, in fact, the totality of nature, the set of natural things that make up the universe.

This includes a series of impersonal rules, such as natural laws, for example. After all, time is inexorable, and that means we will grow old. Living beings die, and that is equally inexorable. Diseases don't care about us, they just happen. And the cosmos doesn't care whether we think it's good or bad - these things are simply part of how the universe works. Therefore, time, death and illness, for a Stoic, are part of God. God, after all, is nature and the universe in its entirety, with its natural rules and characteristics. This totality is wonderful, precisely because it expresses, for the Stoic, a great order, *logos*, of the universe.

In the Middle Ages, the *logos*, the cosmic order, the harmonious order of the universe, was embodied in a personal, exceptional and divine figure: the Christ of God.

Theory, as Clovis explained, is the contemplation of the divine. For the Stoics, this was done through the use of reason, in order to understand the harmony of the universe. With Christianity, this changed radically. For Christians, theory comes about through faith in the divine word (the word of God, brought to us by Christ). In other words, the harmony of the universe is now embodied in a unique and personal God. The Christian God has a personality, wills, intentions and concerns for human beings. And the path to salvation is faith. To understand the universe is to know and have faith in God's word. The world is seen as the work of God's will.

Christian thought was greatly influenced by ancient thought. The cosmological principles of Antiquity and the Middle Ages were strongly based on two major models for understanding the cosmos: the models of Aristotle and Ptolemy.

Clovis has already explained three major characteristics of the Aristotelian universe: it is finite, harmonious and hierarchical. These characteristics remained alive in the cosmological thinking of the Middle Ages. But harmony and hierarchy are now the work of God and reflect his perfection.

There are other important characteristics, which I'll explain below. Some of these characteristics were improved mathematically by a series of thinkers who lived between Aristotle and the Middle Ages. In particular, the geocentric model of Ptolemy (100-170 AD), a contemporary of the Stoics, which was widely adopted and used centuries after his death.

The first characteristic is the immutability of the celestial universe. For both the Greeks and the Christians, the celestial bodies (the dots of light that appear in the sky at night) were eternal and unchanging. This immutability was a great proof of the wonderful order of the universe, as it indicated its harmonious perfection - after all, the cosmos was perfect and nothing could change it. For Christians, this immutability represented God's perfection.

The second is geocentrism. The idea that the Earth, our planet, was the immovable center of the universe. In other words, the other (eternal and unchanging) stars surrounded the Earth, while it always remained in the same place, as the center of everything. Although there were religious reasons behind the Church's adoption of geocentrism, the main reason was that this cosmological model was widely accepted by scientists at the time.

You see, the cosmos for the thinkers of the Middle Ages - and this includes the vast majority of scientists, including physicists - was finite, harmonious (ordered), hierarchical, with immutable celestial bodies that revolved around an immovable center: the Earth.

9

The Copernican revolution

CALABREZ: Everyone has heard of this story: Nicolaus Copernicus proposed the revolutionary idea that the Earth was not the immovable center of the universe - for him, the center was the Sun (a view known as heliocentrism). Nobody believed him. Then came Galileo Galilei, who adopted Copernicus' model and added an important factor: observations with the telescope - a contraption invented by Galileo himself, which allowed for more precise observation of celestial bodies. With his observations, Galileo would have destroyed the previous cosmology (geocentric) and established an updated cosmology (heliocentric).

This was the story the history teacher told my class back when I was a pre-teen. I don't want to say that it's incorrect. But it is, to say the least, an incomplete way of telling the story of the Copernican revolution. It omits fundamental details about one of the most important moments in human history. After all, revolutions aren't simple anywhere - including in science.

To understand the Copernican revolution, we must first answer a question:

How does science work?

To do this, I'm going to share with you the observations of one of the most influential thinkers of the 20th century, Thomas Kuhn. He was a physicist who, for a series of professional and personal reasons, ended up dedicating a large part of his career to studying the history of science. The book in which he published his studies is called *The Structure of Scientific Revolutions* and is one of the most important works of the last century.

So let's get to know this structure of scientific revolutions.

Most of the time, science works according to what Kuhn calls normal science.

Normal science is scientific research based on one or more past scientific achievements. It is focused on solving problems based on a series of assumptions that are not questioned. These assumptions are the result of the past scientific achievements on which normal science is based.

Because of this, the achievements on which normal science is based always have two characteristics. Firstly, they are scientific models that have had enough unprecedented achievements to attract a large number of supporters, drawing them away from other models. Secondly, they are scientific models that are open enough for various other scientific problems to be solved from that previous model.

Kuhn calls this set of assumptions a paradigm. Paradigms govern firstly *the types of questions that are raised.* Secondly, *how these questions are investigated.* Finally, *how the results are interpreted.* From now on, every time I use the term paradigm, I will be referring to this.

Calm down, reader. I know that this purely technical description is difficult to understand. So let's take an example. Once you've understood the example, you can go back to the technical description - and then you'll understand perfectly what Kuhn meant.

Let's go.

A perfect example of a paradigm is Aristotelian cosmology. It has the two elements I mentioned. Firstly, it was an unprecedented scientific achievement, capable of garnering a veritable legion of followers. Secondly, it is open enough for many other scientific problems to be solved.

Another example is the aforementioned cosmology of Ptolemy. Some historians and physicists even argue that Ptolemy's cosmology is an addition to the Aristotelian paradigm, jointly calling them the Aristotelian-Ptolemaic model.

If the success of a paradigm is measured by how long it has been dominant, the Aristotelian-Ptolemaic paradigm is one of the most successful in history. The champion is Aristotle's biology (which only lost its dominance after Charles Darwin's ideas in the 19th century). It's safe to say that Aristotle was the Western thinker who influenced the world for the longest time in practically every field of knowledge. The dominance of the Aristotelian paradigms (cosmology and biology) lasted more than two thousand years.

Now it's easier to understand the technical description I gave earlier of normal science and the concept of paradigm.

Let's go back to the reasoning.

Most of the time, normal science runs smoothly. However, says Kuhn, every paradigm eventually encounters anomalies. Anomalies are scientific results or observations that do not conform to or cannot be immediately explained by the current paradigm.

Most of the time, such anomalies don't cause major problems, so they can be corrected and overcome within the paradigm itself. For example, an anomaly can be the result of a poorly designed experiment, an incorrectly calibrated instrument or a variable that has not been taken into account. After these corrections, the paradigm remains dominant without major changes.

It just so happens that, on rare occasions, anomalies pose a real problem for the paradigm. In other words, they cannot be explained by the current paradigm. But Kuhn observes that, despite this, what usually happens is that such anomalies are ignored, left aside (with some apparently plausible excuse, such as "we'll investigate in the future") or relegated to another discipline ("that's a question for chemistry and not physics", for example).

I'll make a brief parenthesis here to emphasize how *very human* this scientific attitude is and how much it is aligned with the principle of maintaining cognitive consistency that I mentioned earlier. Imagine a scientist who has built his or her career on a paradigm. Think of that scientist looking in the mirror and admitting to himself: "My years of research will be thrown away now that this anomaly has appeared".

This is a reason for great psychological inconsistency. As I've already made clear, our minds hate inconsistencies.

What to do then?

Now, if that scientist comes to believe that it's not a big problem or that it will be solved later, his mind will remain consistent.

But back to the anomalies.

Anomalies (those that pose a real problem to the paradigm) very rarely start to accumulate. In other words, other scientists, in other laboratories and universities, in other parts of the world, begin to arrive at equally anomalous results.

There comes a time when the anomalies accumulate to a point where they can no longer be ignored: "There's no way, there's something wrong with this story".

Scientists begin to admit and publicly disclose the existence of the anomaly. It is here, according to Kuhn, that normal science enters a crisis.

Crises are typically resolved within the context of normal science. In other words, eventually a scientist or group of scientists finds an answer to the anomaly within the paradigm.

At this point, it is important to emphasize a crucial aspect of science, according to Thomas Kuhn: even if normal science is in crisis, this crisis can last for years or even decades. Crises are not necessarily resolved quickly. Quite the opposite. This is because the scientific community generally prefers to remain affiliated with the paradigm, even an anomalous and weak paradigm, rather than having no paradigm at all. In other words, scientists stick to a "bad" paradigm so as not to be left with no paradigm on which to base their research.

A paradigm shift only occurs when an alternative model is proposed: a more robust model, capable of responding to anomalies and continuing normal science. In other words, a paradigm is only overturned by the emergence of a new paradigm.

As we did before, let's look at an example that will make these ideas more concrete.

We have seen that the Aristotelian-Ptolemaic model was a perfect paradigm. It reconciled the order of the cosmos (*logos*) of antiquity with the perfection of God, which was so important to the thinkers of the Middle Ages. There is only one universe, eternal and unchanging. The center of the universe is the Earth. The planets revolve around the Earth on a celestial plane. The stars reside on another celestial plane, immovable and eternal.

The Italian astronomer Nicolaus Copernicus (1473-1543), while observing the stars, made calculations and became convinced that the geocentric model (the Earth is the center of the universe) was incorrect. His early writings were greatly influenced by other thinkers of the time, who also disagreed with the geocentric model. In other words, contrary to what is often believed, he was not the only one to criticize the model. Copernicus deepened and refined his calculations, which culminated in a very important book called *De Revolutionibus Orbium Coelestium* (*On the Revolution of the Celestial Orbs*).

The book was published immediately after his death and influenced many later thinkers.

Giordano Bruno (1548-1600), an Italian philosopher and mystic, was the first to propose a radical idea: the Sun is just one star among infinite other stars, around which various planets (like the Earth) revolve. These planets, for Bruno, had life and complexity just like the Earth does. In other words, Giordano Bruno's cosmos was infinite, with infinite stars and infinite planets around those stars - planets as alive and real as our own. Although he was not a scientist, Bruno is believed to have been influenced by Copernicus' recently published cosmology. Other thinkers contemporary with Bruno, such as the Englishmen Thomas Digges (1546-1595) and William Gilbert (1544-1603), also proposed the idea of infinite stars.

In the 1600s, Giordano Bruno was burned alive by the Inquisition, with a metal point pierced through his tongue and an apparatus preventing him from moving his jaw. The reasons for his condemnation were not strictly linked to his cosmological views - he had questioned various dogmas of the Catholic Church, including the divinity of Christ. But his idea of the cosmos certainly didn't help his defense.

Copernicus' cosmological model did not present calculations precise enough to suggest considerable anomalies in the Aristotelian-Ptolemaic paradigm. Because of this, it was widely rejected by the thinkers of the time (rightly so, in Thomas Kuhn's view). Any anomalies he pointed out were explained within the paradigm itself.

However, some important thinkers were intrigued by Copernicus' work. One of them was a Danish nobleman who was also an astronomer: Tycho Brahe (1546-1601). He made two very important observations that raised anomalies in the dominant paradigm.

Firstly, in 1572, Brahe observed the appearance of a new star in the constellation Cassiopeia, which shone in the sky for eighteen months without changing position. The region of the stars, in the Aristotelian-Ptolemaic model, was immovable, eternal and unchanging. The appearance of a new star was a great anomaly. Today we know that what Brahe saw was a supernova, i.e. a stellar explosion that occurs at the end of a star's life. The remaining effects of this supernova are still being studied today.

Secondly, in 1577 he observed a comet crossing the sky. Based on his calculations, he concluded that the comet had crossed the celestial region of the planets. This region, according to the Aristotelian paradigm, only had circular movements in solid spheres. It was therefore impossible for a comet to pass through it. Brahe concluded that such spheres did not exist, raising serious questions about the Aristotelian model and opening up the question of the orbit of the planets for further research.

During the remainder of his life, Tycho Brahe made enormous contributions to astronomy, making much more precise calculations of celestial movements compared to previous calculations. However, his cosmological model retained the idea of geocentrism. This is a good example of an attempt to resolve anomalies within the paradigm itself.

At the same time, another scientist began to question the Aristotelian-Ptolemaic paradigm: the German Johannes Kepler (1571-1630), who had worked as Tycho Brahe's assistant. After Brahe's death, Kepler used the Dane's observations to make great advances in astronomy. In addition, he was the first astronomer since Copernicus' death to openly adopt his cosmological model - in other words, Kepler defended heliocentrism. But he went further, being the first to propose that the movement of the planets around the Sun is not circular, but elliptical. Although today we know that Kepler was correct, he was unable to carry out the calculations that would properly explain the physics behind the idea.

It was Isaac Newton who demonstrated, decades later, that the laws governing the movement of the stars were in fact close to Kepler's model. These and many other advances in astronomy make Kepler one of the greatest names of the Copernican revolution - and of the entire history of thought. A curiosity: Kepler was the first to use the term "satellite", which is so familiar to all of us today.

Then, once again in Italy, a guy called Galileo Galilei (1564-1642) came on the scene. A brilliant guy, he is considered the father of modern observational astronomy. Some say he invented the telescope. Others say he merely perfected it. The fact is that Galileo's telescope allowed a magnification of 30 times. Nowadays, any telescope you buy online can do more. In Galileo's day, however, this was far superior to any other piece of equipment (call it a telescope or not). With this equipment, he was able to make some critical observations for the crisis of the Aristotelian-Ptolemaic paradigm.

Galileo observed that the Moon had an imperfect surface. In addition, he verified the existence of sunspots. These observations contradicted the idea of eternal and perfect celestial bodies. He also observed that Jupiter was surrounded by moons that orbited around it. This contradicted the idea that all celestial bodies revolve around the Earth. Finally, he observed different phases on Venus, which indicated that its movement was different from that proposed by the Aristotelian-Ptolemaic model.

Anomalies were accumulating, and more and more scientists were realizing the major problems with the orderly and perfect cosmos of Aristotle and Ptolemy. However, the paradigm shift only occurred with the work of the great British scientist Isaac Newton (1643-1727), who unified Kepler and Galileo's model under a revolutionary physical theory capable of explaining celestial movements with mathematical precision according to a heliocentric model, in which the planets revolve around the Sun in an elliptical shape.

I'd like to give you an example of his genius.

Some historians point out that, at the age of 24, Newton saw an apple fall from an apple tree. This led him to ask a question:

If an apple falls, does the moon fall too?

At first glance, it seems like a silly and innocent question. Almost something a child would ask. We adults have a habit of ignoring questions asked by children, believing them to be naive and inconsequential. A child's gaze, however, often reveals profound questions. Don't forget, reader, that Newton was one of humanity's greatest geniuses. His question is brilliant. It carries many of the questions needed to overthrow Aristotelian-Ptolemaic cosmology.

The answer, for him, was "yes". He knew that the acceleration of an object increases progressively as it falls... However, there was no mathematical process for knowing the object's position and velocity at any moment in time.

What did he do?

He invented the calculation.

You know that subject that a lot of people fail at university? The guy invented it to answer the question about the Moon. Some say the apple story is a legend. I don't doubt it. But I also don't doubt that Newton's inspiration came from everyday observations. Science often works that way.

Obviously Newton didn't invent calculus and solve the problem of celestial movements overnight. The summary of his ideas in this regard was published when he was 40 years old in the famous book *Philosophiæ Naturalis Principia Mathematica* (*Mathematical Principles of Natural Philosophy*).

I'd like to stress to the reader that Isaac Newton was a genius. This guy's contribution to understanding the cosmos was one of the greatest contributions a single human being has ever made to the knowledge of humanity. Newtonian mechanics is the basis of all classical physics, which is still studied in schools today. Today it is possible to send a space probe to a moon of Jupiter using the laws developed by Newton. Without him, we wouldn't have reached the Moon or built the International Space Station. Without him, there would be no Einstein and his relativity. Without him, there would be no quantum theory, so important today.

But Newton himself was humble enough to admit: "If I have seen further, it is by standing on the shoulders of giants". Science is a progressive construction, in which new paradigms emerge from the accumulation of anomalies found in previous paradigms. Without Aristotle, there would be no Newton. Without Plato, there would be no Aristotle... I, in particular, am very grateful to all these giants.

In physics after Newton, there were new paradigm shifts. Einstein's relativity is one example. Today, quantum theory is already capable of surpassing the Einsteinian paradigm on a number of issues - and many believe it will be able to surpass it completely in the future.

10

The (un)ordered cosmos: Renaissance, Modernity and Humanism

CALABREZ: The Copernican revolution brought about a radical change in man's view of the cosmos. The order (*logos*) of the ancients, interpreted by the thinkers of the Middle Ages as the perfection and divinity of God, is no longer observed in the universe. There is no *a priori* perfection, that is, a notion of cosmic order that precedes all existing things and on which all things (including physics) must be based and, on an ethical level, conform. The ordered cosmos has collapsed. There is no longer its harmony to inspire us, there is no longer its hierarchy - natural or divine - to which we must adapt.

I don't want to be reductionist here: there were a series of economic, social and cultural changes during the period of the Copernican revolution that certainly contributed greatly to this collapse. The revolution was one of several elements that made up the period that began in the 14th century and culminated at the end of the 17th century with what we call

Modernity. This period of transition, this historical bridge between the Middle Ages and Modernity, is known as the Renaissance.

"Rebirth of what? What was reborn?" the reader might ask.

The answer is well known: the revival of classical values that were widely present in antiquity. In particular, the progressive return of rationality as the guiding element of human life - instead of faith, which was so present and fundamental during the Middle Ages.

However, the ancients saw in the cosmos a harmony (*logos*) to be understood and in which we should draw inspiration in order to live optimally. The collapse of the cosmic order makes this impossible. Try to imagine, reader, living in a world where there is no longer a great philosophical, scientific or spiritual system on which to base your life. Where what we have believed in for millennia has collapsed. Where the universe is no longer finite, perfect, harmonious and hierarchical. The new paradigm makes it clear that the universe is imperfect, chaotic, non-hierarchical, governed by natural forces (such as gravity) and perhaps infinite (as proposed by Newton).

If order is not given *a priori*, if harmony is not an intrinsic characteristic of the universe, how can we contemplate the divine? How to build a theory? After all, the very notion of "contemplating" the divine carried within it the idea of the harmony and perfection of the cosmos. To contemplate it was to understand its order. It was, in a somewhat passive and submissive way, to conform to its perfection. However, when contemplating it now, there is no order - on the contrary, there is chaos.

A need arises. If there is no harmony and coherence, if there is no order in the universe, in order to understand the world and find the best way to live in the world, we cannot be passive. We can't just contemplate and adapt. We must doubt everything that has come before in order to build, with our own hands, an understanding of reality (theory) and knowledge about how to live and coexist in that reality (ethics).

A great movement began that placed responsibility for building a new worldview in the hands of human beings. This means that the Renaissance movement is above all a humanist movement. The collapse of the ordered cosmos brings human beings to the center stage of the universe. There will only be order through work, through active elaboration, through the construction of a better worldview and laws that adapt the world to an order built by us. Natural laws (in the sciences) and social laws (in the city) derived from human effort and not from passive contemplation of the cosmos.

This movement culminated with the Enlightenment in the 18th century - the century of enlightenment, in which human rationality reached a high point. Science progressively adopted the "experimental method" as the main approach to solving problems. The experimental method is still the main driving force behind scientific advances today. It consists of manipulating variables, testing them under different conditions in order to isolate the cause of a specific phenomenon. It is therefore not simply a matter of contemplating reality.

Science now actively manipulates the things of the world, extracting from them the laws that will aid the progress of knowledge and, therefore, the control that humanity exercises over nature.

As Clovis explained, Aristotelian cosmology was teleological, in other words, it was based on the study of ends, the final causes of things. Now, cosmology and all the other sciences are moving towards a perspective of "cause" that is closer to what is colloquially understood as "cause" today. Cause, for us, is the set of circumstances that lead to a certain effect. In this sense, science (and thought in general) becomes more causal - and less finalist.

This brings many changes, including social and economic ones. Aristocratic perspectives, in which a human being was born where they were born because that was their purpose in the cosmos or because that was God's will, no longer make sense. Aristocracy gives way to meritocracy. We are equal, because there are no predefined positions in a harmonious and perfect cosmos. What we are is the result of our free choice.

Slavery began to make no sense. It was in this context that the French Revolution took place between 1789 and 1799, culminating in the publication of the Declaration of the Rights of Man and of the Citizen, popularly known as the Declaration of Human Rights. It was in this context that what we now call the capitalist economic system developed. Again, there were a number of economic and social factors behind this. But there was also the crumbling of worldviews that had reigned absolute for millennia.

The Enlightenment marks a vision that elevates human beings to a level above other animals. Unlike the rationality of other animals, human rationality allows society to "evolve". In the Enlightenment view, a society of human beings today is much more complex than it was thousands of years ago. In other words, human beings are capable of perfecting (improving) themselves over time, of evolving as a society. By comparison, a society of bees or termites is essentially the same as it was thousands of years ago. These observations are central to the work of the Enlightenment philosopher Jean-Jacques Rousseau (1712-1778). The ability to perfect oneself over time is what he called "perfectibility".

The central message of the Enlightenment is human freedom. We are free. We are not determined by a cosmos, be it natural or divine. Our freedom should not be used to try to conform to a cosmic perfection, because there is no such perfection.

Moreover, we are not determined by an animality, by a bestiality, by a *nature* - as other animals are. As the philosopher Jean-Paul Sartre (1905-1980), a 20th century humanist, said, almost replicating Rousseau's words: "Existence precedes essence". In other words, the human essence is not the result of an animalistic nature that we are born with. That's something other animals have. Human beings, on the other hand, are free. This freedom means that everything we are (our essence) is the result of our choices. First we exist (by choosing freely). What we are (essence) comes later, as a consequence.

This idea was already found in the "blank slate" of the philosopher John Locke (1632-1704). For him and many other thinkers of the time, human beings are born as blank slates. There are no mental contents pre-inscribed in our nature. There is no innate psychology. It is our free choices that will fill this sheet of paper. Our minds, ideas and knowledge are the fruit of perception and experience. It is experience that will build our essence. And human experience is, by definition, free.

11

The deconstruction of Humanism

CALABREZ: It's not surprising, then, that a revolution occurred in the transition between the 19th and 20th centuries with the work of three great thinkers, each in a different field of activity. Friedrich Nietzsche in philosophy. Charles Darwin in the natural sciences. And Sigmund Freud in the sciences of the mind.

Remember the Enlightenment vision. For it, the great cause of what human beings are, and also the cause of what they do, is their freedom and the proper exercise of the faculties of reason. The ideals of humanism, rationality and freedom govern the Enlightenment vision. As such, human beings are different from all other animals - and their superiority is possible precisely because of these great ideals.

The thinkers I mentioned above will deconstruct these ideas, each in their own way.

Nietzsche (1844-1900), a German philosopher, challenged the idea that human rationality was the liberating thing that thinkers before him claimed. For him, we have replaced the old idols (the cosmos, the *logos*, God and religious authority) with new idols.

But which new idols?

Precisely the ideals of freedom, rationality, science, humanism, etc. The problem, for Nietzsche, lies in the *idealization of* these visions. By idealizing worldviews, we create transcendental values - values considered superior to everything else. His philosophy will try to deconstruct this idealization. The proposal is that by placing ideals above everything, by placing certain values on a transcendental level, we are placing them above life. As such, we continue to "believe" in new idols. Idols that are higher than the only thing that really exists: life.

A contemporary of Nietzsche, the English naturalist Charles Darwin (1809-1882) proposed an idea. A "dangerous idea", in the words of American philosopher Daniel Dennett. Darwin's idea, like the ideas of the other thinkers I'm quoting here, had a huge number of ramifications and a gigantic impact on all subsequent thought. His idea is the perfect example of a new paradigm, as I defined it earlier. Today's advances in the field of genetics are possible because of Darwin's initial idea that all living beings derive from the same common ancestor and have changed through a continuous process that he called "natural selection".

Freud (1856-1939), an Austrian neurologist, proposed a radical idea - going against a whole tradition of thinkers who claimed that human thought is conscious, free and rational.

And what is that idea?

It's one of the most popular: the idea that the vast majority of our psychological processes are actually unconscious. In other words, we are unaware of most of the things that motivate our thoughts, affections and behaviors.

All these theoretical models are revolutionary, each in its own field. But they all have one thing in common: they deconstruct the idea that human beings are special, free masters of their destiny. We are not fallen angels, but primates who have risen and now walk upright. We are not fully aware of what motivates us and the causes that surround us. We are much more animalistic, much more determined, much less free, much less of *a blank slate* than the Enlightenment thinkers would have liked.

12

Stoic philosophy vs. contemporary philosophy

CLÓVIS: The Stoics understood philosophy as a great concern of the intellect, the aim of which is to enable anyone to live better. The distance from today's philosophy is enormous.

Philosophy today is a set of texts, a set of ideas and writings, books and treatises, courses, and all this materializes in discourse, discourse that generates more discourse, that confronts discourse in the form of debate, and the truth is that anyone interested in philosophy today is confined to thinking about a few ideas and showing them through words.

For the Stoics, philosophy was all about practice. Intelligence was at the service of a happier, less frightened, less distressed life of flesh and blood. And one of the things they thought was too disruptive in our lives was giving a damn about other people and what they think of us. It's impressive how the Stoics tried to prepare us against the comments about us, against the gossip we're always subjected to, and to train us, they would provoke these situations and, by facing them, they would lose their fear and become resistant.

The big question is: if classical philosophy was so concerned with life in the flesh, what happened to turn philosophy into this compendium of texts, treatises and ideas that have little or nothing to do with our daily lives? Here's a great observation: between the Stoics and us, we went through centuries and centuries of thought dominated by disciples who claimed the discussion about life for themselves, for theology, for the teachings of God and the prophets. For these disciples took reflection out of philosophy. Whether that's good or bad, don't ask me. But philosophy lost this prerogative and was limited to a conceptual discussion, far from happiness, far from the good life, far from salvation - far, therefore, from all the concerns that were once strictly philosophical.

13

Poetic naturalism

CALABREZ: Before I go any further, I'd like to make a comment. Since I started talking about the transition between Antiquity and the Middle Ages, I've done a lot of summarizing here. I have intentionally omitted a number of key points in this whole historical process. I've simplified the thinking of complex authors. I've left out many fundamental thinkers. I've skipped over important ideas to get here.

An attentive reader might say: "You talked about the Enlightenment without mentioning Kant! That's almost heresy!".

I tend to agree, but I'll explain: this dialog is not a perfect historical record of human thought over the centuries. My aim is didactic, in other words, to lead the reader to understand a certain "thread", a certain logic in the progression of ancient thought to what we understand today as the cosmos.

In the recommendations for further reading at the end of the book, we provide many avenues for those who wish to delve deeper.

To the more experienced readers, already familiar with the history of thought, I ask you to understand this choice. For reasons of time and space, I've had to restrict myself to what I believe to be the most fundamental aspects of this complex - and fantastic - story. All so that we could finally get here.

And where is "here"?

This is today. The contemporary world. I want to share with you, the reader, a contemporary cosmological vision. It's not the only one, of course. But it's one that, in my opinion, elegantly brings together the moment in which we find ourselves today.

• • • • •

There are those who, on reading how ancient thinkers saw gods in things, might say: "What a bunch of idiots! Calling the sun a god! We know that the sun is a star. We know its physical and chemical characteristics. What nonsense!".

The same can be said for the fervor with which the thinkers of the Middle Ages clung to geocentric astronomical models, and so on...

I would then like to make it clear that there is no such thing as "knowledge" in nature.

See what I mean: there is no such thing in the universe as "knowledge", which has its own substance or is made up of substances that have a place on the periodic table. Knowledge has no matter, no energy, no physical reality. Knowledge is not somewhere in the universe waiting for human beings to capture, imprison and understand it. Knowledge is a construction. Knowledge is a human production. It is not an *a priori* fact of the world.

Protons, neutrons and electrons, *quarks* and the Higgs field, for example, are all examples of *a priori* data about the world, the foundations of nature (according to what we know today). Knowledge is the way we describe this data and integrate it into one or more visions of how the world works.

Like all human production, knowledge will be strongly influenced by everything that is genuinely human. Greed, fear, envy, laziness, anger and so many other things.

One example: there is no shortage of cases of fraud in the history of thought. Scientists - sometimes renowned - have been caught falsifying data to make the results fit their hypotheses. Another example: reluctance to abandon a paradigm is common in the history of science. As we have seen, careers are built on certain paradigms - and overthrowing them almost always means overthrowing (or, at the very least, setting back) the careers built on them. We must always remember that these careers are lives. People who want prestige, who have shame and who need to feed their families. Human beings.

This obviously doesn't justify any behavior. We should strongly repudiate the scientist who cheats, we should strongly criticize the scientist who clings to outdated paradigms. However, situating the production of knowledge as a human enterprise allows us to better understand why these things happen.

They happen because they are human things.

Despite all this, despite the imperfection and fallibility inherent in every human endeavor, we must remember something fundamental. The thinkers of Antiquity, the Middle

Ages, the Renaissance and Modernity, the contemporary thinkers (some call them post-modern), all of them, even with all these human limitations, were guided by one great intention: to explain how things work.

To this day, this is the great intention that guides us. Me in psychology and neurosciences. Clóvis in philosophy. Both of us in the classroom, as teachers.

Notice the term I used: explain. It means that human thought will always *talk about things*. Create discourses. Create ways of talking about things in the world in order to explain them.

There are many ways of talking about things. They always have been, and some say they always will be. But they are governed, at least in the history of rational thought, by a few major rules. Without them, we wouldn't have gotten this far. Without these rules, we wouldn't be able to replace the old ways with "better" ways of explaining things (in other words, ways that explain the world in a way that is more coherent with how it actually works).

The first rule is the notion that not all ways of talking about the world are the same. There are better ways and there are worse ways.

But what makes them better or worse?

The best ways are useful - and that means they are consistent with each other and with the world.

On the other hand, the worst ways are not useful. In scientific jargon, we say that they are "wrong" or "false".

This means that they are not consistent with the better ways and are not consistent with the world.

The second rule is the idea that our purposes *at the moment of explanation* determine the best way to talk about the world.

Let's delve deeper into this, as it may seem strange at first glance. As we've been doing all along, we'll use an example.

The example will be the same as the one I used before: the Copernican revolution.

Before the revolution, there was one way of talking about the world. This way of talking about the world was the Aristotelian-Ptolemaic model. In that world (i.e. at that *moment of explanation*), all the ways of knowing the world (astronomical observation, mathematical calculations, etc.) were relatively coherent with each other and were coherent with what was observed in the world. They were therefore the best way of explaining that world.

With the revolution came a new way of talking about the world. There were technological advances in telescopes and the development of more precise mathematical calculations, which culminated in Newtonian mechanics. As a result, the previous way of talking about the world was no longer coherent - neither with this new model, nor with the world now observed. The Aristotelian-Ptolemaic model became an unhelpful model or, in other words, a wrong model, a false model. The new Newtonian model proved to be coherent with all the other models, which in turn were coherent with the observations of the world at that time.

Centuries later, Albert Einstein's model emerged. He introduces new ways of talking about the world. These ways are coherent with each other and coherent with the world at that time. Precisely because of this, they became a better way of talking about the world. The same thing has been happening with quantum theory more recently.

We see the same movements in biology.

Aristotelian biology, the dominant paradigm in the natural sciences for two millennia, was the best way to explain the different forms of life on Earth. When Darwin and the ideas of common ancestry and natural selection emerged, as well as the first genetic theories (beginning with Gregor Mendel), Aristotelian biology became an unhelpful way of explaining the biological world, giving way to evolutionary biology (which remains to this day, with the necessary improvements and extensions, one of the most relevant paradigms within the biological sciences).

However, you see, these two good ways of talking about the world - quantum theory and evolutionary biology - are fundamentally different.

If I ask a physicist what a brain is, he may well reply: "Nothing more than a collection of elementary particles that obey the natural and immutable laws of physics".

Is he wrong? Of course not.

But in this context, at this *point in the explanation,* this is not the best way to talk about the world. Here it's more useful (more coherent) to talk:

The brain is an organ that functions as the center of the nervous system in all vertebrate animals (and many invertebrates), operating as a biocomputational machine that has evolved according to the process of natural selection, being selected so that organisms respond in biologically more advantageous ways (ensuring a greater chance of survival and procreation) to the challenges imposed by nature.

It can thus be seen that evolutionary biology is more coherent with our objective at this point in the explanation.

We can say that this is a *poetic* perspective on understanding the world, because it allows for multiple ways of talking about it. Ways that will be more or less useful depending on the context, the moment of explanation.

• • • • •

What's more, with the progressive scientific advances from modern times to the present day, evidence is accumulating of what is known as "naturalism".

This is not a new vision. It begins in philosophy. In a way, some pre-Socratic thinkers can be considered the first naturalists in the West. Aristotle shows strong characteristics of naturalism in his thoughts. Stoicism is perhaps the philosophical school of antiquity that comes closest to naturalism as we understand it today. Many argue that, after the Middle Ages, in the 17th century, the thought of the great philosopher Baruch Spinoza is an example of naturalism. In post-modern philosophy, Nietzsche can be considered a naturalist.

But what does "naturalism" mean today?

Naturalism essentially means three things.

Firstly, that we are only capable of understanding one world: the natural world. Secondly, that the world evolves according to unbreakable patterns: the laws of nature. Thirdly, that the only reliable way to learn about how the world works is to observe how it works. This observation of the world, however, is not merely passive - it often requires extremely active stances, such as the construction of intricate experiments to demonstrate the existence of elementary particles, for example.

Many great scientists adopt a naturalistic approach to understanding the world. The ideas of Albert Einstein, Carl Sagan, Lawrence Krauss, Leonard Mlodinow, Michio Kaku, Neil deGrasse Tyson and Stephen Hawking are, among many others, examples of naturalistic perspectives.

I strongly recommend that readers seek out texts, videos and books by these great thinkers. With the exception of Einstein, whose work is extremely difficult to understand, all the others are able to explain some of the most fantastic, unbelievable and surprising discoveries of contemporary cosmology in a way that is not so complex - but extremely elegant and profound.

I also recommend watching the TV series *Cosmos*. There is an old version, presented by one of the most charismatic figures in the history of science, astrophysicist and cosmologist Carl Sagan, and an updated version, equally excellent, presented by the famous Neil deGrasse Tyson, also an astrophysicist and cosmologist.

This perspective of understanding the world (naturalism), therefore, combined with the aforementioned poetic perspective of the many possible ways of talking about the world, makes up a philosophical stance called "poetic naturalism".

The term poetic naturalism was proposed by American physicist and cosmologist Sean Carroll. The ideas I'm going to describe here can be found in greater detail and depth in his book *The Big Picture*, released in 2016 and unfortunately not yet translated into Portuguese.

Some readers may be thinking that poetic naturalism is a necessarily atheistic vision, i.e. one that totally excludes the possibility of God or gods.

It's not true.

Although there are many atheist naturalists, there are those who don't believe in supernatural interference in our universe (in other words, the universe is strictly governed by natural laws), but who believe in the existence of a superior force behind the absurd and marvelous complexity that governs the cosmos. This is known as deism.

There are those, moreover, who can find no other explanation for such complexity than a creator God. At first glance, naturalistic views and faith in God seem mutually exclusive. However, there are examples, both in science and outside of it, of individuals who have integrated both into their lives. Galileo Galilei and Isaac Newton are two thinkers who did this.

14

Laplace's demon

CALABREZ: Poetic naturalism has important implications for how we see the world. After all, if the natural world is governed by unbreakable rules (the laws of nature), this means that by knowing all the natural laws, we will be able to know the cosmos completely.

The French mathematician and physicist Pierre-Simon, Marquis de Laplace (1749-1827), proposed a mental experiment that takes this idea to the extreme. According to Laplace, if there were an intelligence, an intellect vast enough, capable of understanding all the natural laws and also knowing all the variables that determine the state of the universe at the present moment, this intellect would be fully capable of accurately predicting the future states of that universe.

Laplace's contemporaries found the name "vast intellect" too dull and preferred to call it a demon - Laplace's demon.

I know it can be difficult to grasp the idea, so I'll use a more tangible example. Laplace's demon could be understood as a supercomputer. Imagine a computer capable of solving all existing equations. You enter a piece of information (the complete mathematical state of the universe at this instant). The computer makes a calculation (based on the laws of physics). A result is generated (the state of the universe at the next moment, i.e. in the future).

If you've seen the movie The Ma*trix*, you'll remember that the world inside the Matrix was determined by pre-programmed mathematical rules. In the second movie of the trilogy, the protagonist Neo meets the Architect. He is the creator of the Matrix and knows all its operating rules, all the variables that determine its present state. As a result, he is able to make exact predictions about everything that will happen in the future of the Matrix. The Architect is a modern version of Laplace's demon. If you haven't seen the *Matrix* trilogy, I recommend you do - it's excellent and raises intriguing philosophical questions. The dialog between Neo and the Architect is very interesting.

I want to make one thing clear: nobody in their right mind, not even the most famous physicist, not even Stephen Hawking, claims that we know all the natural laws - and even less that we know all the variables that determine the present state of the universe. There are many things we don't know. There are questions that *we know that we don't know*. There are probably many more questions that *we don't even know we don't know*.

Thus, Laplace's demon is a mental experiment, i.e. logical reasoning about an experiment that is impossible to carry out in practice, but with consequences that can be explored through the imagination (with the help of the scientific tools we have).

Laplace's demon teaches us a great lesson, widely accepted by contemporary cosmologists, because it is perfectly aligned with the mathematical models that explain the world at the level of the fundamental laws of physics.

Here's the lesson: the universe is determined by natural laws and, if we know these laws, we will know what determines the states of the universe. By knowing the variables that determine a present state, we will know both what its previous (preceding) state was and what its subsequent (proceeding) state will be.

This is a perspective known as "determinism", which usually accompanies naturalistic views. Spinoza's philosophy, for example, is both naturalistic and deterministic.

Determinism simply means that the present state of a system is determined by its previous state. Knowing the present state, therefore, allows us to know both the preceding (previous) state and the proceeding (subsequent) state. Contemporary cosmology generally considers that the cosmos works in a deterministic way.

At this point, many may think two things.

First: determinism means that there is no free will. We'll talk about freedom in the third part of the book.

Secondly: does determinism seek to identify causes and effects in the universe? The answer is yes and no.

The idea of cause and effect, so important to science (Aristotelian and post-Aristotelian) doesn't make much sense today - at least not on a fundamental physical level, i.e. on the level of the fundamental natural laws that govern the universe on a microscopic level.

"What do you mean the idea of cause and effect doesn't make sense anymore? Everything has a cause!"

I know this is a rather difficult idea to swallow. I'll try to explain it as didactically as possible. And if you think it's too complicated so far, get ready: it gets a lot worse.

15

The direction of time

CALABREZ: First of all, let's define "direction". When we say that time has a direction, we mean this: *time always moves forward, never backwards.*

With this, we are saying two things.

Firstly, that the past is different from the future. Direction, in this case, implies a difference between two points (past and future), based on a reference (the present).

Secondly, that this difference is asymmetrical and irreversible. In other words, nothing in the future can change the past, because it is the past that determines the future. The past has a greater influence on the future than the future has on the past.

Let's apply the concept of direction (difference, irreversibility and asymmetry) to space.

Imagine that you are an astronaut floating in the vacuum of space, far away from any planet, star or other celestial body. In this place there is no direction. In other words, there is no "above", "below", "behind" or "in front". It's easy to accept this idea. There is only direction in space if there is a reference point. "Above *what*?" As there is no reference point in the vacuum of distant space, there is no pre-fixed direction of space. To put it more bluntly: floating in space, any direction you point to will have equal content. All positions are symmetrical. You won't be able to say "up there, down here".

It's obvious that this doesn't happen when we think about time. Everyone with a healthy brain agrees on which direction of time is "yesterday" and which direction is "tomorrow". A great example is memory. We remember what happened yesterday, but we don't remember what will happen tomorrow. The future can be predicted (as meteorologists do), but it cannot be remembered. Moving from the present to the past is a totally different movement from moving from the present to the future.

Now comes the hairy part of the story.

On a microscopic level of the fundamental laws of physics (such as Newton's laws, Einstein's laws and quantum field theory), *time has no direction*. In other words, according to these laws, there is no difference, no asymmetry and no irreversibility between past and future. The laws of physics treat the directionality of the present to the past in exactly the same way as they treat that of the present to the future.

Let's understand this story.

Imagine two simple systems, which you probably studied in physics class at school: the movement of a pendulum and the movement of the Earth around the Sun.

Both systems are governed by physical laws. Although invisible, these laws are capable of perfectly predicting the movement of the pendulum and the translation of the Earth. If I record a movie of these movements and show it to you, I guarantee that you won't be able to tell whether the movie is being played backwards or forwards. The directionality of time doesn't matter for the laws governing these movements!

"But Pedro, of course there is a directionality. The pendulum and the Earth have a directionality. Just because I couldn't discern it while watching the movie doesn't mean it doesn't exist. It just means that I couldn't identify it!"

If you thought that, don't worry. It was the same thing I thought when I came across this idea. But physics has an answer for that too.

If we look at the equations governing the movements of the pendulum and the Earth, we can see that they are *reversible*. If we reverse the speed of the Earth in the equation, it will move *exactly* backwards *and symmetrically* in relation to the opposite movement. There is no asymmetry, no difference, no irreversibility between forward and backward, past and future, in these equations. And this doesn't just happen in these equations, but in all equations in physics - with just one exception.

Summary of the opera: at the fundamental level of the invisible physical laws that govern the microscopic universe, *time has no direction*. As I said, there is only one exception, which we'll study next.

16

The cosmos tends towards disorder

CALABREZ: Now we need to reconcile this radical idea with what we observe in our experience of the world. If, on the microscopic level of the fundamental laws of physics, time has no direction, how can we explain the fact that, on the macroscopic level of the observable world in which we live, time obviously has a direction (difference, asymmetry and irreversibility between past and future)?

As I said, the directionality of time does not exist in the laws of physics. With just one exception: the second law of thermodynamics.

This law observes that, in an isolated system, the total entropy of the system will always remain the same or increase over time. However, there are no perfectly isolated systems in nature - all natural systems interact to a greater or lesser degree.

The only isolated system would be the universe itself - if we consider that our universe doesn't interact with other universes, which many physicists say it does. I'm not going to get into that, otherwise it'll get too complicated. Let's accept, for the sake of reflection, that our universe is an isolated system.

Therefore, the second law of thermodynamics can be described as follows: the total entropy of the universe will always remain the same or increase over time.

"I don't understand anything! What the hell is entropy?"

Entropy is synonymous with disorder.*

"But what is disorder?"

Let's take an example.

When we look at the macroscopic characteristics of a system, we know that they are not a perfect representation of the microscopic characteristics. Many different microscopic arrangements between atoms can result in the same phenomenon observed macroscopically.

To understand this, imagine a cup of coffee. At the microscopic level, there are several possible arrangements between the atoms that make up the coffee molecules. Many of these arrangements will result in the same thing when we observe the macroscopic world: a cup of coffee. However, they are fundamentally different arrangements at the microscopic level.

In other words, *the same macroscopic observation can be the result of many different microscopic arrangements between atoms and molecules.*

* Note by Pedro Calabrez: some researchers criticize the use of "entropy" as a synonym for "disorder". An alternative would be "uncertainty" - which is also criticized. I opted for the original term used by Ludwig Bolztmann, who proposed the second law of thermodynamics. "Disorder" is also the term used by Sean Carroll, author of the cosmological vision presented here.

So what is entropy (disorder)? It's the number of microscopic arrangements that result in the same macroscopic observation. Actually, it's the logarithm of that number, but that doesn't matter for our purposes.

Well, we say that a system is not very entropic (not very disordered) when we notice that its macroscopic observation has a small number of possible microscopic arrangements between atoms. Conversely, a system is very entropic when we notice that its macroscopic observation has a large number of possible microscopic arrangements between atoms.

Let's go back to the second law of thermodynamics: the total entropy of the universe will always remain the same or increase over time. Now you understand what this means: in our universe, the number of possible microscopic arrangements that generate the same macroscopic phenomena tends to increase.

One observation: it is possible to reduce the entropy of a system within the universe. A perfect example of this is when we cool the temperature inside the fridge. But the natural consequence is an increase in the general entropy of the universe - in the case of the fridge, heat will be produced at the back, which is highly entropic.

I know this idea may seem abstract and useless. But it is grand, extremely important and has radical implications for how we understand the cosmos today.

Let's look at the implications.

FIRST IMPLICATION: the cosmos is doomed to "chaos".

Chaos here is synonymous with "great disorder", which in turn is synonymous with "great entropy".

If the entropy in our universe never decreases, but only stays the same or increases, this means that the universe will, at some point in the future, reach the maximum state of entropy. When the universe reaches this maximum level of entropy, it will enter a state that physicists call equilibrium. In the state of equilibrium, there is no further increase in entropy. Remember: there is only directionality of time in the second law of thermodynamics. In other words, there is only directionality of time when there is an increase in entropy. Because of this, when the universe reaches its maximum state of entropy (equilibrium), *time will no longer have any direction*.

Today, scientific data suggests that this is precisely the path the universe is taking. Obeying the second law of thermodynamics, the universe is expanding and diluting in space. Eventually, many billions of years from now, all the stars will die. Some will become black holes, and all the black holes (as Stephen Hawking proposed) will evaporate. What will be left of the cosmos will be a great void on all sides.* There will be no more increase in entropy. There will be no things. There will be no time. There will be no consciousness.

SECOND IMPLICATION: the cosmos derives from a moment of very low entropy.

* Note from Pedro Calabrez: I'm not considering the multiverse theory here. However, it is important to point out that, although our universe tends towards emptiness, there is the possibility of new universes emerging from it.

If in the state of maximum entropy (equilibrium) there is no direction of time, this means that we live in a universe with relatively low entropy.

"Regarding" what?

To a previous state, in which entropy was even lower. And before that, entropy was even lower...

We can continue this regression until we reach an initial moment, around 13.7 billion years ago, when the universe existed in a state of very low entropy. That moment is the Big Bang. A moment of great order (low entropy), but also of great instability.

THIRD IMPLICATION: this is what makes it possible for the universe, as we know and experience it today, to exist.

It is thanks to this characteristic of the universe (the progressive increase in entropy) that the phenomenon we call "time" exists, as we perceive it in everyday life. In other words, it is thanks to it that time has a direction.

Returning to the previous analogy: here on the surface of the planet, we can perfectly identify the asymmetry between the spatial directions "above" and "below". This is possible because we live close to an object of great influence: the Earth.

Similarly, we only know the differences in the direction of the past and the future because we are close to an event of great influence: the Big Bang.

As we have seen, an astronaut in a vacuum will no longer have any notion of spatial direction. All directions have the same content, they are all symmetrical. Following the same analogy, a state of equilibrium does not allow a notion of the direction of time. Past and future do not exist in a universe without an increase in entropy.

Therefore, every irreversible physical change that depends on the direction of time, such as the evolution of the universe, the formation of galaxies and systems, the emergence of life, brains, the fact that we can't "unscramble" a broken egg? In short, everything we call the world or reality - all of this is a process that can only occur because we are in a state of progressively increasing entropy, but low enough to allow for the complexity of the universe.

FOURTH IMPLICATION: order and complexity are different things.

The reader may question the previous ideas, saying: "If the universe is progressing towards chaos, towards disorder, why does life exist? Why is there consciousness? Why are there stars and solar systems and galaxies? In other words, why is there so much complexity? Doesn't complexity depend on order?"

I've already explained in detail what order and disorder are. Order is when a low number of arrangements (combinations) between atoms is capable of producing the same macroscopic reality. Disorder is the opposite, when a high number of arrangements produce the same macroscopic reality.

Complexity is something else. By simple we mean a system that requires little information to describe. By contrast, a complex system is one that requires a lot of information to describe. In other words, complexity is the degree of difficulty (amount of information required) to describe a system.

Let's go back to the coffee cup. Suppose I pour milk over the coffee, very carefully, slowly, so that the glass is divided exactly in half. On the top half, milk. The bottom half, coffee.

Let's think about the rearrangements of atoms I can make in this system. If I change the arrangements between the coffee molecules, it will still be coffee. If I change the arrangements between the milk molecules, it will still be milk. Only if I change the arrangements of the coffee molecules, replacing them with milk molecules, will I have a macroscopically visible change. This is why this is a low entropy system, because only a small number of arrangements between atoms (changing milk for milk, or coffee for coffee) generates the same macroscopically observable phenomenon (milk on top, coffee underneath). We also say it's a simple system because it's not difficult to describe: it's a symmetrical distribution of milk on top and coffee underneath.

Now suppose I put a spoon in the cup and start stirring, mixing milk with coffee. What has changed? We still have milk at the top and coffee at the bottom. But in the middle there are liquid clouds of coffee and milk mixing together. I can still change the arrangements between milk molecules at the top, just like before. I can also change the arrangements between coffee molecules at the bottom, just like before. But now something new appears. Inside these liquid clouds where milk mixes with coffee, if I change the arrangements, swapping coffee molecules for milk molecules (or vice versa), it won't make that much difference anymore. In other words, the entropy of the system has increased, as there are now a greater number of arrangements that result in the same macroscopically observable phenomenon (milk at the top, coffee at the bottom, coffee with milk in the middle). The system has also become more complex, because in order to describe it I would need to explain exactly how the waves and swirls of latte mix and differ from each other.

If I keep mixing the coffee with milk, the entropy keeps increasing, i.e. the number of arrangements of molecules that result in the same macroscopic phenomenon keeps increasing. When I finish mixing, the liquid is uniform, with the brownish hue we all know. This is the maximum state of entropy of this system, because if I rearrange any coffee molecules, replacing them with milk molecules anywhere in the cup, it won't make any difference - the observable macroscopic phenomenon will remain the same (coffee with milk). This is the equilibrium state of the system. Note, however, that the state of equilibrium makes the system simple again, because we need little information to describe it: it is a homogeneous mixture of coffee and milk.

This is a pattern observed in physics: as entropy increases, so does complexity. However, when entropy reaches certain levels, although it continues to grow, complexity begins to decrease. This is what will happen to the universe.

We are lucky enough to live at a time when the levels of entropy in the cosmos are low enough for the complexity of the system to be high. Galaxies, solar systems, planets, life, brains, consciousness and self-consciousness are only possible at not too high levels of entropy. We live in an age when coffee and milk are beginning to mix.

As the entropy of our universe grows, there will come a time when its complexity decreases, culminating in a highly entropic but terribly simple chaos: the empty vastness where there is no time or any complex systems. One day, the café au lait will mix completely, becoming homogeneous.

FIFTH IMPLICATION: cause and effect only exist in the macroscopic world.

If you've understood everything I've explained so far, it's now easy (or less difficult) to understand what I said back there: cause and effect don't make sense in the microscopic world of the immutable and invisible laws of physics. After all, in this world there are no causes or effects. The only thing that exists are patterns.

A great way to understand this idea is to think of a sequence of numbers: 1, 2, 3, 4, 5 and so on. We know that 3 comes after 2, and that 1 comes before 2. But that doesn't mean that 2 is the *cause of* 3, or that 1 is the *cause of* 2, or that 2 is the effect *of* 1. Nor that 2 is the *effect of* 1. I think you get the idea. These are patterns, universal and immutable rules that govern the universe.

Causes and effects only exist in the macroscopic world. If you come home today and find a goat in the middle of your living room, you'll immediately think about the possible causes that brought a goat into your living room. After all, goats don't spontaneously appear in the living rooms of apartments and houses.

Suppose that, after finding the goat, you call a physicist friend and ask what caused the goat to be in your living room. Your friend replies: "The cause is the immutable and invisible laws of physics".

Is he wrong? In the general sense, no. Unless you believe in a spirit or something - a supernatural entity that has a huge hard-on for putting goats in people's living rooms. Otherwise, what brought the goat into the room certainly obeyed the laws of physics.

But that's an unhelpful answer to the question. In the macroscopic world, the observable world in which we live, causes and effects are important. In the macroscopic world, causes are descriptions of the circumstances that led a phenomenon to occur.

When a crime occurs, we look for the criminal - the cause of the crime. When a mistake occurs, we look for the cause of the mistake. In the observable world in which we live, it is perfectly natural (and useful, according to our poetic naturalism) to talk about causes and effects.

That's why, for various sciences such as psychology and sociology, causes and effects are still useful and appropriate ways of talking about the world. Psychological and sociological phenomena, for example, depend on the direction of time.

When we talk about the invisible physical laws that govern our universe on a microscopic level, cause and effect no longer make sense, because there is no direction of time. Only patterns. In fact, some of these patterns are, to use Spinoza's term, "causes of themselves" - in other words, the nature of these patterns can only be conceived as existing.

A classic example is the speed of light. From Einstein's calculations, we know that nothing can travel faster than the speed of light. It's mathematically impossible. Then you turn around and say: "Oh, Pedro, but that math of yours, those numbers and equations and laws that physicists discover? That's all on paper. In reality, things are different!".

Well, that's what experimental physics is all about. It turns out that in experiments carried out in the large particle accelerators that exist today, scientists are able to accelerate particles up to 99.997% of the speed of light - but no more than that.

This is a strong indication that Einstein was right, that this is an unbreakable pattern in the cosmos. But there is no cause for it. It's simply the way things are. There is no way to demonstrate a cause for the universal patterns inherent in the functioning and relationship between things in the world governed by the microscopic laws of physics.

We can, of course, discover new patterns that better explain other patterns. But even so, at its most fundamental level, the universe is determined by a series of immutable natural patterns - the laws of nature.

• • • • •

Dear reader, if you've made it this far and understood all the ideas, the most difficult part of the book is behind you. From here on in, things will be a little less complicated.

You may have gotten angry at the use of the terms "order/disorder", "chaos" and "equilibrium". In that case, don't be mad at me - be mad at physicists.

I've tried to explain highly complex concepts as simply as possible. I know that for some these ideas may seem harsh, difficult, too closed. Unfortunately, there's no way to make them simpler in written form - if you do, you run the risk of misrepresenting them. As already mentioned, at the end of the book there is recommended reading for each section. It's worth a look.

We'll still have some difficult ideas by the end of Part 2, but in my opinion, nothing compared to the idea that time may have no direction. So here we go.

17

A pale blue dot

CALABREZ: The path we've followed so far has been a brief introduction to the great cosmologies - conceptions and visions of the cosmos - from antiquity to the present day. The most important cosmologists in the world today are physicists. Most people know names like Stephen Hawking and Neil deGrasse Tyson.

Why are they important? What makes them important?

I consider "importance" here to be the impact of their research and teaching on society in general and science in particular.

Earlier, I described a naturalistic view of the cosmos. The natural world evolves according to unbreakable patterns: the laws of nature. The only reliable way to learn about how the world works is to observe how it works.

Whether you agree or not, naturalism is the standard *modus operandi* of science today. By this I mean that *all* the major scientific paradigms that are active are naturalistic. Without exception. All high-impact scientific journals (such as *Nature* and *Science*) approach the world in a naturalistic way. All the important cosmologists I've mentioned present naturalistic views.

This bothers a lot of people. Many think that science is saying that religion or spirituality are unnecessary. There are indeed scientists who defend this stance.

But I don't think that's true.

What I've learned from naturalism is that, when looking for the best ways to talk about the world, we should strive to make these ways coherent with each other and coherent with what is observed in the world.

To do this, you have to doubt. Doubt everything.

Imagine a world without the attitude of doubt. Without investigative motivation. Without the constant intention to understand things better. No openness to throwing out obsolete ideas and adopting better ones.

Without all this, we would still believe that the Sun is the god Ra, as the Egyptians did. Or Helios for the Greeks, Tonatiuh for the Aztecs, and so on.

I'm not trivializing the importance of myths. Characterizing the Sun as a god was once the best way to talk about the world. Myths say a lot about who we are and especially about who we once were. However, talking about a sun god today is no longer the best way to explain how the world works. It is not consistent with the observations we make of the world with the tools of science. The Sun is not a god. It's a star. We know what stars are, what they are made of and how they are born and die.

The scientific stance does not seek to provide absolute truths. Scientific truths are provisional. They are the best explanation we have for that phenomenon at the time. There may be better explanations. If we find them, we'll change the way we talk about the phenomenon. If we don't, we'll keep looking.

We live in a universe *full of* mysteries.

There are many examples.

The universe is expanding rapidly, and we don't know exactly why. There is "dark energy", or "ghost energy", causing this expansion. There is also a type of matter that we can't identify with any of our current scientific resources. We only know of its existence because of the "footprints" it leaves behind: the gravity it exerts on other types of matter. Scientists call it "dark matter". An interesting detail: dark energy and dark matter together account for 95% of the mass/energy of the observable universe.

What happens inside black holes?

What came before the Big Bang?

What exactly was the Big Bang?

These and many other mysteries are bound to baffle anyone. There are so many things we don't know, so many things we may never know. The field of possibilities opened up by science is very vast.

I really like the allegory of the "island of knowledge" proposed by physicist Marcelo Gleiser. For him, we live on an island where knowledge accumulates progressively. The ocean around the island represents our ignorance. The island tends to grow, as we accumulate more and more knowledge as time goes by. Our knowledge gets bigger and bigger. Consequently, the island gets bigger and bigger.

It turns out that the bigger the island gets, the bigger its borders will become. And this will increase the island's contact with the ocean of ignorance. In other words, the increase in knowledge entails a necessary increase in *our awareness of our own ignorance*. And there is no end to this process: there will never be a time when we build a computer with the capabilities of Laplace's demon.

Perhaps, by the time you are reading these pages, years will have passed since the publication of this book and some mysteries will have been unraveled. If this has happened, I'm sure that many new mysteries will have arisen. We are doomed to mystery and we need to find comfort in this idea: we are not capable of knowing everything. This is not defeatism. Admitting our ignorance is only sad for those who have delusional claims to greatness. Admitting our ignorance allows us the humility to turn the page and start again, abandoning obsolete worldviews or admitting that we were wrong all along.

We are limited. Firstly, by the tools, instruments and theories of the times in which we live. But we are limited above all by the human cognitive apparatus itself. Our brain is a machine. Inevitably, there are things it won't be able to understand.

We must always be humble.

Our Sun, the source of our energy and life, is just one of the hundred billion stars that occupy our galaxy, the Milky Way. Until 2016, scientists estimated that the observable universe contained between 100 and 200 billion galaxies. Today, following new observations by the Hubble telescope, that number has risen to 2,000,000,000,000. That's right: two trillion galaxies. Remember: this is the observable universe. There are parts of the universe that we are not yet able to see.

But let's take it easy, because in 2018 the James Webb Space Telescope - Hubble's successor - will be launched. It's incredible to imagine what the new discoveries will be.

In the midst of this indescribable immensity, in a galaxy among two trillion observable galaxies, close to one of the galaxy's hundred billion stars, there is a small blue planet. Our young planet, 4.5 billion years old. After all, the Big Bang occurred 13.8 billion years ago. On that planet, at a specific moment in the cosmos, when there was a direction to time and complexity... At that moment, due to a series of highly improbable events, something called "life" emerged. It's a fleeting moment, because one day there will be no more life. There will be no more past or future. Stars will die and black holes will evaporate. But in this special, fleeting moment, life is possible. More than that, intelligent life is possible. Consciousness and self-awareness are possible. You and I are possible.

Human beings - a species that is two hundred thousand years old. Sounds like a lot. But imagine the existence of the universe. Imagine the entire period of the universe's existence fitted into a single year. A cosmic calendar. The Big Bang occurs on the first minute of January 1st. The moment I'm writing this book occurs at midnight on December 31st. The Milky Way is formed on March 16th. Our solar system is formed on September 2nd. Do you know when humanity was born? At 11:52 p.m. on December 31st.

Two hundred thousand years seems like a lot to someone who lives a measly hundred years. But they are almost nothing in the face of the vastness of the cosmos.

On February 14, 1990, the Voyager 1 space probe completed its primary mission: to study Jupiter and Saturn. In 2012, it left the solar system. The first human spacecraft to enter interstellar space. But in 1990, it took a photo. A *selfie* in space. One of the most famous photos in history: a dark immensity. In the middle, hard to see, a tiny dot. A pale blue dot: the Earth, photographed six billion kilometers away.

From this distance, the Earth may not seem very interesting. But it's different for us. Consider that point again. It's here. It's our home. It's us. It's home to everyone you love, everyone you know, everyone you've ever heard of, every human being who has ever existed, everyone who has ever lived their life. The totality of our joys and sufferings, thousands of confident religions, ideologies and economic doctrines, every hunter and gatherer, every hero and coward, every creator and destroyer of civilizations, every king and commoner, every young couple in love, every mother and father, every hopeful child, every inventor and every explorer, every teacher of ethics, every corrupt politician, every "superstar", every "supreme leader", every saint and every sinner in the history of our species lived there - in that speck of dust suspended in a ray of sunshine.

Earth is a very small stage in a vast cosmic arena. Think of the rivers of blood spilled by all those generals and emperors so that, in glory and triumph, they could be momentary masters of a fraction of a point. Think of the infinite cruelties committed by the inhabitants of one corner of this pixel against their equals in another corner. Think of how frequent the disagreements between them were, how thirsty they were to kill each other, their fervent hatreds. Our attitudes, our imaginary self-importance, the delusion that we have a privileged position in the universe are challenged by this pale point of light. Our planet is a solitary speck in the great cosmic darkness that surrounds us. In our obscurity, in all this vastness, there is no indication that help will come from elsewhere to save us from ourselves.

Earth is the only world we know of so far that is capable of harboring life. There is nowhere else, at least in the near future, for our species to migrate to. Visit? Yes. Settle down? Not yet. Whether you like it or not, for the moment, Earth is where we have to make our home.

It has been said that astronomy is a humbling and character-building experience. Perhaps there is no better demonstration of the folly of human vanity than this distant image of our little world. For me, it reinforces our responsibility to be kinder to each other and to preserve and cherish our pale blue dot, the only home we've ever known.

These were Carl Sagan's words at a public lecture at Cornell University in 1994. *Pale Blue Dot* is also the title of a book by Sagan. A recommendation: search for the video on the internet to hear this beautiful text in the author's voice. A giant whose shoulder serves as a support for all of us to see further.

• • • • •

In the midst of all this, here we are. Me writing, you reading. Both of us reflecting on all these incredible things.

Do you have any idea how rare and special that is? We were born with a brain capable of appreciating all the elegance of the cosmos. A brain capable of contemplating and understanding the complex vastness of the universe. A brain that can philosophize about existence and think about itself, trying to understand how we ourselves work. A brain that allows us, above all, to be able to build a better world tomorrow than the one we have today.

We must always be humble. But as well as being humble, we should be grateful. This is a gift given to us by nature. A blessing - perhaps the greatest blessing it is possible to receive within nature today. Some will thank God, others the gods, goddesses or nature itself. Regardless, be grateful, reader. For you are alive and you have a brain that, without a shadow of a doubt, is the most complex machine in the known universe. If that isn't sacred, I don't know what is.

This brings us to the greatest mystery of the cosmos: how is a biological machine weighing around 1.3 kilograms capable of doing all this?

18

Brain: a cosmos within the cosmos

CALABREZ: The study of the nervous system of living beings in general and of the brain in specific is carried out by a series of scientific fields that come together under the name "neurosciences". Affective neuroscience, cognitive neuroscience, computational neuroscience, molecular neurobiology, biopsychology and many others.

Studying the human brain has been part of my daily routine for years. Despite this, every time I stop to think about the brain, I'm amazed again - just as I was when I first opened a neuroscience book.

If you were to hold a human brain in your hands, I guarantee: you wouldn't be impressed.

Here we have a meatloaf whose mass varies between 1.2 and 1.3 kilograms. That's a little more than a carton of milk you buy in the supermarket. What's more, it's not very big: it fits in the palm of your hand. The texture is strange and hard to describe. It's half jelly, half sponge. It's like a kind of tofu cheese, but much firmer.

Nothing impressive, right?

Now think: although the brain makes up an average of 2% of a human being's body mass, it consumes around 25% of their energy. This means that, despite its small volume and mass, the brain does something very important for us - after all, it consumes 1/4 of what is one of our most precious resources, energy.

Like any biological apparatus, the brain is made up of cells. Different types of cell make up the brain, but the cells most responsible for brain functions are called neurons.

Each brain has an average of 86 billion neurons. This is a recent figure, obtained thanks to studies carried out by Brazilian researchers. Before that, it was believed that the brain had around a hundred billion neurons. That's the number I used in my classes and lectures. That's the great thing about science: we learn new things and abandon obsolete ideas.

Neurons are cells that receive and transmit information between themselves; therefore, they make connections. On average, each neuron makes between one thousand and ten thousand connections with other neurons. These connections occur at microscopic contact points called synapses.

Let's calculate how many synapses there are in each human brain. There are 86 billion neurons and between 1,000 and 10,000 synapses per neuron. The result: *between 86 and 860 trillion synapses in each human brain*. Remember the number of galaxies in the observable universe I mentioned earlier? Two trillion galaxies, according to the latest estimates. In other words, there are more connections in the human brain than there are galaxies in the cosmos.

•••••

You often see pictures of brains around. Most people today know what one looks like. However, people hardly ever stop to appreciate and respect a picture of a brain.

It is thanks to the workings of your brain that you are reading these words and understanding what they mean. Your thoughts, plans and dreams for the future, as well as your affections, memories and experiences - all emerge from fantastically complex electrical, chemical and magnetic patterns that occur in the brain. When your brain is altered, you are altered.

The use of alcohol and other drugs is a perfect everyday example. There are more striking examples: a small injury to the brain can completely change your personality. This doesn't happen if you damage any other part of your body. If you've ever fainted or undergone general anesthesia, ask yourself: what was the world like during that experience? You know the answer. There was no world. You had the experience of a world that "switched off". Because, in a way, the apparatus that produces your conscious experience of the world has been "switched off". The activity of your brain is responsible for who you are. This includes the construction of the reality in which we live.

The world is not sad. But it's not happy either. The world is not difficult, beautiful, stressful or frightening. *The world simply is*. A collection of matter and energy dancing to the music we call "natural laws". The values of the world are our production. The production of our brain.

One day, leaving work, the world was stressful. After a couple of beers, the world became less stressful. You see, the world remained the same. What changed was the brain.

I'd like you, the reader, to reflect the next time you see a picture of a human brain.

That brain was a life. Like mine and yours, full of ups and downs. There was love, but there was also hate. Joyful moments, smiles and belly laughs. Sadness, anguish, tears and days when I didn't want to get out of bed. Laziness to go to work, excitement at good news, longing for someone's hug. Some certainties and many doubts. Curiosity, deep reflections and existential questions. All of this contained in 1.3 kilograms that fits in the palm of your hand.

Everything we know about the cosmos, every worldview that has ever existed, from prehistory and ancient myths to contemporary quantum physics, has been produced by human brains. All the great thinkers we've talked about here owe their ideas to the workings of this spectacular biological machine.

Our little brain is a gigantic cosmos within the cosmos.

Or would it be the other way around? After all, there would be no idea of a cosmos if there were no human brains. So we could say that it's actually the universe that lives inside this fantastic cosmos called the brain. To understand it is to understand ourselves. To walk through the brain is to visit the roots of who we are. An important journey. Perhaps essential for a fully human life.

19

Being born and growing up

CALABREZ: A giraffe can stand up shortly after being born. Zebra cubs are able to run 45 minutes after birth. Dolphins are born swimming. In contrast, human beings are born fragile. The human brain is born incomplete. Human babies are the most fragile of all mammals. It takes us a year to be able to walk. Another three years or so to articulate thoughts that allow us to communicate with each other more or less efficiently. Many more years before we can reproduce and live on our own. We are born totally dependent on the people around us. Some people, in fact, take this very seriously and stay at home with their parents long after the gray hairs start to appear.

At first glance, it seems like a huge disadvantage for us.

Imagine being born with your brain "ready", like other animals. Or at least "semi-ready"! That would be incredible!

Let's take it easy.

This primary advantage that other species have over us brings with it a tremendous disadvantage. A brain that is born "ready" or "semi-ready" is undoubtedly capable of turning itself around more quickly. For this to happen, it must be a pre-programmed brain, born with a series of pre-inscribed programs.

This is great for the animal's survival in the ecological niche in which it was born. But it comes at a huge price: adaptability. Take the animal out of this niche, and it will have great difficulty adapting and surviving.

When was the last time you saw a polar bear in the forest? Or a zebra in the snowy mountains of Norway? Or a caribou living in the desert?

On the other hand, human beings have a great capacity for adaptation. We have managed to survive in the most varied ecological environments. From terribly cold environments like the Arctic to terribly hot environments like deserts. We survive in the dryness of the cerrado and the extreme humidity of the Amazon rainforest. At high pressures, near the sea (and even in it), and low pressures, on mountain tops.

This is only possible because we are born with an "incomplete" brain - one that comes with fewer pre-programmed things, allowing it to mold itself according to the experiences it is subjected to.

I warn you.

This may remind some readers of John Locke's idea of the blank slate. The idea that we are born as a blank slate. Without a nature, without an *a priori* essence.

This idea is incorrect. Like all animals, we have a nature. We have biological pre-programming. We are deeply influenced by our genes. Psychologist Steven Pinker, a professor at Harvard, wrote a book called *Tábula rasa: the contemporary denial of human nature*. An essential book for understanding this issue.

Today we know that nothing is derived from experience alone. Just as nothing is derived from biology alone. Everything is the result of the relationship between biology and experience.

Think of a pianist. He's playing a beautiful sonata. You come up to him and ask: "Is this music coming from you or from the piano?".

We quickly realize that the question doesn't make sense. Music is the result of the relationship between piano and pianist. Both are necessary.

The same can be said about human beings. Nothing is exclusively the result of our nature, our biology, our genes. On the other hand, nothing is exclusively the result of our choices, the experiences we have lived through, the (social, cultural) environment in which we were born. Everything is a relationship between biology and experience.

Although we do have a nature, we are different from other animals in this respect. We have a greater window of flexibility to adapt to the environment in which we are born and develop (and the experiences it provides). This obviously involves our choices. We are freer in this sense. Something that Rousseau, in his own way, had already said.

• • • • •

The neurons in a human baby's brain are scattered and disconnected. There are billions of synapses already formed, of course. But a transformation is taking place. During the first two years of life, the baby's neurons begin to establish new connections at a dizzying speed. Around two million new synapses are formed every second in a baby's brain. By the age of two, a child has approximately double the number of synapses found in the adult brain.

At this point, this explosion of new connections gives way to a process called "synaptic pruning". Just like pruning a plant to make it leaner, this process reduces the number of synapses.

But which synapses are pruned and which remain?

Synapses that are useful, i.e. that actually participate in brain circuits, are maintained and strengthened. In other words, these connections become stronger. Unused synapses are discarded.

In a way, the brain we have today was polished from the possibilities that were already in it when we were a few years old. From the brain's point of view, what we are today is largely defined by what has been removed - and not by what has been added, as is often imagined.

Throughout our childhood, our brain adapts to interact more efficiently with the fundamental aspects of the environment in which we grow up. One example of this is language. As we are exposed to different language systems, our brain adapts to the predominant language system in the environment. There's nothing to stop it being more than one language system.

For example, the brain of an adult born in Japan and exposed exclusively to the Japanese language for the first few years of their life will have difficulty discerning the "r" and "l" sounds - which we easily distinguish in Portuguese. This is because these sounds are not distinct in Japanese.

The principle here is simple. At birth in Japan or Brazil, a child will hear and respond equally to the sounds of both Japanese and Portuguese. Over time, the ability to hear sounds particular to the native language will improve, while the ability to hear sounds other than the native language will become worse.

But there's nothing to stop us learning new languages even when we're adults. And this doesn't just apply to languages, but to *any kind of learning*. The human brain is highly malleable. Our brain is capable of refining its connections - creating, strengthening, loosening and abandoning synapses throughout our lives. This malleability is called "neuroplasticity". We often say that the brain is plastic. This means that the brain never stops developing, right up until our last day of life.

However, there are more critical periods of plasticity, when the brain is more malleable; therefore, more subject to changes and influences from the environment. The brain is extremely sensitive in the first three years of life (including the intrauterine period). From then on, it remains highly malleable throughout childhood. In adolescence, this malleability is reduced and, between the ages of 20 and 25, the brain reaches its mature stage - with its lowest levels of plasticity, which remain relatively stable throughout the rest of adult life.

•••••

We've just seen that the "incomplete" brain we were born with brings an enormous advantage in terms of adaptability. This neural incompleteness is accompanied by two major characteristics of the human species.

first characteristic: we are a highly social animal.

In 1943, a famous psychologist called Abraham Maslow published a scientific article in which he described a *hierarchy of human needs*. In other words, he pointed out the most fundamental needs and how the less fundamental ones were built only after the most basic ones had been met.

This hierarchy of needs became very famous and is still used today by some teachers and books. It is typically presented in the form of a colored pyramid, known as Maslow's pyramid.

For Maslow, the primary level of human motivation is the satisfaction of physiological needs (water, air, food, sleep, rest).

After satisfying physiological needs, human beings focus on security needs. This involves personal security, financial security, health, well-being, safety from accidents and illness.

Once the need for security has been met, human beings move on to the need for love and belonging. For Maslow, this involves friendships, intimacy and family.

If the needs for love and belonging are properly met, then the human being will seek to satisfy the needs for esteem - which involve self-esteem and self-respect.

Finally, when all the previous needs have been fully met, the human being will dedicate themselves to satisfying the needs of self-fulfillment. At this level, the individual will seek to be the best they are capable of being, to express their maximum potential. This potential varies between individuals and can be achieved in the most diverse areas of life, such as the arts, business, family, etc.

Maslow's pyramid is often used to demonstrate human needs and motivations. However, despite its fame, this hierarchical model has a major problem.

The problem is due to the fact that we are mammals - and all mammals are born relatively incomplete. At birth, mammals are incapable of looking after themselves. They are even incapable of taking care of the most basic physiological needs, such as food and safety.

This is true for all mammals, but it's especially serious for the human child. As we have seen, the human baby is one of the most fragile offspring in nature. Without the care of parents and family, the child is unable to feed and protect itself. It is unable to meet the most fundamental needs of the pyramid.

In other words, the big mistake in Maslow's hierarchy is forgetting that, as mammals, *our main need is social.* We need people to survive, we need the support, affection and security that only other human beings can offer. And we don't need this on a whim, out of mere desire. It's a necessity for survival. Without it, we die in the first days of life.

The great primary human need, the greatest of our needs, is the need for social support. This is a key survival factor - and it means that it will be a top priority for our brains.

We now know that the human brain's highest priority is to think about other people. You can test this now: try calculating the percentage of your thoughts that involve other human beings every day. You'll quickly see our top priority: social life.

All of this is directly linked to our survival. We don't have horns or claws. We're not strong. We don't run particularly fast. We look like a very average animal if you look at our physical prowess.

But the greatest human feats are not physical: they are mental. And, as I said before, the mind is what the brain does. A complex mind is only possible with a complex brain.

In terms of survival, are human beings physically half-assed? Yes.

Despite this, we do have one strength: we manage to come together and, through a highly flexible and adaptable union (which naturally requires great intelligence), solve problems unimaginable for any other species.

•••••

The brain is made up of layers of neurons. The top layer, which covers the deeper layers, is called the cerebral cortex. The structures of the cortex, i.e. the cortical structures, are largely responsible for cognitive processes such as language, abstract thought and rational planning. These are the processes that fundamentally differentiate us from other animals, including other primates.

There is a thin layer that covers the cortex. It is the uppermost layer of neurons in the brain, called the neocortex, new cortex (from the Greek νέος, or *néos*). It is the most evolutionarily recent structure in the brains of animals. Only mammals have a neocortex.

Comparative studies of primates (including humans) suggest that one of the main reasons for the increase in the primate neocortex over the course of evolution was precisely the need to accommodate primates in larger, more complex societies.

Let's understand this with an example.

Imagine a society of primates millions of years ago. This society, for whatever reasons, survived efficiently. The number of group members increased, making the society populous, with a large number of individuals. The individuals who, through random genetic mutations, were born with a greater volume of neocortex, were able to cope more efficiently with the complexity of the environment - and thus able to survive and procreate more effectively. This trait (larger neocortex) was then passed on to future generations. Progressively, a larger neocortex ensured greater survival in increasingly complex environments.

It turns out that there is nothing more complex than the social world. Interacting with other intelligent beings, knowing who is friend and who is foe, learning to win allies through communication...

It seems that social life was one of the main reasons why primate brains (especially the cortex and neocortex) became progressively larger throughout evolution. Living together in complex societies is a key survival factor - more important in today's nature than attributes such as strength and speed.

No wonder no other animal does this as well as humans. After all, we are the most intelligent animal in observable nature. Social activities occupy the vast majority of human daily life.

We are the most social animal on the planet.

• • • • •

Now that you've understood the first fundamental human characteristic (our social nature) that accompanies an "incomplete brain", let's move on to the second - which is very serious and can be very sad.

second characteristic: the first years of life are decisive - for better or for worse.

In 1965, Nicolae Ceaușescu was the General Secretary of Romania, the highest leader of the communist country. A year after taking office, Ceaușescu introduced laws banning abortion and any form of contraception throughout Romania. The reason? To increase the population and the workforce. A "celibacy tax" was applied to families with fewer than five children. Women with more than ten children were given the title of *heroine mothers* by the state. Special government agents, gynecologists known as "menstrual police", inspected women of childbearing age to ensure that they were producing as many children as possible. In addition, harsh laws were put in place to make divorce difficult - marriages were only dissolved in exceptional cases.

The result: the birth rate exploded.

Poor families, unable to care for their children, gave up custody of the children, who were sent to public orphanages. As the number of orphaned children grew, the government built more and more orphanages.

Ceaușescu was ousted in 1989, the year in which Romanian orphanages accumulated 170,000 abandoned children. In the 1990s, the Western media had access to some of these orphanages. Photos of the inhumane conditions in which the children lived made headlines all over the world. The babies had only a few minutes of human contact a day, only at feeding time. The rest of the day they were left alone in their cribs, without any stimulation for their brains. Caregivers were told not to play or interact with the children - it was believed that this would spoil them. When they grew up, they lived a mechanized life. They wore the same clothes, had the same haircut and queued to use plastic pots as toilets.

This scenario was nothing new in Europe in the 1960s. Especially after the end of the Second World War in 1945, due to the large number of adult deaths, hundreds of thousands of orphaned children lived in similar or worse conditions. It's important to note: millions of children around the world are still subjected to this kind of reality today.

These children often have serious developmental problems - which continue into adulthood. The problems mainly involve social and emotional development. A common behavior exhibited by children with these conditions is an "indiscriminately friendly" attitude - they jump on laps, hug, kiss and easily become attached to total strangers. At first glance, it seems cute - but we now know that it's a common compensatory mechanism in neglected children, which often accompanies serious problems in emotional relationships in adulthood. But it doesn't stop there: the IQ I. of children subjected to these conditions is often well below average. Brain studies show that they have considerably reduced neural activity.

I hope, reader, that you have understood the seriousness of this. Contrary to what many people think, it is not only physical abuse that causes serious harm to a child's development. Several studies have shown that emotional abandonment and neglect are also associated with a high risk of children developing psychiatric disorders, such as depression and anxiety.

When I say that social contact is a necessity, I'm not using the word lightly. It literally means that it is necessary. In psychology, "attachment theory" (or "bonding theory") has been demonstrating since the 1950s that a newborn baby needs to develop a close relationship (which involves contact, affection, physical and emotional support) with at least one primary caregiver. Without this, their social and emotional development does not occur normally.

It's biological, it's written into our nature. We are not a blank slate. We share this characteristic with other mammals - especially primates.

The primary caregiver is often the biological mother. But not necessarily. Our cultural development allows us to reshape family structures. Many people have primary caregivers who are not the mother, such as fathers, grandparents, uncles. And also those without any genetic link.

Children who are adopted and removed from orphanages and receive healthy care and support tend to recover to varying degrees. The younger the child, the better the recovery. Remember the windows of neuroplasticity I explained earlier. The most critical, without a doubt, is during the first three years of life. It's no wonder that children up to two years old who live in situations of neglect, when taken in by a family, tend to develop normally. From then on, the extent of the damage is linked to age: the later the child is taken into care, the worse.

But these cases occur with children who have already been born. And before that? What role does intrauterine development play?

• • • • •

The year was 1944. The Second World War was drawing to a close, and Europe was going through one of its darkest moments. During the fall, German soldiers blockaded western Holland, preventing the entry of fuel and food. After the Nazi blockade came winter - one of the harshest ever experienced in the country. The cold froze the water in the canals. Food became scarce. People survived on a diet of thin soups, eating around five hundred calories a day. To give you a measure of comparison, a Big Mac has 490 calories.

In May 1945, the blockade was lifted and Holland was liberated by Allied troops. It is estimated that during this period, known as the "hunger winter", around twenty thousand people died - mostly elderly people. Tens of thousands fell ill.

But there was another group that suffered terribly from the impact of the winter famine: the forty thousand or so women who were pregnant at the time. The fetuses developing in their wombs did not escape unscathed from the conditions to which their mothers were exposed.

Some of the effects were immediate: there was a significant increase in the number of miscarriages, stillbirths, birth complications and deficiencies due to nutrient deprivation.

But the effects didn't stop there.

The children who survived to adulthood had higher rates of obesity, diabetes and heart problems. They were men and women with higher glucose tolerance (a precursor to diabetes), high blood pressure and cholesterol problems. There was a significant increase in the risk of psychiatric disorders, such as schizophrenia, schizoid/schizotypal personality disorder and affective disorders (depression, for example).

What happened to these fetuses? Why did nutrient deprivation lead to so many problems in adulthood?

The answer at first glance is obvious: fetuses are in a critical period of development and need full nutrients and calories for this development to take place optimally.

But beyond the obvious, there is a reality that few know about intrauterine development.

Problems such as cardiovascular dysfunction and obesity typically stem from continuous excess. We know this well: the *fast-food* world today is seeing the rates of these ailments rise dangerously.

It turns out that the adults who were born during or immediately after the winter famine didn't necessarily commit excesses. Without living in excess, such evils still arose. Why?

It seems that the intrauterine period is a time when the baby's body - and that includes the brain - is adapting to the world into which it will be born. The idea is to be born as adapted as possible for survival.

And how does the baby do this?

Capturing information from the mother's body and adapting to it.

When we think of intrauterine development, we usually think of putting headphones in the mother's belly so that the child can listen to Mozart. But it's much deeper and more visceral than that.

If the mother is malnourished and ingests low amounts of calories, the fetus will develop in order to live as well as possible in a world lacking in nutrients and calories.

The children of the Hunger Winter, despite having developed in hungry and malnourished wombs, were born into a world of abundance. What for us is a healthy amount of calories and nutrients was too much for them, for their bodies.

The result: individuals who lived relatively healthily showed health problems typically found in people who live in continuous excess.

The importance of the intrauterine period of development is critical. Everyone knows more or less about the damage caused by the consumption of drugs - including cigarettes and alcohol - during pregnancy. But I repeat: the issue is profound and visceral. *Everything that happens in the mother's body is experienced to some extent by the fetus.*

We know that stress, depression and anxiety during pregnancy increase the risk of a series of problems for the neurobehavioral development of the fetus - which, in turn, lead to an increased risk of health damage throughout the life of the child and the adult who will be formed.

The first years of life are fundamental to what we will become as adults. And the period we spend in our mother's womb isn't just included in this developmental window - it's absolutely fundamental.

• • • • •

We've seen the importance of development in the first years of life.

Before I go any further, I'd like to warn you.

Looking after children isn't easy. Quite the opposite: it's a boring, tedious, tiring process. But there's a super-simple way to make a fussy child sit still: put a *tablet* in their hand and give them a packet of cookies, chocolate or snacks.

Giving a child food containing sugar before the age of three should, from the point of view of the brain, be considered a crime. The same can be said for sodium (salt) artificially added to food. After that, until the age of eight or so, it is still highly recommended that you don't feed children artificial sugar or foods containing it.

But that's impossible! All my friends at school eat garbage!

Here I recall the words of my great friend and neurologist Fabiano Moulin: "Today's world confuses the ordinary with the normal."

It's common for children to eat sugar, be sedentary and spend most of their time looking at cell phone, *tablet* and computer screens. It's common, but it's not normal. Normality, for our bodies, is distorted by the current routine in which we live.

As a result, we are creating a sick society. Childhood obesity rates are rising dangerously. Studies show an association between excessive use of social networks and psychiatric disorders such as depression. There is even an academic term for it: *Facebook* depression. Another example: evidence is accumulating that suggests potential problematic effects on the brain, as well as an increased risk of mental disorders, from excessive consumption of pornography.

Remember: common is not necessarily normal.

Take care of your child. This includes affection, emotional and material support. It also includes providing your child with healthy development - highly enhanced by proper nutrition, regular physical activity, quality sleep, time to rest, play, explore the world and an active social life.

It also means setting limits. Knowing how to say "no". Knowing how to make agreements and stick to them. Many parents feel guilty about not spending enough time with their children. Because of this, they are highly permissive. Imagine a child who has never heard "no", who has never had limits imposed and demanded, who has never had to postpone an immediate pleasure in order to achieve something greater in the future. That child will grow up thinking that the world owes them obligations. They will believe they are special and better than other human beings. They won't be able to stand the harshness of the world when their face inevitably hits a metaphorical floor.

We must never forget that it's important to fall in order to learn how best to get up and move on. And we only fall when the world frustrates our steps and expectations, putting potholes and obstacles in our way. Educating also means reminding our children of this harsh truth.

20

Maturing

CALABREZ: Years pass. Childhood and its delights, the worlds that each new interaction with reality reveals to us, are left behind. The slow, very slow passage of time disappears - and with it go the days that, as an adult, will be remembered as long, long, long. To be a child is to experience a succession of spectacular surprises with every interaction with things that in adult life we will consider banal.

As we grow up, part of the world becomes smaller, because our imagination is smaller. Largely because of a castrating upbringing. But also by a developing brain. Memories are formed through novelties, breaks in expectations and emotionally striking events. All this is increasingly rare as we enter maturity. As we grow up, another part of the world opens up, and the longed-for freedom welcomes us, cold and frightening, while also bringing us breaths of lightness and enchantment.

We've grown up.

We've reached that terrible stage of human life: adolescence. Terrible first of all for parents. Studies show that this is the phase that gives the most work. Not only that: it's during the children's teenage years that the couple's levels of satisfaction with their marriage plummet.

The parent of a teenager would probably reply: "I don't need to be a scientist to know that!".

I can imagine.

But as well as distressing parents, adolescence is also a very difficult time for young people.

We have to ask ourselves: what the hell is going on in teenagers' brains to make them... well, to make them so *teenage*?

Notice, reader, that adolescent has become an adjective. But I'm not talking about its use to designate a phase of life. No, adolescent is used to designate a certain type of behavior - a set of attitudes, a certain attitude towards the world and people.

"You're acting like a teenager!", says the wife to her husband who, for whatever reason, has committed an imprudent act.

Let's understand this story.

• • • • •

When you enter adolescence, your body goes through a period of great change. Floods of hormones alter its appearance, progressively building up the characteristics of the adult body. In the brain, invisible changes mark a moment of transformation of considerable importance. These changes profoundly alter who we are and our relationships with the world and other human beings.

The onset of puberty brings a second blossoming of new cells and synapses, creating new pathways through the brain. This moment is followed by about a decade of new synaptic pruning - in which the brain reinforces useful pathways and discards weak and little-used connections. These changes take place especially in the prefrontal cortex, which has already been mentioned. As a result, the volume of the prefrontal cortex decreases by around 1% a year during adolescence.

The first consequence is the emergence of a new experience of the *self*, of the *psychological self* in the adolescent and, with this, an ever deeper experience of self-consciousness.

The medial (middle) structures of the prefrontal cortex (mPFC) become active when we think about ourselves, especially when we think about the significance and emotional impact of a situation. As we become adolescents, the PFCm becomes increasingly active in social situations, with peak levels around the age of 15.

The result is known to everyone who has ever been a teenager: during this period, social situations have an enormous emotional weight, with markedly intense stress responses when we are exposed to other human beings - especially those we admire or who are important in our group.

This stems from a new and impacting experience of the "psychological self", which leads adolescents to be very concerned about what others think of them. The adult brain, adapting to this "psychological self", progressively tends to worry less about the gaze of others. In adolescents, however, this is a novelty and takes on great importance.

In addition, the reward structures (motivation and pleasure) show increased activation in the adolescent brain - an activation equivalent to that of adults. However, the dorsolateral (front and side) structures of the CPF, which are necessary for the ability to control impulses and curb emotions, take a long time to mature and are only "adult" in their twenties. In other words, adolescents have an adult reward system (pleasure and motivation) that coexists with an infantile ability to curb impulses and emotions. As a result, adolescent behavior tends to be riskier, especially when faced with things that provide pleasure - such as drugs, sex and adventure.

Car insurance companies didn't need neuroscience to realize this. Insurance costs for young people have been higher than for adults for decades.

Finally, studies show that, in the adolescent brain, structures involved in social considerations (such as the CPFm) are more strongly connected with other brain circuits responsible for transforming motivations into actions (the corpus striatum and its circuits). This has led researchers to suggest that this is why adolescents' risk-taking behavior tends to be more likely when they are close to their friends and especially to relevant members of their social group.

The adolescent brain only fully matures between the ages of 20 and 25. I'm sure that many adults reading these words have already thought: "When I was a teenager, I was a bit of an idiot...".

Now you know: yes, you were - and so was I!

Joking aside, I think it's wrong to call it idiotic. After all, it's not a matter of free choice, but of a brain that developed and inclined us to certain decision-making patterns that were markedly different from those typically displayed by adults.

This is not to say that teenagers are not free to choose the paths they take in life. As I've already said: nothing is just biology. However, it is impossible to understand adolescence without understanding the biological characteristics of the brain at this stage of development. It's safe to say that, on average, a teenager doesn't have the same decision-making faculties as an adult. There will be exceptions, of course. However, by definition, exceptions do not make up the majority of cases.

• • • • •

Many people think that after the age of 25, when the neural revolutions that marked adolescence come to an end, the brain is "ready". They therefore believe that there will be no further changes during adulthood. This perspective was adopted even by scientists decades ago.

Today we know that the brain continues to change and take on new forms throughout life. This is fundamental to understanding the changes of adult life and, above all, to understanding that we are never "ready". As we shall see, this has serious implications for our well-being and health.

In 2006, a study investigated the brains of cab drivers in London. For those of you who have never visited London, it's important to note that although it's a very interesting city, its streets are a real labyrinth. It is one of the most complex collections of urban roads in the West.

To receive a license to work as a taxi driver, candidates must pass a rigorous test called *Knowledge of London*. To give you an idea of how difficult this test is, the preparatory training lasts four years. Aspiring taxi drivers must memorize London's roads and all their combinations - covering 320 different routes through the city, 25,000 streets and avenues and 20,000 points of interest, such as historic sites, hotels, police stations, etc.

The results of the study are not surprising. The brains of taxi drivers showed greater volume (compared to non-taxi drivers) in a structure called the hippocampus. We've known for a long time that the hippocampus is very important for the brain's memory system - and that includes so-called spatial memory, i.e. our ability to remember places in space, such as addresses and the location of the car in the *mall* parking lot.

This is just one example of how our brains create new roads throughout life. Aspiring taxi drivers begin their journey of getting to know the streets of London in adulthood - and yet we notice profound changes in their brains.

• • • • •

This brings me to the most important point in this discussion: the way we conduct our lives.

As we mature, our bodies change. Metabolism is progressively reduced, and this means that eating a whole pizza, as we did when we were teenagers, has more serious consequences and can lead to what scientists call "belly fat".

Our responsibilities increase and with them the number of activities we have to distribute our time between. Increased stress is a consequence.

Changes also occur in the brain. Adulthood brings a considerable reduction in novelty. As a result, time seems to pass more quickly. We often look back and say: "Wow, it's December already, I haven't even seen the time go by!".

With the weight of the responsibilities of adult life and the reduction of the hormones that kept us energetic, vigorous and full of vitality in our youth, comes a great laziness - of everything. Laziness especially to face things that challenge us, that force us to expend energy.

Two obvious examples: learning new things and practicing regular physical activity.

To explain the big problem with all this, I'll use the example of Alzheimer's disease, which is so well known and feared. It's a fatal and extremely difficult disease, not only for the patient, but also for the people who are watching their loved one's personality, memories, decision-making and, ultimately, life gradually fade away.

Look at this data very carefully, reader:

A major study carried out by Alzheimer's Disease International estimated that between 2015 and 2050, the proportional increase in the number of people suffering from dementia in six of the seven countries that make up the G7 (Germany, Canada, the United States, Italy, France and the

United Kingdom) will be 104%. In the countries that make up the G20 (which includes Brazil) this increase will be 196%. In the rest of the world, the increase will reach 247%. Some studies suggest that in developed countries (not necessarily the richest), such as Scandinavia and Japan, the number of cases will decrease in the future.

What does that mean?

It means that dementia, the result of diseases such as Alzheimer's,* are not completely inevitable. On the contrary: wealthier countries are able to promote better brain health, reducing the prevalence of this type of disease - which, unfortunately, is still growing proportionally over time.

Imagine an adult between the ages of 30 and 40. We can consider them young, of course. This is when the accumulation of certain proteins in the brain begins. This accumulation will later result in a progressive and irreversible death of neurons. The consequence is Alzheimer's disease.

There is genetic determinism in Alzheimer's disease. But I'd like to remind you, reader, of what I said before: nothing is just genetics and biology, just as nothing is just environment and experiences.

Part of Alzheimer's is the responsibility of the individual and also of the society in which they lived and made their choices.

Let's look at some examples.

* Note from Pedro Calabrez: Alzheimer's disease is now the leading cause of dementia in the world.

Learning a second language can delay the onset of Alzheimer's disease by up to five years.

Why?

A second language is literally a re-signification of the whole world inside your brain. Table is no longer just table. Now it's table and *table*. Apple is no longer just apple. Now it's apple and *apple* - and so on.

Being bilingual is a great way to create new roads in the brain - and here's the key point: creating new roads in the brain is one of the best ways to keep it healthy, active and functioning well.

I can give other examples: an engineer who learns poetry, an actor who learns mathematics, a neuroscientist who learns philosophy, an accountant who learns painting...

I think you get the idea. New roads. New languages.

• • • • •

Once a student came up to me and said: "Professor, I don't want a man who works out his body anymore! I want a man who works out his brain!".

It's become an exam question. Point out the error in the student's sentence.

The mistake is so obvious that many people don't realize it. The brain is part of the body, just like your thumb, liver and nose. However, we are under the illusion that body and brain are separate entities. Consequently, we believe that the same is true of mind and brain. This is a terrible mistake for the health of our brains - and therefore our minds - throughout our lives. Remember the phrase that has been repeated more than once in this book: the mind is what the brain does.

The perfect example of this is regular physical activity (at least three times a week). We now know that this practice is one of the best ways to prevent depressive episodes. It is also extremely effective in combating anxiety and many other mental disorders. It's not surprising to learn that people who are physically active throughout their lives have a reduced chance of developing Alzheimer's disease by up to 50%.

The Mediterranean diet, so famous and studied by science, which fed all the great Greek thinkers, significantly reduces the chances of developing Alzheimer's disease by more than 30%.

Do you know what the worst possible diet is for your brain (and heart)? The one where you eat a lot of red meat and a lot of simple carbohydrates. Let me give you an example: rice, beans, steak and French fries. The Brazilian diet is very unhealthy, contrary to what people often think.

Another important thing for brain health that is extremely neglected: sleep. We now know that sleep is crucial for maintaining brain health. Poor sleep kills.

By all this, I mean that the maturation of the brain until the end of our lives is, to a certain extent, in our hands. In every *fast food* you eat instead of salad and vegetables. In every red meat steak instead of fish or vegetable protein. In every laziness that makes you stay on the sofa instead of going for a run in the park or working out at the gym. Every time you choose to interact with things you're already used to instead of learning new things. Every night you choose to work instead of lying down and resting your brain...

One Big Mac at a time, one bad night's sleep at a time, one day on the sofa at a time - and you're condemning your brain to a much greater risk of falling ill and ultimately dying.

• • • • •

"But I don't have time!"

This is one of the most common phrases uttered by adults around the world.

I imagine, reader, that you have 24 hours in your day. That's the same amount of time I have, and every other human being in the world has. The phrase "I don't have time" is a very common self-deception.

Tell the truth: "It's not my priority!"

Obviously, we have people who don't have the minimum conditions of dignity and health. People who depend on two or three jobs and many long journeys on public transport to put food on the family table. These people unfortunately have no way of prioritizing their own health - let alone acquiring knowledge. We have to improve other much more fundamental social and economic conditions to give them better opportunities. It's not a question of free choice.

Curiously, I don't hear "I don't have time" from these people. It's executives and entrepreneurs, for example, who usually say this. People who deliberately choose to exchange their health and the company of their loved ones for a fistful of money that in the future will probably be used to pay for hospital expenses.

Nowadays it's increasingly common for people in their forties, those who say "I don't have time", to suffer heart attacks. When they survive, the doctor says: "Either you change your routine, eat better and exercise, or you're going to die".

When you leave the hospital the next day, you're on the treadmill at the gym at 7am. For lunch, a big plate of salad, lots of whole grains and a fillet of fish.

It seems that now she has the time she didn't have before. But we know that's not the case. Health has simply become a priority.

• • • • •

Death is inevitable. The path we will take until then, not so much. Our choices sculpt a better or worse brain to withstand maturing and the passing years. We can live - and die - a little healthier. A little more dignity and freedom. After all, illnesses imprison. They stifle life and the possibility of being what we want.

But death itself is difficult. What can you say about it? The brain stops working. There is no more neuronal activity.

I confess: death terrifies me. It's my greatest fear. That's why I try to live. That's why philosophy.

21

Death

CLÓVIS: I often ask in my classes: "Do you remember suffering before you were born?". And the answer is obvious: "Of course not!".

There is no memory, neither of suffering nor of anything else, because memory is always of experiences and there are no experiences before life.

If that's the case, why fear death?

The fear of death is always in life, it's a thing of life, it's a thing of those who are afraid. Death is nothingness, and in nothingness there is neither life nor suffering. How can you fear a situation without suffering? There seems to be a symmetry between what there was before we were born and what there will be after we die. This is what the Roman philosopher Lucretius suggests, who philosophized in a beautiful poem in Latin, *De Rerum Natura,* which means "the nature of things". Here's what Lucretius says: "Remember now and consider how the ages of eternity that elapsed before our birth were nothing to us. Here, then, is a mirror in which nature shows us the time to come after our death. Do you see anything terrible in it? Do you perceive anything gloomy? Does it not seem more serene than the deepest sleep?".

Well, the argument establishes a singularity between pre-natal non-existence and post-mortem non-existence. Both are simply states in which we don't exist. Lucretius also notes that we don't fear the time before birth - the time in which we don't exist. Thus, the time after death justifies a similar affection.

My friend, we could always think that it's not exactly the same, couldn't we? After all, before we were born we hadn't gone through life. So death is always the end. A loss. And then I think there's no possible comparison between what existed before we lived - when we didn't know what it was like to live - and what will exist after we die. Because if life was good, its end is always regrettable. So I keep thinking what I've always thought: dying is very bad when it puts an end to a joyful existence, but it's not so bad when it puts an end to a life of suffering.

• • • • •

It's very difficult to talk about death from a philosophical perspective - when a loved one dies or when someone we don't have much against dies - because philosophy arose to deal with a problem that is precisely finitude. And the problem is not the finitude of existence, but the fear of it.

I imagine that for many people, the idea that there is no suffering before birth means that there shouldn't be suffering after death either. And if there is something after death,

I have nothing to say about it. Or perhaps what I do have to say is that I hope very much that there will be something very good after death, but I'm afraid that it will coincide too much with what I would like to see happen. And when we take for granted what we would like to happen, we call it an illusion.

So I would prefer to say that for those who die, it's just an interruption that leads to the end of an existence and the end of self-awareness. Naturally, the regret is for the life not lived, but the life not lived is nothing to the person who dies. There is no possibility of reflecting on what could have been, but wasn't for the person who died; therefore, death in the first person is simply nothing.

The ideas that we never meet death because either we are and death isn't there, or death is there and we aren't - which are the classic reflection of the Seneca-style Stoics - are nice from the point of view of poetry, but they do nothing to refresh our fear of dying. I personally think that what greatly increases the anguish and sadness in the face of death is an individuation, an exaggerated singularization of each one of us. In other words, if we considered ourselves more part of a whole that remains and less of an autonomous individuality, death would be less cruel.

Imagine little wooden figures standing next to each other and inert. Then imagine a bag of some kind of powder that you sprinkle on each of them and, as you do so, the little figures are endowed with an energy of existence that allows them to move, think and speak. The same powder you put on one doll is also put on the other and the other, and so perhaps it will become clear that the energy that makes me live is of the same nature, of the same kind as the energy that makes you live.

We could call this bag of dust God, if you like. And we could also imagine that all the dust that was in the bag is already spread on the little wooden figures and also on plants, animals and everything that lives. At a certain point, the effect of this dust wears off, and then what happens is that it is rescued as dust, which will be spread on other things, allowing them to exist too. This creates a kind of cycle: some of the dust is scattered, some is going back into the bag to be put on other things, and there is always dust being distributed so that inertia becomes life.

Thus, the end of the dust in a particular unit of this collective is a kind of blink in the functioning of the whole. It's as if you were watching television and, for a hundredth of a second, there was a power cut. It's a slight turbulence in the progress of the whole, in such a way that we could also say that all the time there will be dust scattered and dust being picked up again. It's clear that dust comes and goes. This dust that is God, which is all energy - energy that comes and goes, that increases and decreases.

These little figures interact with each other and the energy increases a little here, decreases a little there. Sometimes the plant dies, losing its energy so that the doll can eat it and increase its own. And so does the animal.

If you think like that, you might have fairer expectations of what it means to live. I would recommend that you think about the conditions of our birth. You must have learned at school that there are trillions of sperm and that one of them hits the target. And that's you. In fact, improbability begins at fertilization and, I don't know why, throughout our lives we forget this improbability, that of staying alive. Life requires a lot of things to go right, but all it takes is for one of them to fail and the chances of life ending are very high.

Throughout our lives, by living with others, we're led to believe that at least we'll live to be eighty. And that's the unfortunate thing, because when someone dies at 49, we think there are 31 more to go. The mistake is in the expectation, not in the death. What's surprising is that people haven't realized that the error is one of estimation, not the end of existence. The end of existence is more than predictable, more than logical, more than normal.

In reality, suffering is the result of a mistake. If every day we were convinced that staying alive is a mystery, an improbability, a rarity, and that each new day lived, far from being an obvious certainty, is the opposite of that, the result of an incredible coincidence of factors that can fail to happen at any moment, there would be two things: firstly, we would be less surprised by death and, secondly, we would value life in all its moments.

One example: as we were writing this book, the plane belonging to Federal Supreme Court (STF) minister Teori Zavascki crashed. Unfortunately, there were no survivors.

I, like all Brazilians, was appalled by the fact that someone who was such a warrior - and that's regardless of any preference on my part - so confident in himself, such a fighter, with a large family, should die like that. There's no way that someone like me, in my 51 years, who for some time now has been in one place every day, fighting to bring my speech, my ideas and in doing so trying to contribute to people's lives, often picking up these unsafe pieces of junk, couldn't put himself in the shoes of those who died in the accident. But perhaps I'm a victim of the same error of expectation that I denounce so much. Because philosophical discourse is one thing, but our lives, which are very much like anyone else's, are another.

So let's take advantage of every thought, enjoy every moment, because one day this improbability will be false. One day the rule of mismatch will impose its yoke. And then, well, it will have been what it was and it will have been worth the seconds of laughter and sharing.

•••••

Death isn't bad in itself. It's bad as an expectation. I remember, as a child, asking my father if, when we died and were in the coffin, it would really be dark, if it wouldn't be distressing to close the lid and stay inside. My father would reply that we wouldn't realize it. It's just that the idea of sleeping implies waking up afterwards, but in the case of death, you won't wake up anymore. We always end up getting distracted by this kind of conversation, because it's interrupted, we order a pizza and pretend that everything is fine.

But the Stoics really believed that death is nonsense because we're part of a really cool thing. The problem with the fear of death is believing that you are worthwhile in your own right. When you understand that you're part of something that will never end, you can rest assured that you'll continue to participate, because, as I've already mentioned, part of you could become a doorknob or something else.

I don't know if this reflection is satisfactory for humans like us. We call it salvation to reduce the fear of death. If you say that I don't have to be afraid of dying because I'll end up turning into fuel or a boar's testicle, well, frankly, that's not a very exciting speech. Between becoming a boar's testicle and staying in a dark coffin forever, I honestly don't know which is better.

The Stoics believed that overcoming the fear of death could be achieved through a few stratagems that make it easier to understand that you are part of a contraption that is eternal and that, therefore, you are a fragment of eternity. Death is therefore no problem.

One of the perspectives they give us is descent, and you see a piece of yourself in your children, be it in the way they look, their ears, their size or the way they speak. It's clear that going from father to son guarantees you eternity.

Look, let's face it, these guys are pretty cool, their initiative is good, saying that I shouldn't fear death because my daughter has eyes the same color as mine is nice, I appreciate the initiative, but it's such a lame firepower that it's embarrassing.

There are other ways to try and break this deadlock and understand that you're gaining an eternity.

•••••

Let's talk about the second perspective given by the Stoics for overcoming the fear of death. What a great tip: become a hero. That's right, become a hero. You didn't read that wrong. And do you know why? Because if you become a hero, they'll keep talking about you even after you're dead. And then it will be as if you hadn't died because you're still alive in the narratives. And if those stories are written down, your name will appear on the pages of books, newspapers and magazines, and you definitely won't have died. The coffin, the wake and the funeral will be an illusion. You will be alive in libraries, alive in the reading of everyone who is interested in your story. Isn't that nice?

Hannah Arendt, a great 20th century thinker, deals with exactly this in a text called "The Crisis of Culture", in which she says: "The hero is as if he hadn't died because, through writing, he gains a kind of survival, a kind of eternity".

Well, I'm trying hard here, and of course they're talking about me. If they say something bad about me, that's fine, because I'm guaranteed to survive. You don't have to speak well. I think getting bad press is easier than getting good press. So you don't have to be a hero. You just have to be remembered. You can be a terrible scoundrel. If he's in the books after he's dead, it's all the same. I really think that's the way it is.

Anyway, that was the disappointing reflection of the moment. Let's face it, trying to convince me that I don't have to fear death because after I'm gone they'll keep talking about me, reading about me in written narratives, well, spare me.

•••••

For those who are 15 or 20 years old, the fear of death doesn't haunt them. But after 50, wow! The calculation that can be made today, at 50, is the following: "Up to 70 we can guarantee it, after all, medicine has evolved," the fool thinks. "If you're lucky, you'll make it to 80".

It's just that life will be strong from 50 to 60. Ten years to go. And do you know what ten years is? They're nothing. After 60, nothing works anymore. In fact, between you and me, you're already functioning like a blinker when you're 50: it works all the time, it doesn't work all the time. My eyes work, my ears work - I'm deaf, so I use feedback during lectures so I can hear myself. Vixe! Lumbar, sciatica, what about sex? It takes a cosmic combination to have any kind of guarantee.

The Stoics had every reason to think about it. They spoke of descent, of heroism. And they have a third way out: when you fit into the cosmic order, you live in the present, and that's an interesting promise. That instant is worth itself, there's a reconciliation with the world, in such a way that you're not obliged to think about what has already happened, what we call the past - because it doesn't exist except as a memory, recollection or thought of what has already happened - and you're also not obliged to think about what will happen, because the real is enough. And that's exactly how it is.

When you're spearfishing in the Mediterranean, the beauty of that landscape makes you want it to last forever, it's worth it in itself, it's wonderful, you can't think of anything else. Since I've never been spearfishing, let alone in the Mediterranean, I've used this example just so those of you reading this can imagine.

There are certain situations that are spectacular, like a beautiful naked woman. What are you going to think about in the past or the future? What you want to do is feel her up, seduce her. When reality is spectacular, there's no past or future.

I, for example, love mocotó. And I have a friend, Chico, who prepares a spectacular mocotó; when I taste the mocotó he makes, my mind thinks of the mocotó, my mouth eats the mocotó, my stomach prepares itself to receive the mocotó. Everything is mocotó. There is an alignment in the mocotó, and I don't think about the past or the future. The same happens when I give a talk. I get involved, the lecture enchants me, I only think about the lecture, totally focused, and so I have no reason to think about the past or the future. And I can assure you: when you don't have to think about what's going to happen, you don't think about death and you finally overcome that stupid fear of dying.

Make your life attractive, exciting and fascinating every second, and you won't remember that you're going to die. And the victory will be final.

Long live the Stoics! Fuck the fear of death! How am I supposed to think about death when I'm so focused on these reflections? Fuck death! This is the lesson of Seneca, Epictetus and Marcus Aurelius.

22

God

CLÓVIS: People have always wondered whether God exists, and many have come to the conclusion that their own intelligence is incapable of solving this enigma. We wouldn't have the rational competence to decree with certainty that he exists, nor that he doesn't exist.

Pascal suggests a stratagem to resolve the standoff. And this stratagem is very self-interested. You see, Pascal was a mathematical genius, the guy who discovered the area of the ellipse. And he did philosophy, back in the 1600s, in a work called *Pensées*, in which he proposes the following: what do we gain by betting that God exists?

Well, if we bet that God exists and he really does, we win eternity and apparently a very nice, very comfortable eternity, far from all the evils.

But what if God doesn't exist and we bet that he does? Then we gain nothing. But also, says Pascal, we lose very little, because, after all, what does God demand of us? One or two deprivations in the earthly world, in this life of flesh and blood, in this life of the world of life. And Pascal asks what would be more advantageous: to lose an eternity full of nice things or to lose one or the other piece of junk in a finite and deteriorated world? His answer is that it's more advantageous to bet that God exists because, if he does and we bet on him, gee, it'll be forever!

Now, if it doesn't exist, what we lose is one or two fits of rage, the impossibility of shooting someone in the head who's giving us a hard time or possibly going out gallivanting and cheating our victims.

You've understood Pascal. For my part, I don't know if I'd take that gamble, after all, depending on the god, there aren't that many deprivations. And betting that life is just this, in a world that is just this, and going for broke, could be a good thing.

I leave you with this reflection. If you want to read Pascal's *Thoughts*, you can find them on the newsstand.

• • • • •

For those who believe that God exists and that he is kind and powerful, one question often bothers them: if he is kind and powerful, how come he allows so much evil in the world?

Either he's good, but he can't do anything about it and so he's not powerful, or he's powerful, but he's evil because he doesn't do what he could do to stop so much evil.

The question seems embarrassing, but philosophy answers it with lightness, grace and intelligence: if God is creator, then he creates something other than himself. If he is perfect and created the world, if the world were perfect, God would not have created anything other than himself and there would only be God. In order for there to be something other than God, he had to create something other than himself. Therefore, if he is perfect, he creates something imperfect. So, if God is love, he can only have created something other than love: hatred. If God is peace, he can only have created war. If God is beauty, he can only have created ugliness. If God is intelligence, he can only have created stupidity.

In this way, we begin to understand evil in the world. If evil is imperfection, God lets the world be imperfect so that the world can be the world. And here is another question: what is the point of creating something different from oneself? Why does God accept this reduction? After all, God plus the world is worse than God alone.

The answer is that God accepts this imperfection out of love. Out of love for his creature. So think with me: my class isn't perfect because the perfect class would be given by God. If God guaranteed the perfection of my class, there would only be God's class and there wouldn't be my class. For Professor Clóvis' class to exist, for Professor Clóvis to be able to exist, God must allow the imperfect class. If God guaranteed the perfection of the world, he would always be in our place, after all, we are imperfect. If God guaranteed the perfection of my class, it would be God teaching the class and not me. Therefore, in order for Professor Clóvis to exist, God must allow it, he must withdraw, he must accept this diminishment. And God accepts this diminishment out of love. And out of love, he lets Clóvis be Clóvis, so that the teacher can be himself with all his imperfections.

What applies to my class applies to anything else. God could guarantee the perfection of everything, but then there would only be God. Everything would be God. Everything would be perfect, and the world wouldn't exist. That's why God's love for us and God's relationship with his creature is reminiscent of the footprints in the sand on the beach: they indicate that God has already been there, but has left so that the world can be as it is. He left so that you can exist as you. He left so that we can all be different from each other to the extent of our own specific imperfection.

•••••

There are many problems with believing in a transcendent god. The big question is: when God recommends something to us, does he recommend it because it's good? Is it good for its own sake?

In this case, we have the competence to identify what is good and we recognize that what God has recommended is really good. Or is something good only because God has recommended it? Is everything he recommends good by trade?

Let's look at the first possibility: God only recommends what is good, and what he recommends is good in itself. Now, my friend, in this case, our intelligence can identify what is good, it can discern how we should act, it can identify what is not good for us. Our intelligence guarantees us the possibility of attributing value to things in the world, as well as value to our behavior. And if we are intelligent enough to do this, if we have morals - since morals are intelligence at the service of the good life - then God would be a little too much. We ourselves would be enough.

Let's now imagine the second hypothesis: the thing is good because God said so. If he hadn't said it, it wouldn't be good. What makes things good is the fact that God has recommended them. Thus, everything would depend on his recommendation and we wouldn't need intelligence to identify what is right and what is wrong, we wouldn't have the competence of reason to attribute value to things in the world. And we would have no morality.

Well, you realize the difficulty. We're at a crossroads. Either things are good in their own right and God is in charge, or things depend on God to be good, in which case we are amoral, mindless creatures who are incompetent to solve our problems.

23

The illusion of immortality

CALABREZ: We live under a terrible illusion of immortality. Or perhaps a convenient forgetfulness of our mortality. People come up to us on our birthday and say: "Congratulations! Another year of life!".

That's wrong. It's one year less.

More experiences, more memories, more achievements, more interactions with the world? It could be.

More years of life? No.

Someone might disagree: "Well, that's another year of life lived!"

What does that mean, reader? Where does this "year of life lived" add up? There's only one answer: the year lived is added to memories. Our personal memories in our brain. Also the physical memories we keep outside of ourselves, in the world: photos, movies and the like.

For the brain, time is made up of the past (memories) and the future (plans and dreams). With each passing year, we have more memories. With each passing year, we have less time to achieve our plans and dreams. Ageing is by definition an exhaustion of the time at our disposal. After all, death is a certainty. Every moment is a step towards it.

We may believe that there is a life after this one, reader, but you must agree with me: this life here, now, is unique - and there will never be another opportunity to live it.

• • • • •

One year less every year. This is perhaps the most stoic of lessons. *Memento mori.* Remember that you will die.

And anyone who hears me say that might think: "What a sad thing! That's a horrible way of looking at life!"

No. I totally disagree.

It's sad to reach the end of your life, look back and realize that you wasted your precious time and energy on people and projects that weren't worth it. It's sad to regret not having made the most of it, not having tried, not having taken a chance.

In relationships, for example. Friendships, relationships, marriages, family relationships - it doesn't matter. In all of them, we tend to adapt. For years, the person is there, within our reach. But we adapt. We get used to their presence and have the terrible illusion that things will always continue as they are. We stop thanking them, valuing them and investing our energy in the relationship. We start to treat the person as if they were always going to be there.

Until one day the person leaves.

Sometimes by force of nature. Nothing remains. Unfortunately, neither does health. It's the only certainty we all have, says popular wisdom.

Sometimes of their own volition. After all, one day people get tired. Tiredness, exhaustion - from being treated with disregard or not having their presence properly valued.

That's where *it* comes in. The most common feeling in the void left by those who leave: regret. For not having done this or that. For not having appreciated. For not being grateful. For not having been there. For not having tried.

At the root of regret is a bad kind of hope: the kind that comes from the verb "to hope". The repentant person is usually (or was) hopeful. They waited for things to change, they waited for the opportunity, they waited for courage. They waited instead of acting. Instead of doing something different.

Regret is one of the most common feelings we encounter inside hospitals - from where many unfortunately don't return.

This scene has already been seen by many doctors:

An elderly man suffers a stroke. His son, a young man in his forties, is waiting for news. The doctor approaches him and says: "Unfortunately, based on the images of your father's brain, the condition is irreversible".

At that moment, you see a grown man start to cry like a child. In tears, in a desperation that breaks the heart of any human being capable of empathy, he says: "But doctor, I had a fight with my father twenty years ago. We haven't spoken since. I really wish I could talk to him again and say goodbye!".

But unfortunately it's no longer possible. There's nothing left to do.

But the father was there for decades. Within reach of a phone call. Within reach of a hug and an apology.

This brings me back to my initial point: one of the great roots of this is the illusion of immortality. We believe that we will live forever. Conveniently, we forget about our own death. As a result, we fall into a delusion that opportunities will always be there, within our reach.

Imagine a world in which we were truly aware every day that every minute is a minute less, that every moment is an investment. A world in which we remembered every day that one day we will close our eyes and they will never open again. A world in which we accept the idea that the hug we gave our mother and father may have been our last. That the kiss we gave our spouse might be goodbye.

If people were aware of the finiteness of life on a daily basis, I believe we would eliminate much of the pettiness and small-mindedness we find in everyday things.

Aware of your mortality, perhaps you wouldn't fight in traffic. Perhaps you wouldn't cling to small, insignificant details to fight with the people in your life. Maybe you'd stop complaining about trivialities at work and take advantage of the opportunities you're given every day.

Life comes to an end. That's why we should be grateful to nature every day for having given us the opportunity to briefly stroll through this universe. Above all, we should be grateful for the opportunity to walk through the cosmos while possessing, within us, the most complex brain in existence - the only brain capable of learning about itself, reflecting and seeking to live better tomorrow than we do today.

Part 3

LIVING AND SOCIALIZING

1

Love and passion

CLÓVIS: Let's talk about falling in love, passion, enchantment. There are certain worlds that make us happy. These worlds suit us. When they appear in front of us, they transform our physical-chemical composition, increasing our potency, our energy, our libido. It's normal that, having caught this experience, having brought this feeling into our consciousness, we want to repeat the dose. This is what Spinoza calls love. Joy when it is accompanied by an awareness of its cause. And then we start looking for what we think will make us happy. Well, only those who don't want it don't see it: a relationship of dependence is established. We come to believe that if the thing we think will make us happy isn't around, joy becomes impossible and sadness is probable.

Money allows many of these things to stay around. There's no doubt why we go after money so greedily: to ensure that things that make us happy can stay close by. In this way, if the sea makes us happy, money allows us to have a house on the beach; if the mountains make us happy, money allows us to have a house in the mountains; if a rabada makes us happy, money allows us to have a good restaurant; if a comfortable car makes us happy, money allows us to enter the dealership with pride.

Things get complicated when our joy becomes dependent on encounters that money can't guarantee. This is what happens when the cause of joy is someone's presence. When a person is the cause of our joy, we have to rely on their willingness to stay close to us. The strategies we use to do this don't always work, and we're at the mercy of a set of decisions we can't control. And when our joy depends on decisions we can't control, we become their slaves. Our soul oscillates, our body becomes unbalanced, everything is revolutionized in us. My friend, the chances of this not working out are quite high.

Lucretius considered this to be the worst of situations and recommended a relentless fight against it, advising that we try to identify their defects, their imperfections, in the one who supposedly makes us happy: "Force yourself to find imperfections in the one on whom your joy depends so that you can resist and, by resisting, avoid such dependence." The big problem - which perhaps Lucretius knew but didn't want to say - is that one of the first things that happens is our immediate inability to identify imperfections in the one we love. The big problem - which perhaps Lucretius knew, but didn't want to say - is that precisely when we are falling in love, one of the first things that happens is our immediate inability to identify imperfections in the one we love.

It's really ugly. That's why our society ends up teaching us, second by second, that frivolous relationships are one thing and great enchantments are another. And in this post-modern world, we are increasingly encouraged to maintain frivolous relationships. The new technologies make it too easy, people quickly become replaceable, not least because they're all very similar on WhatsApp lists. As for their most distinctive characteristics, well, sometimes you don't even have time to get to know them, because there's always another, another, another on the list to entertain you.

Some don't adapt to postmodern society. They're card-carrying modernists. Late representatives of the 19th century. To them, my solidarity in suffering and pain.

• • • • •

This is a kind of experience that has always intrigued me. I don't know if you've ever been in love. Passionate like that on all fours, thinking about the person 24 hours a day.

The situation I'm going to try to analyze is that of falling in love, of enchantment, in which there is still no kind of courtship, no kind of relationship. You want it to happen. You're in the midst of seduction, but nothing has happened yet. If I had to compare this situation to something else, I'd compare it to a rollercoaster. When you ride a rollercoaster in a park, what happens? You have experiences you don't control: you don't control where the ride goes, when it goes up, when it goes down, the speed it acquires at different times, you don't control the radical nature of the experience, the intensity of the sensations you feel. Well, when you're in love it's more or less like that. You don't control the intensity of the sensations you feel, you're adrift, at your mercy.

Let's imagine a first moment when you're with the person you love desperately. Joy can happen - remembering that joy is gaining the power to act. In that moment of pure joy, you're next to the person and you're fine. It's almost an experience of spirituality. The person speaks, expresses themselves, acts, runs, and this touches you, does you good, is enough for you, and you find yourself joyful. It's joy in the midst of so much passion.

However, you may experience other feelings with your loved one. As well as joy, you may feel hope. And what is hope? It's also a gain in power and its cause is what you imagine. Realize that now you're presupposing what's going to happen from then on, you're thinking about living with that person, being that person's boyfriend, being that person's husband. And while they're there, acting, you create a future scene in which you'll relate to them and, as well as joy, you feel hope. But here's a comment: joy plus hope is worse than joy alone.

Why?

Because every hope is inseparable from its opposite: fear, the fear that it won't happen, the fear that the person will never date you, that the person will never be yours. Hope and fear are two sides of the same coin. They are essentially the same thing. If, during that meeting, you imagine a shared future or a future of separation, there will be hope and there will be fear. And, of course, it will be less cool than just joy.

Here's what can happen when you're with the person you're in love with.

Well, let's imagine now when the person is not by your side. You think about them, and then a lot can happen. There won't be the joy of the loved one's presence. There could be sadness at the absence. But let's be clear: absence is not the cause of any affection. Absence is nothing, and nothing cannot be the cause of anything. In fact, what makes you sad when the person isn't there is the reality you encounter. It's when you go to the bakery without the person. When you go to the movies without the person. When you go to the restaurant without the person. What causes sadness is reality, but reality separated from the person you'd like to be with. And this feeling is even sadder when you've already been with that person in the places you revisit. So, of course, a first experience is pure sadness.

But when you're separated, far from the person, you can also feel hope: you can imagine being with them, you can imagine their presence. And you can feel fear: you imagine never meeting them again. You realize that joy and sadness, fear and hope are all part of the life of someone in love. You oscillate as if you were on a boat.

And here's another observation: throughout the history of thought, there are very few thinkers who think that this life of falling in love is a good life. Philosophy has always been suspicious of all emotions that you can't control. Philosophy hates rollercoasters, because you're at the mercy of what happens and you can't control it.

When the Greeks talk about ataraxia and Eastern philosophy talks about the Zen state, they are referring to life situations in which you control the causes of your emotions. A lot of philosophy, if we were to continue with the amusement park metaphor, considers the good life to be a merry-go-round. Nothing unexpected happens on it. The horses go round and round, and you know exactly what's going to happen. The good life would be like a trip in a rowing boat around an island in a lake with no waves, it would be the complete mastery of the causes of emotions. Strictly speaking, it's the opposite of the rollercoaster that enslaves you, that subjects you to this maddening seesaw between joy and sadness, between opposing emotions such as fear and hope. Take, for example, when you're with the person you want, you're overjoyed, and then they say: "My boyfriend is very intelligent".

That's it. You go from joy to immediate fear of never being able to have that woman's love. You realize that you can't control her initiative to talk about her boyfriend, and this initiative causes you to go from joy to fear. Suddenly, she says: "But even though he's very intelligent, he's violent. He doesn't want me to work, he doesn't want me to develop.

You move from fear to hope. Again, you are not in control. Again you are at the mercy of a discourse whose cause you have no access to. The vast majority of philosophers are horrified by this.

And you're curious to know what I think about that? Then I'll tell you: I think that if your life is one of ataraxia, as the Greeks would have it, or Zen, as the Eastern philosophers would have it, and you control all the causes of your affections as if you were circling an island in a lake without waves, well, that's what I call absolute boredom, which is the ideal of philosophy. And believe me, if someone comes along with a rollercoaster that's nice to try out, you might be on the verge of getting hit in the back. I think there are some really cool roller coasters where the equation between fear and hope, between joy and sadness, can be favorable. I think that's the best possible situation: a moderate rollercoaster, because some are very difficult.

There are some bets you shouldn't make, such as making your happiness conditional on becoming president of the United States. It's preferable that you change the condition of your joy, because the chance of that happening is very remote. I know that a banana can fly without external impetus, but if your joy depends on becoming president of the United States, it's possible that sadness will become sovereign. It could also be the case that you fall in love with Isis Valverde or Reynaldo Gianecchini. And then you might have to suffer a little until you drop the ball and find a more plausible rollercoaster. That's what I think: no lake without waves, no rollercoasters that are too radical. I'm Aristotelian and moderate. That's my opinion.

CALABREZ: Passion, when we look at the brain, resembles a state of great motivation and pleasure, with characteristics of temporary dementia, stress, obsession and compulsion.

Love is probably the feeling that has most instigated human thought over the centuries. All the great mythologies and religions have discussed love in depth. In philosophy, love has been present since the beginning, as Clovis shows us. In art, the omnipresence of love is indisputable. Just think of Shakespeare or even today's cinema, where even in dinosaur and alien movies the scriptwriters try to squeeze in some romance.

But far from being something metaphysical, something outside the concrete world, love is a manifestation of brain functions. Today we know that romantic relationships generally begin with a first stage of high intensity and short duration that we usually call infatuation.

But what happens to our brains when we're in love?

Like any emotion, passion is regulated by what we call endocrine factors, in other words, it involves a series of hormones and neurotransmitters, which are nothing more than chemical substances. These substances have an effect on the functioning of the body in general and on the brain in particular.

Firstly, studies show that two hormones play an important role during passion: oxytocin and vasopressin. These hormones play various roles in the human body. In the case of passion, they function as neuropeptides - in other words, small compounds that act locally on various brain circuits. The action of oxytocin and vasopressin in the brain during passion is associated with attachment, the connection formed between the couple. It is also associated with the preference that the person in love has for *that specific person,* in a way "ignoring" the others.

This means that, during infatuation, we are extremely attached to the person we fall in love with. What's more, that person will stand out, be more prominent, more important, more relevant to us than any other person. This explains some of the feeling we get that that person is unique, that no one can replace them.

We also find oxytocin and vasopressin receptors in a brain circuit we call the reward system. We already defined the concept of reward in Chapter 2 of the first part of the book. However, let's define it again briefly to remind ourselves.

We can start with some examples of highly rewarding stimuli: caloric foods (ice cream and dessert, for example), some drugs (such as cocaine) or even certain challenges to our brain (such as a very exciting movie or book).

From this we can see that reward primarily involves motivation. In a motivated state, our body compels us to keep doing what we're doing - or to do more of what we're already doing. Think, for example, of you being hungry. You order a coxinha. It arrives. You take a small bite. Proving to be a person of sound mind, you start biting off the end. To start eating the coxinha any other way is almost heresy.

Jokes aside, let's get back to the process.

At the very moment of the bite, you realize that your body is inclining you towards a subsequent behavior, in other words, compelling you to a new action. And what is this action? It's obviously to take and eat another bite. And another... Until, of course, you are satiated. That's motivation. This *inclination to keep doing what we're doing - or to do more than we're already doing.*

Reward also involves pleasure. By this, I mean that the reward also involves the positive subjective sensation associated with the motivating stimulus. In this case, the pleasure of eating the coxinha, the delicious sensation, the deliciousness of the coxinha.

• • • • •

The brain's reward system largely involves the action of a neurotransmitter called dopamine. Like the hormones I've already mentioned, dopamine has a number of different functions in the human body. In the case of passion, it is associated with a motivational state. Passion is a hyperdopaminergic state. This means that it is associated with a heightened experience of reward. In other words, infatuation generates motivation and pleasure when we come into contact with the stimulus - in this case, the stimulus is the person we are in love with.

It's important to note that physical contact isn't necessary to generate this motivation and pleasure. It's enough to think of the person, remember them or some aspect of them, and the emotion comes. Emotions can be triggered by mere mental content, such as an idea or memory.

Passion, then, is a hyperdopaminergic state. This explains why we are extremely motivated when we are in love. At the beginning of a relationship, we seem to have energy and desire for everything. Sexual desire (specifically for the person) is high. We want new experiences, to travel with the person, to explore different places, to please the person in every way. What's more, being with the person and thinking about them are extremely rewarding experiences. They motivate us and give us pleasure.

• • • • •

Another substance involved in passion is serotonin, also a neurotransmitter. Like all the substances I've talked about here, serotonin is associated with a number of functions in the body. One of its important roles in the brain is in regulating mood. The most popular antidepressants interact with the serotonergic system.

When you're in love, your serotonin levels drop. Interestingly, there is another condition in which we observe drops in serotonin levels: obsessive-compulsive disorder, known as OCD.

Realize that infatuation has both obsessive and compulsive characteristics. Obsession involves invasive, recurring thoughts and a strong fixation on the idea of the person. You're at work, in traffic, taking a shower, watching a sitcom, and the idea of the person pops into your head, regardless of your will. Very similar to obsession.

What's more, when you're with the person you're in love with, you want more and more time with them, there isn't enough time, and that time you spend with them makes you feel joy, comfort, relief from anxiety. This is very similar to compulsions.

It's no wonder that recent studies suggest that people who take antidepressants known as "serotonin reuptake inhibitors" (substances that increase serotonin levels) have less intense symptoms of passion.

There is another hormone involved in infatuation: cortisol, typically associated with stress responses. Cortisol levels rise during infatuation. When we fall in love, we become anxious, insecure and feel euphoric. The heart beats faster and stronger, the digestive system changes (have you noticed that when you fall in love and the person is around, you don't feel hungry?). Our energy increases, we become hypervigilant (i.e. sleepless). These symptoms all arise when we come into contact with stressful stimuli. Elevations in cortisol may explain why they occur during infatuation.

• • • • •

Finally, one last interesting thing happens during infatuation. There is a change in a brain structure called the prefrontal cortex, which I've already talked about. This structure, which is immediately behind our forehead, is inhibited during infatuation.

In the first part of the book, I talked about a substance that inhibits the prefrontal cortex: alcohol. You thought that was strange, because the last thing you feel when you drink is inhibited. But that's because, among the many things the prefrontal structures are responsible for, is the ability to curb our impulses, hold back our desires and anticipate the future consequences of what we do now. In other words, these structures are involved in planning and decision-making.

With the prefrontal inhibited, our desires and impulses come to the surface without so many brakes, and the ability to think about the consequences of our actions is diminished. That's why drunks tend to make stupid and inconsequential decisions. Remember my friend wrapped in aluminum foil.

With the brain in love, prefrontal inhibition also occurs. That's why making big decisions in love is often a bad idea. You may have seen that people who are extremely passionate often make bad decisions, such as getting their girlfriend's name tattooed on their left buttock.

In this sense, passion has the characteristics of dementia.

This is why passion, when we look at the brain, resembles a state of great motivation and pleasure, with characteristics of temporary dementia, stress, obsession and compulsion.

•••••

None of this takes away from passion's beauty and charm. Being in love is one of the most incredible experiences there is. If I could, I'd be in love all the time. Who would have thought that being a bit "demented" could be so enjoyable!

However, I must emphasize one last characteristic of the neurobiology of passion. Passion is fleeting. Studies show that its chemical and functional effects on the brain disappear after 12 to 24 months.

We can look at it realistically and coldly. You only fall hopelessly in love because one day you find yourself, and the passion goes away. You only fall out of love with someone because one day you hit the ground - and wake up to reality. I think a lot of people reading these words have already experienced this.

In a different way, we can look at it more poetically, as Vinicius de Moraes did. May passion not be eternal, since it is a flame. But may it be infinite as long as it lasts.

The chemical and neural processes responsible for passion are fleeting. But that doesn't exhaust love. As I said at the beginning: love is typically divided into two different phases. Infatuation is usually the first, of high intensity and short duration. Sometimes, when infatuation ends, a process of attachment continues. Many will call this process love in fact, denying that infatuation should be called "love".

As a teacher, I don't like to use love and passion as different things. I prefer to think of passion as a stage of love. Often, it's the first stage. Sometimes love develops into a second stage. Sometimes the stages are reversed. Sometimes love ends when passion ends. Sometimes love starts without passion, going straight into the second stage. We often have moments of passion during this second stage.

Researchers often call the first stage *passionate love* and the second stage *companionate love*. This second stage is made up of a strong bond of union, which becomes stronger and stronger over time. It involves deep commitment, affection, care, security and trust between the parties. However, it is a more difficult relationship to maintain: there is no longer a flood of hormones and neurotransmitters that keep us motivated and attached to the person. This second stage is less intense and lasts longer.

Lasting relationships require effort. They are a construction in which each party must seek, day after day, a better and stronger connection. Like the health of the body, built day by day, in which we reject the immediacy of *fast food* and laziness, relationships are built through efforts of attachment, gratitude and appreciation.

• • • • •

Falling in love is not a choice.

Some will say: "Yes, it is! I chose to fall in love."

All I'm saying is that the choice we have about passion is the same choice we have about other emotions and feelings. Can you choose not to rejoice when you receive good news? Or choose not to be afraid if a shark appears when you're diving? Emotions and feelings are not derived from choices. Only behaviors are subject to choices.

So I repeat:

Falling in love is not a choice. Building a relationship is. A daily choice, continuous effort, active construction - and therefore the fatal victim of laziness. There is no greater death sentence for a romantic relationship than accommodation and laziness, which lead to a reduction in the effort to maintain and strengthen bonds. Accommodation is death.

•••••

There's something contradictory about love.

On the one hand, it's not always reciprocated. When I say that I would be in love all the time, I'm considering a reciprocal passion. Unrequited passion can cause indescribable anguish.

But suppose that love was reciprocated.

Relationships end one day. It may be during the first moments or after years of companionship. Eventually, we will die and leave the person we love - or they will leave us first. Separation is almost always difficult and painful. In the second part of the book, we saw how important social relationships are for our health.

It's no wonder then that this is reflected in the functioning of the brain. When going through a process of separation or rejection, studies indicate that the same brain circuits responsible for mediating physical pain (such as breaking a leg or being punched in the face) are activated. There is something similar in the brain between physical and emotional pain. In other words, *physical and emotional pain are to some extent processed by the same brain circuits.*

So the term "heartbreak" seems appropriate. I'm sure many readers have gone through terrible emotional pain - and would rather have a broken leg than go through that.

To love is to sign a sentence that will most likely condemn us to these sorrows sooner or later. At the end of a relationship, in separation or divorce, or - at the latest - in the mourning of loss.

On the other hand, not loving means living smaller. Giving up something that is literally a human need: the warmth of another human being. I'm not just talking about romantic love, but in a broader sense, including friends and family. After all, the same sorrows apply here. Without this love we literally die. The studies are clear: quality social relationships are the most important factor for human well-being, even associated with individual health. We need attachment.

That's the contradiction. We need to love in order to live better. Life, however, condemns us, sooner or later, to losing the person we love - a loss that will be the source of great sadness.

When we love, we trust that the joys will be great enough to overcome the eventual and probable sadness of separation or loss. Perhaps now it makes more sense that, in the first stage of love, we become "demented". Then we don't think about such things. We don't imagine such sadness and we don't question this trust.

CLÓVIS: We all know that sadness exists. Sadness is what we feel in encounters with the world that hurt us. It stems from chance encounters. Our power decreases every time the traffic lights close and we're in a hurry, every time we have a stomach ache, every time we suffer humiliation at work. These sadnesses are the result of encounters that might not have happened. And the world presents us with new sorrows every day.

But this reflection is not about those sorrows. It's about a suffering that doesn't depend on life's circumstances. A suffering that never leaves us. A suffering that stems from the fact that we are desirous, that we constantly seek permanence in a world that flows. The fact that we always want joys to translate into happiness, for loves to last forever, for good times to be repeated eternally. This pretension blasphemes the world of life, where nothing remains.

Wanting to live forever in a life of traffic is fighting against the very essence of our existence, the cause of our deepest suffering. So be sure: suffering is not the attribute of a life badly lived, it is not the result of mistakes, it is not punishment for something we have done now or in other lives. Suffering is inherent to life, it is essential to life. Without suffering, life doesn't exist either. Suffering is to life as chocolate is to chocolate cake, chicken is to chicken soup, bananas are to bananas, guava is to guava.

• • • • •

What would you choose between clinging and getting fucked or living a life of shit without attachment?

Attachment is the hope of repeating today's joy tomorrow and, therefore, a kind of certainty in the possibility of stretching out an instant of gaining power and joy. There's an extra difficulty, and the problem isn't just that the object of attachment deteriorates, changes, falls apart in the air. The problem is that when you meet someone and feel joy, you say with the lightness of ignorance: "Armando made me happy".

What could be behind the word "Armando"? It's actually a collection of complex, sometimes contradictory, disparate attributes. Armando doesn't mean anything. A person, after all, is a collection of characteristics, so you need to know what about Armando made you happy. If you don't do this analysis, you may be surprised to find that the same Armando who supposedly made you happy in the past has characteristics that will now make you sad. Sometimes a person has a beautiful smile, a lovely hug, is capable of unheard-of caresses, and at the same time is selfish, stingy, morally clumsy, capable of atrocities. All in the same Armando, in the same person.

Often we get attached because we feel happy, we buy a big packet that comes full of strange oranges. Or have you never bought a box of strawberries in which the top layer was the most beautiful, large, attractive, and when you got home and took off the first layer, the ones at the bottom were crumpled, blemished, even bitten? Sometimes Armando is like that: on your first meeting, he shows you the top strawberries. You're happy, you get attached and, as you get to know him, the bottom strawberries appear.

Some might think: "Oh, eat the top strawberries and throw away the rest!".

They probably didn't understand that it was an allegory, a kind of didactic device to compare attachment to a person. If they had, they wouldn't have considered this solution. After all, when they become attached and want to eat only the top strawberries and throw away the rest, they might want to warn the victim first. The victim of the amputation, of the discrimination, of the splitting of what is a sweet and good strawberry from what is a rotten strawberry, right?

So what is the cause of joy? It's almost inevitable that a person will be able to be happy and sad almost at the same time. To cling to it, therefore, is to buy sadness and, what's worse, to sponsor an encounter with sadness by putting it in the house. How many times do we make a mistake when it comes to identifying the cause of our joy?

Ah, my friend! It's that story about the girl who goes on vacation in Punta del Este. There she has a moment of joy when she meets an Argentinian from Buenos Aires. She believes he's the cause of her joy. So she brings the Argentine here, welcomes him at Cumbica and, already on the Marginal, thinks about going back to the airport and returning the guy, because she makes a late and desperate discovery: when she was happy on *New Year's Eve* in Punta, it was for another reason - maybe the city, the sunset, being on vacation, because the hotel was nice, the food was good - but not for the Argentine. But he was the only one she decided to put in the house. Oh, dear! Really sad! We almost always cling to packages that have everything. Yikes! Sometimes it's too late, and the next thing you know, sadness is already on the bed, in its bathrobe, just waiting for you.

If you want to have a moment of illusion, just turn on the television, because that's what it's made for, to deceive. So is the rest of the world. Advertising will not fail. There will be no shortage of illusion.

Life as it is, only here, in reflections.

•••••

Trust, on the other hand, is certainty. And certainty is a privileged relationship between what we think and the world. When we are certain of something, we maintain a relationship of knowledge with the world. The certainty of trust is a certainty about things we can't verify. We can be sure of the rain right under the rain. We can be sure of something when it's right in front of us.

That's not what trust is. Trust is a certainty without being able to verify it, without being able to establish empirical proof with the world. It can be an ethical value. In this case, the certainty is not about the sunset, or even about the rain. Trust is an ethical value when it has as its object someone's behavior. You are certain that someone will act in one way or another, you are certain of someone's conduct even without being able to verify it. Trust is super-important in relationships, after all, behavior is still going to happen. When you hire someone, when you decide to be friends with someone, when you marry someone, what matters is what will happen from then on. And what will still happen, by definition, cannot be verified. Therefore, in relationships there needs to be trust.

We can trust someone because we know them a lot, because we know that they have a certain regularity and because they always do something in a certain way. This is a trust based on previous experience. But of course, one day they might do something different and surprise you.

There is another kind of trust. It's the certainty about the other person's behavior even without previous experience, even if the other person has never done what they promise to do. This trust is more noble. It is trust in someone who has never managed to do something, but who we are sure will succeed. It's a trust that belies the past, it's the open door to future behavior. The behavior of someone you trust even if you have no reason to.

• • • • •

In the second part of the book, we saw that for Stoic thought it is possible to overcome fears and find a world that satisfies us, that relieves us of thinking about what has already happened and what will happen, overcoming the fear of death and living fully. But what is this world that invites us to full reconciliation? What is this world that is so good that it makes us overcome the worst of fears, the worst of obstacles to a good life?

This world is what we love, it is the object of our love. That's why I have no doubt that love is the solution to the fear of death, because when love exists, the present is enough. And when the present is enough, the future doesn't ask to enter our minds. And when the future doesn't cross our minds, there's no need to think about the moment of our death. And fear disappears.

So you have to get real, in both senses: you have to realize that only the world right in front of you is capable of meeting this need and preventing you from having to think about the future. You have to give the world a chance. This is what Nietzsche calls amor *fati,* love for the world as it is, as it is perceived by you and not as you would like it to be.

When you live according to how you'd like things to be, you're giving your mind space. It contains the things you would like them to be. If you always contrast the world with what you would like it to be, it will never be good enough, giving you room to think about pasts and futures.

Love more. Love the world as it is. Reconcile yourself with reality. I'd like to quote here a phrase by Professor André Comte-Sponville, who is admittedly stoically inspired, which is fantastic: "Regret a little less" - that's the past - "hope a little less" - that's the future - "and love a little more" - that's the present moment, what we're living right now. If the past doesn't ask to pass, if the future doesn't impose itself, the present will be enough. The present that is enough is the one we love, the present that is the object of our love, the greatest of our feelings, the main of our emotions, the salvation from the fear of death.

CALABREZ: In addition to these important considerations, it seems to me that there are two other elements that must be taken into account in love.

First of all, admiration. There is no love without admiration. Passion almost naturally makes us admire the person. Even if we don't admire their intellect or personality, for example, we can admire their beauty. When we move on to the second stage, companionate love, admiration becomes even more important. When admiration runs out, the flame of love threatens to go out, the bonds loosen, the connection between the parties diminishes.

Another element I spoke about briefly is care. "Those who love, care", goes the popular saying. In fact, caring and loving seem to go hand in hand.

But we need to be rigorous. What does it mean to admire? What does it mean to care? Have we confused admiration and care with a mixture of desire and joy?

CLÓVIS: Admiration is what we call a particular state of our mind, of our imagination. Your mind is active all the time, even when you sleep. As you go about your life and encounter the world, the world offers you inputs that stimulate the mind's activity, and you make connections, associations. When, for example, I come across a book, depending on the type, it makes me think about class, it makes me think about work. There are other books that make me think of entertainment, of rest. By observing things all the time, they make us think of things which, in turn, make us think of other things, and these connections continue until new stimuli determine new chains.

What about admiration? Admiration is an abrupt interruption of these connections. It's when an element of reality that we are contemplating doesn't find a connection or association hook in us. Then there is a sudden paralysis of mental activity. We call this paralysis admiration. It's important to realize that admiration is a consequence of the disposition of our ideas, our ability to think and imagine. It is therefore an interruption caused by a gap in our mind, a lack of a hook. This means that admiration is not caused by the world we contemplate. If our repertoire were different, if our ideas were different, obviously our willingness to think would be different, and the worlds that cause us wonder would be different.

Realize that when you say that something is admirable, you are saying that you were perplexed, paralyzed, unable to make associations in the face of a world you have just seen. But this world that has brought you to a standstill is not admirable in itself, because if the observer had been different, perhaps it would have been connected and admiration would not have occurred. We must remember that admiration in itself is neither good nor bad. It's just a fact, a reality of your mental activity.

Admiration can be accompanied by joy. It is joyful when the interruption of the mental nexus of chaining generates a gain in the power to act.

Admiration can be sad. In this case, at the same time as we find ourselves powerless to move forward in our mental activities, we lose heart, we shrink back, we shy away from life.

We often look at someone and say: "Hey, are you traveling?". We put our hand in front of the person's face to indicate that they are in the world of the moon, they are somewhere else, but not there.

That's right. When we say that someone is traveling, it's perfectly possible that they are engaged in an intense activity of imaginative connections. It's perfectly possible that this person is far removed from admiration. But it's also true that when we're in awe, imaginative inertia makes us look like travelers. So when you observe someone distracted, it's very difficult to know whether they seem distracted because they're in awe or because they're in intense associative activity.

It's worth remembering that admiration is often produced by observing someone's behavior. In that case, at that moment, that person is the cause of our admiration. Let's be clear: this is not necessarily a good thing. Firstly, it stems from a gap that is yours, the observer. Secondly, it can be accompanied by a deep sadness, a profound "diminishing" inertia. This is what happens when we admire evil.

But how is it possible to admire evil? When we admire, isn't it necessarily something we think is good?

Of course not. Evil can paralyze, it can block our mental activity and therefore be worthy of our paralyzed admiration.

• • • • •

Now, about care.

Once, talking to a friend on the phone, as we were saying goodbye, he said to me: "Take care".

And I replied: "You too".

I hung up the phone and wondered what that meant. "Take care of yourself. " We could imagine an easier situation: one person takes care of another. What does that mean?

Basically, caring implies an affective shielding on the one hand and the promotion of other affections on the other. When you look after someone, you try to make the world hurt them as little as possible. You prepare the world to reduce sadness. When you look after someone, you try to give them joyful encounters with the world, you try to prepare the world to make them as sad as possible and as happy as possible. Of course, this involves many things.

You can, for example, take care by offering nourishment, providing joyful encounters that leverage power, like well-prepared rice and beans. When you take care of someone, you prevent them from eating things that make them sad, you take care of nutrients that could cause harm. When you take care of someone, you make their bed, you tidy the covers, and all of this is care for the world, so that the world can rejoice.

At the end of the day, caring for someone is a very complicated emotional equation that requires 24 hours of attention to everything that can hurt in the world. Taking care of someone is a difficult task, because the world is cunning and crafty when it comes to making people sad.

But that's taking care of someone. Now, can I take care of myself? That would imply that I could discern the things that can make me happy and sad. It would require my intelligence to be at the service of my affections. It would require me to have the ability, by anticipation, to find things in the world that might make me happy and get rid of those that might make me sad. Taking care of yourself requires an incredible ability to anticipate the affective outcome of encounters with the world. Taking care of yourself is not easy, because you are alone in the face of a world that always surprises and rarely in the sense of joy. Taking care of yourself means being careful with your affections, using your intelligence to avoid what we only assume might make you sad.

Taking care of yourself can be full of mistakes, because we will only avoid worlds that make us sad because of previous experiences. We're only going to look for worlds that make us happy because of previous experiences, and everyone knows that previous experiences don't repeat themselves. Sometimes, because we were sad one day, we missed the chance to be happy; because we were happy one day, we missed the chance to avoid sadness.

Taking care of yourself is not easy. I think it's what we try to do all the time. We use our intelligence to find happy worlds and avoid sad ones. But intelligence is in short supply in the face of such a complex world. The world will always be much more difficult than our ability to anticipate it, diagnose it and identify what suits us and what doesn't suit us. Taking care of ourselves is just an attempt doomed to failure because, if it succeeded, we might never die.

2

Freedom

CLÓVIS: There's a lot of talk about freedom. The word "free" is on everyone's lips. But what can be free? Which substance is free?

You know that bitter is an attribute of chocolate and that it would never be an attribute of a bedside table or a coat rack. To say that a coat rack is bitter is absurd.

What is free? What can be free? Someone will say:

You can be free.

But that's too vague. After all, what is free in a person?

The first thing about a person who can be free is their actions, their conduct. The imprisoned individual is deprived of many behaviors and many actions. The second thing is in our thoughts; we can think whatever comes to mind, without limits. The third thing that could be free in us is our desire. What we want for ourselves. Is it? Are we free to want? Are we free to desire? Or does desire impose itself on us? Or do we watch our bodies desire without being able to do anything about it? Does desire tyrannize us? Is desire our greatest bondage?

• • • • •

Talking about freedom brings us back to a beautiful concept from 20th century philosophy, which is the concept of bad faith. I often joke in lectures that there are always two of us. I'm referring to ourselves as bodies that desire, that feel, that rejoice, that suffer, that think, but I'm also referring to us as the consciousness we have of ourselves, our bodies, our sensations and our thoughts. In this way, when you see that you've put on weight, there are two of you: the fat person and the person who realized that they had. When you have a blow job, there are two of you: the blow job and the embarrassed person.

Shame is a particular form of sadness. We already know that sadness is always a loss of power, a decrease in our power to act. Shame is a sadness with a very special cause, it's an attribute caught in itself, it's a sadness that we give ourselves.

We can be saddened by what happens in the world, we can be saddened by other people, we can be saddened by events. Shame is always a sadness caused by ourselves. It's the flagrancy of a misalignment. It's when we perceive a behavior, a conduct, a thought that is incompatible with our identity, with what we believe ourselves to be, incompatible with the characteristics we believe to be ours. This misalignment makes us lose face, makes us sad, makes us blush, makes us feel ashamed.

Shame is a privileged tangent between the body and the soul. In shame there is the conscious and rational flagrancy of a shameful attribute in ourselves. And in shame there is also body, cell, hormone, sensation. Shame is the noble intertwining of reason and passion in sadness. It is therefore a privileged moment to realize how much our reason depends on our passions and how much our passions depend on what we think.

With every behavior we have, we can have some conscience. We can rejoice in what we do - which we call pride - and we can be saddened by what we do - which we call shame. The possibility of thinking about ourselves, of having self-awareness, is a condition for our freedom. Those who don't think about themselves shy away from the freedom of their conduct; after all, they act without discernment about other life possibilities. The more you become aware of yourself, the more you will realize how different your life can be and the more you will realize your own freedom.

And what is bad faith? It is the denial of this duality, the denial of self-consciousness, the denial of freedom. Those who act in bad faith are always justifying their behavior not by their own discernment, not by their own choice, but by the fatuity of encounters in the world, by the inexorability of life's circumstances. Those who act in bad faith deny that they could have acted differently, deny that their life is made up of choices, deny that they are where they are, but that they could have chosen to be somewhere else. Therefore, those who deny freedom and choice end up denying their own humanity. Those who act in bad faith make a point of making the cat their idol.

• • • • •

Much of our presence in the world is not the result of any decision; it is merely a reaction to the things that happen in front of us. However, part of our existence is made up of deliberate behaviors chosen from among many others that seemed worse. These choices are always complicated. When it comes to choosing the best course of action, when it comes to throwing away what we're not going to do, the equation is complex.

We often use moral rules. Moral rules are based on moral principles, i.e. benchmarks of conduct that seem important to us, that seem to have value and that we would like to guide our lives. For example, we are cordial to people because cordiality is important to us. We tell people the truth because it is important to us. We are loyal to our partners because loyalty is important to us. What happens, however, is that when it comes to making decisions, many of these principles come into conflict.

Imagine that someone comes back from the hairdresser, someone you like very much, and you don't really like the result. At that moment, you're torn between telling the truth and helping the person with their next choice of *style*, or telling them you liked it in order to be kind, to be polite. You realize that there is a conflict here between politeness and kindness on the one hand and the truth on the other.

Other times, when you're intimate with other bodies under the sheets, you don't get the best of sensations. Someone gives you an unpleasant bite, something that you may believe to be pleasurable, but which you don't like very much and you're left wondering whether to say you like it or tell the truth.

Each behavior can be the object of conflict and trouble. There's the colleague who cheats, and you find yourself in doubt as to whether to be loyal to the colleague or tell the teacher the truth. You are a civil servant and you receive an offer that will allow you to provide your loved ones with a more dignified material life in exchange for facilitating a privilege for a corrupt agent. You wonder why you shouldn't give the people you love a materially better life in the name of a society you've never actually seen or even met.

As you can see, moral dilemmas are part of our lives. Therefore, much more than having moral principles and rules, you need to think about establishing a hierarchy between them, because only this hierarchy will allow you to choose among the principles those that will truly guide your life.

CALABREZ: That makes me think of Socrates. He was sentenced to death and imprisoned. He therefore had his right to come and go totally impeded. We could say that Socrates lost his freedom. However, it seems to me that Socrates was freer than many men who today have ample opportunity to move wherever they want.

Another example that comes to mind is more recent: the Frenchman Jean-Dominique Bauby. He was an actor, writer and editor-in-chief of the prestigious fashion magazine *Elle*. In 1995, at the age of 43, he suffered a devastating stroke. The result was what in neurology we call "locked-in syndrome". As the name suggests, the patient is trapped in their own body, unable to move, speak, breathe...

When he woke up in hospital, Bauby could only move his left eyelid. However, the mental faculties of patients with locked-in syndrome generally remain intact. Memories and the ability to think, for example, are not impaired. This imprisonment - an intact mind inside a paralyzed body - can be considered a terrible loss of freedom.

Here's the paradox: even in prison, unable to move, Bauby wrote a book. Using only the blink of his left eyelid, with the help of a person who ran his finger over the alphabet, again and again, for each letter. He composed and edited - inside his head - the beautiful book *The Scaphander and the Butterfly*, which was adapted for the cinema in a film of the same name.

We can also think of Stephen Hawking in terms of this kind of freedom. At the age of 21, he was diagnosed with amyotrophic lateral sclerosis - a neurodegenerative disease that progressively paralyzed his entire body. Today, Professor Hawking communicates through a computer. A sensor captures movements in his cheek - the only muscle he is still able to control. Enclosed in a wheelchair, he is responsible for some of the most important ideas in astrophysics in recent decades. One example is the aforementioned evaporation of black holes.

How many people are free to move, run and jump - but have minds incapable of taking flight, of creating and reflecting, of thinking differently, of deconstructing and reconstructing ideas? I'm talking about prejudiced people and scoundrels, for example.

It's natural for me, when talking about freedom, to think of the freedom of the mind. The freedom of Socrates, Bauby and Hawking.

This might lead the reader to think that the mind is an entity independent of the body. In other words, it floats freely, regardless of the conditions of the body. Apparently, this is a mistake. "Descartes' mistake", as neuroscientist António Damásio put it. The mistake of dualistic thinkers, who consider mind and body to be separate and independent things.

There are documented cases of affable and friendly people suddenly displaying aggressive behavior, even murdering family members or friends. When they examine these people, doctors discover tumors pressing on structures in the brain associated with emotional processing. If the tumor is removed, the person returns to a friendly state - and falls into tears, in a mixture of regret and horror, when they realize that they have killed a loved one.

I've already talked about Alzheimer's disease in the second part of the book. It's a sad and debilitating disease. The patient loses their memory, decision-making ability and reasoning. They also suffer from emotional changes, depression and apathy. Their personality changes. Their behavior changes. Their mind gradually wastes away, causing suffering for family members too, who witness the changes. In short, the person ceases to be who they were. Alzheimer's disease is associated with the accumulation of a certain type of protein, the tau and beta-amyloid proteins, which cause the degeneration of neurons. In other words, brain structures die.

The psychopath's brain is different from yours and mine. They have dysfunctions in a series of circuits. Psychopaths are incapable of feeling empathy, affection or shame, for example. When you see someone suffering, you suffer with them (unless they are your enemy). Psychopaths don't feel this empathy, this shared pain - their brains are incapable of it.

Depression, bipolar disorder, obsessive-compulsive disorder, panic, attention deficit disorder, schizophrenia. All of these were once considered "psychological" illnesses, i.e. illnesses of the mind - unrelated to the body. Today, some of the greatest advances in understanding these (and many other) illnesses is in the study of the patient's brain dysfunctions and also genetics.

Alzheimer's sufferers don't have the freedom to remember things. A person suffering from depression doesn't have the freedom to feel happy and motivated. The person with a tumor (as mentioned above) doesn't have the freedom not to feel angry. The psychopath is unable to feel empathy, just as you are unable to see the infrared light coming from your remote control.

They are imprisoned, limited, cut-off minds. In other words, sick minds. I repeat once again the phrase of the great Harvard professor Steven Pinker: "The mind is what the brain does". And the brain is part of the body, just like the nose and stomach. The mind exists in an intimate relationship with the brain and, therefore, with the body.

Sick bodies are associated with sick minds. Look at Plato. He lived for eighty years at a time when there was no such thing as a toilet or antibiotics. He was an athlete. As I said earlier, his name, it is believed, was Aristocles. The nickname Plato means "the broad", "broad-shouldered". He ate well. The famous "Mediterranean diet" is to this day one of the healthiest we know. He slept at night - after all, there were no electric lights, *smartphones* or Netflix. He also remained intellectually active until his last days.

If you remember Chapter 20 of Part 2, you'll realize that these are fundamental practices for maintaining the health of the body in general and the brain in particular. They prevent anxiety, depression, Alzheimer's and strokes. Freedom of the mind is closely linked to freedom of the body. A sick body condemns the mind to imprisonment. Free minds need healthy and free bodies.

If Socrates hadn't had his body imprisoned and killed, how much more could he have done for human thought?

Bauby died shortly after the publication of his book. He only survived to publish it with the help of hospital machines.

Imagine if Plato had lived a sedentary life filled with stress, smoking, *junk food* and Rivotril. Perhaps symptoms of dementia would have appeared early on. Would he have written *The Republic,* a masterpiece of human thought (completed when he was over 50 years old)?

•••••

The reader may have concluded that an adult, with a healthy body and mind, can be totally free.

Could it be?

Unfortunately, everything indicates that this is not the case. The vast majority of what you and I think, desire, feel and do is the result of mental operations to which we have no access. In science, we call this world the "unconscious". Leibniz, Schopenhauer and Nietzsche, for example, already spoke of unconscious processes (without using this name). But it was the brilliant and revolutionary Sigmund Freud who named and made famous the idea that we are unaware of most of the mental processes that take place within us. The sciences of the mind today help us to understand the dynamics and gears of the unconscious.

If you're sitting reading this book, I bet you're not aware of the pressure the seat is putting on your buttocks. Now you are - just because I drew your attention to it. Before, it was a totally unconscious process. You're not aware of the mechanisms that control your blood pressure, heart rate, breathing, peristalsis and so many other things.

But this is not restricted to apparently "mechanical" physiological functions. Our desires, decisions and judgments are often beyond our conscious control. I'll give you a few examples (all derived from scientific studies):

A supermarket put four French wines and four German wines on the shelves. For each French wine, there was a German equivalent (in terms of grape, price and dryness/ sweetness). On alternate days, the supermarket played French and German music. On the days with German music, 73% of the wines sold were German. On French days, 77% of the wines sold were French. After the purchase, the participants answered a questionnaire which showed that they had not noticed the influence of the music on their preference.

In another study, participants holding a cup of hot coffee tended to describe certain people as more generous and caring than participants holding a cup of cold coffee (and describing the same people). The researchers offered them gifts so that they could choose whether to keep the gift for themselves or give it to friends. Participants in the group holding the hot coffee cup were significantly more likely to choose to give the gift to friends.

When researchers forced people to feel disgusted - with a bad smell or a disgusting movie - they tended to make harsher judgments (of what is good and bad, right and wrong) than people who were not disgusted.

Participants in a study who filled in the survey questionnaire next to a tube of hand sanitizer tended to have more conservative political views than those who filled in the questionnaire without the tube.

One study found that *strippers* received significantly higher tips when they were ovulating than when they were not ovulating and that tips were even lower when they were menstruating. *Strippers* taking the contraceptive pill, on the other hand, showed no variation.

I could go on and fill an entire book on the various ways in which our decisions, desires and behaviors are influenced by unconscious factors...

But I'll end with just one provocation: studies indicate that the brain initiates a behavior seconds before we think we've decided on that behavior. In other words, from the point of view of brain operation, the belief that we have decided occurs after the decision has taken place (unconsciously). For these and other reasons, many researchers believe that free will is an illusion. And these are not small people. I'm talking about some of the most respected scientists in the world, from universities such as Harvard and Oxford.

I'll let you, the reader, sort that out. For my part, I'll just say that freedom is much more complex and probably much more limited than our everyday sensations of free will make it seem.

A provocation: is anyone free to be a scientist and contribute to knowledge as Einstein did? Do we all have the freedom to coach soccer and play as well as Lionel Messi?

CLÓVIS: In any human activity it's easy to see the combination of talent - ability, natural gift - and effort - dedication and perspiration. What is the most valuable behavior? The one determined by talent, by natural gift - by virtue, as Aristotle would say - or the behavior that results from effort, dedication and perspiration?

It's interesting to note that effort is the result of each person's will, decision and deliberation. When we make an effort, we could not make an effort. Effort is a decision, it's what we call willpower.

Not talent. Talent is a given of nature, a gift, a natural resource that we inherit at birth. Talent is imposed on us, we don't choose it, we don't decide. Talent is what it is.

The hard worker might not be, but the talented person has to be. We are experiencing a crisis in the value of talent because the idea of merit - or meritocracy, which is so popular in the professional world and in organizations - always implies the possibility of acting differently, the possibility of not being what you are. Every merit presupposes a meritorious decision and that's why there is applause for effort, dedication, blood in the eyes and a knife in the teeth.

Effortless talented behavior, on the other hand, is often seen as the result of an injustice in the natural distribution of resources and is therefore not always applauded. In the artistic world, talent is still recognized. Outside it, you're expected to work from sun up to sun down. Talent has given way to effort. This is normal in a society that sees equality as its fundamental ethical principle; after all, when it comes to making an effort, we're all at the same starting point. If the ruler is effort, we start from the same place, but if the ruler is talent, there is an inequality of principle that we can never overturn. That's why we applaud effort, even if it's mediocre, tied up and stuck.

This is clear in sport. Two brothers, Raí and Sócrates, made history in Brazilian soccer. Sócrates was pure talent and zero effort. Raí, some talent and a lot of dedication. In the end, Sócrates was a much better player than Raí, but the latter was much more applauded and venerated with titles than Sócrates.

CALABREZ: This can even lead us to a question of justice. After all, it doesn't seem "fair", in the current sense of the word, for some people to be born with so much (natural talents such as intelligence, sporting prowess, beauty, etc.) and others with so little. The distribution of talents in nature is radically asymmetrical. And social asymmetries are considered unfair by many people today. Many even bring this into the economic sphere: some are born with almost nothing, while others are born billionaires.

But justice is not a fundamental concept of nature. There is no particle called "justice" alongside *quarks* and the Higgs boson. Justice is a certain way we use to refer to the relationships between human beings and the world.

CLÓVIS: Natural attributes, the resources that nature bequeaths to each person, end up being a legitimizing factor for the exercise of a certain power, at least in ancient thinking. Imagine an individual who was born with a physical problem, a handicap. This individual is poor in natural resources, at least some of them. Then they will be perceived as inferior. This means that, in the social hierarchy, they will have to obey rather than command and will be condemned to a position of submission in relation to those who are naturally superior to them.

When it comes to thinking about a just city, the Greeks have a very clear opinion on the matter: the city's resources must allow everyone to stay in their place and must allow people with more talent, with more of nature's legacy, to develop their resources towards excellence. In this way, the just city for the Greeks ends up reinforcing traits of strength and power that pre-exist in everyone's natural condition. Aristotle leaves no room for doubt: "To whom must we give the best flute? Well, the best flute to the best flutist". The talented individual by nature must have the most expensive resource.

We must also provide schooling, a condition for improving thinking, for those who are already naturally gifted at thinking. This means that the just city ends up reinforcing what nature has already distributed in an unbalanced way. You'll agree that in the modern world many of us think quite the opposite: the just city must correct the inequalities of principle, it must make life easier for those who are naturally weaker. In this way, those with disabilities can count on a series of facilities that are applauded by everyone - or almost everyone. The aim is for the blind to be able to get around easily, for the wheelchair user to be able to take the elevator without difficulty and for everything to be in place so that the individual with some difficulty can have a life on a par with the life of the person who has no difficulty at all, the most gifted by nature.

In conclusion, what the Greeks called a just city is more or less the opposite of what we call it. At least as far as the relationship with natural attributes is concerned. For the

Greeks, a just city is one that puts the naturally gifted in a position of superiority and in a position to pursue excellence, and the naturally deprived in a position of never leaving the place that is naturally theirs.

CALABREZ: It seems to me that, at least on this issue, today's world allows us more freedom than the old world.

The world is less and less inclined to support aristocratic models in which the essence of the individual is determined by their "natural" place of birth. In their legislative systems, societies seek to offer opportunities in a more balanced way to their citizens, taking into account the discrepancies between them - one example is accessibility for people with disabilities.

That is undeniable. However, I'm bothered by the view that the world today is *completely* free. That we can be and live as we please. In a species as social as *Homo sapiens*, full individual freedom is necessarily a delusion. There is no individual without society. Therefore, there is no full individual freedom.

Perhaps the biggest indication that we're not so free is how much we change in the course of a single day to try to fit in with what other people expect of us...

CLÓVIS: One distinction that seems relevant to me is between a simple choice and a decision. Sometimes they can seem to mean the same thing. But a choice is a simple realization of the superiority of a means, a strategy, an action for achieving a certain end or objective. The one who chooses believes that he or she has mastered the extent of the consequences of each of the possibilities considered and thus, logically and rationally, realizes that one of them is more likely to allow the desired objective to be achieved.

We could say that, in the case of this rational choice, there isn't really a choice, since the selection of the most convenient alternative is the result of criteria that are completely imposed on the person acting.

On the other hand, a decision requires the identification of the best alternative among several possible paths, without the decision-maker believing he or she has mastered all the variables or all the possible consequences of the alternatives under examination. Whether it's because they don't have enough time for this assessment, or because the effectiveness of each of the possibilities depends on supervening events, i.e. chronologically after the decision has been made - the act of deciding goes beyond a mere observation. It therefore requires personal commitment and risk-taking.

We can give two examples.

If you want to lose weight and you have two types of food at your disposal with the right nutritional values, you should logically opt for the less calorific one. This is a mere observation.

But those who want a long career in the same company and have to decide between several alternatives have no control over the management and human resources policies of the years to come - especially in times of so much transformation. This individual is forced to make a decision, to take a risk, because they will have to identify and adopt an alternative without controlling everything that will affect the success or failure of the decision.

We can say that almost all of our major existential crossroads are a matter of decision and almost never a matter of rational choice. This is because almost always the conditions we have to identify the path we will take do not allow us to exhaust the variables at stake, condemning us to a certain uncertainty, to taking great risks and to being accompanied by an anguish that will be faithful to us.

That's why we may have to expect our educators, both in the formality of school and in the informality of life, to prepare young people to decide, much more than simply to choose.

A complicating element of every existential decision lies in the possible and probable conflict between what we believe to be our most intrinsic characteristics and what society expects of us. We believe we have talents, aptitudes, tastes, desires, inclinations and appetites that are our trademark. Society, in turn, establishes the conditions for the manifestation of each of these elements that define us.

This makes the necessary adaptation between the material and social conditions of existence and what we believe to be our definition potentially painful. Society was already there when we were born, believes it has an acquired right and can't tolerate chronic heresy, otherwise it won't guarantee a minimum of order and conviviality. It's very likely that we'll have to make our decisions based on repressive instances whose forcefulness we ignore, at least partially.

You go to the theater, and the actor or actress plays a role, embodies the character, pretends to be someone they're not. They finish the play and go back to being who they are, their true selves.

You take the children, go to a birthday party, find yourself talking to other parents and start to realize that you're playing the role of father or mother well, talking about paternity or maternity, filiation, acting like a father or mother, warning your child - after all, you're at a birthday party full of annoying people who demand a certain paternal or maternal attitude from you. You leave, go to bed and the next day you go to your mother-in-law's house, meet up with the whole family and find yourself once again acting out and saying typical family things, talking to brothers-in-law. Sunday passes, you wake up on Monday, go to work and find yourself looking like a good professional in front of the Japanese executives who are there waiting for your *performance*. In a suit and tie, you play the role of the effective executive. On Wednesday, you go to the soccer match in the evening, you're a fan and you play the role well, you shout, you scream in the stands.

Then one day you think: mask at the theater, mask at the party, mask at the mother-in-law's house, executive mask, fan mask, mask, mask, mask... Could it be that behind all these masks there is a non-mask? An essence? A real me? A real Clóvis who isn't a professor at USP, who isn't a speaker at a company, at a sales convention, who isn't the one who meets with executives to sell his consultancies, who isn't the one who has breakfast with his daughter and is always close to his children? What is behind all these masks, all these characters?

Maybe nothing. Maybe we're just faceless masks. Characters in search of an actor who doesn't exist. Characters in an eternal theater, and behind them, only emptiness. Just a blind force, an energy without purpose, without cause. Only will. The rest, masks. Faceless masks. Permanent pretenses. Sometimes with greater, sometimes with lesser awareness. It's what we call different degrees of cynicism for a life in which we adapt like actors hiding the emptiness of their own being. After all, where would the real me appear? In the vase in the morning? Is it really? Or bathing alone? Or perhaps in the middle of the ocean, sailing?

Vixe! More or less sophisticated masks of someone who struggles to believe they are something, but who is nothing but a character in an endless theater.

What now, my friend? Suck on that mango.

CALABREZ: I can't imagine a more masked society than the one that lives in a world of social networks. I think the name "profile" is appropriate when referring to our pages within the networks. Facebook profile, Instagram profile. After all, a profile implies, by definition, that there is another side - a hidden side to what we are seeing.

People invest an enormous amount of energy in turning themselves into shop windows. We live in a world full of walking mannequins.

Silicone-enhanced breasts, anabolic-fueled muscles, faces paralyzed by botulinum toxin, smiles surgically constructed at the orthodontist, hair implants, bellies and buttocks liposuctioned and - why not? - "liposculpted", make-up, tattoos, hair dye, navel *piercings* and wherever else is appropriate, artificial tanning, clothes, accessories, cell phones, trophy boyfriends to show off to friends... All of this is carefully designed to produce a profile, a showcase of oneself, for people to click on, like and share. All this in the name of an apparently free, complete and happy life, open to the world through the global window called the internet.

In fact, studies show that looking in the mirror and feeling good is an important contributory factor to well-being. This means dressing and adorning yourself the way you want. Owning your own body is very important.

The problem is when this becomes an existential rule. When absolutely everything is appearance, only appearance. When we build our lives, including our bodies, based on a desire for constant approval. We ignore any deep reflections on ourselves, because all that matters is showing ourselves to be special in the eyes of others. And that's the snowball: becoming special, more and more special, makes us want to get closer and closer to perfection, and perfection is a great illusion.

You know that celebrity who looks so perfect in their Instagram photos? We forget that they have diarrhea from time to time. That friend of yours who's always smiling his

28 white teeth off at parties, surrounded by perfect people? Some days he's sad and doesn't feel like getting out of bed.

Or the photo of that statuesque body, without any imperfections, that makes you think "I wish I had a body like that"? Well, that body exists! It takes dozens of clicks to find the right light at the right angle. Perhaps with the help of some anabolic steroids and a pinch of Photoshop. This body exists somewhere else, but not in this real, flesh-and-blood world where we live.

I don't mean that the internet is evil. I just want to point out an ambivalence. Nothing is purely positive, just as nothing is purely negative. I think the internet has brought us enormous freedom. Greater perhaps than any previous technology.

One example: today we are able to speak out and denounce things that for a long time went under the radar, such as prejudice and discrimination. Another example: if we had depended on the mass media (such as TV, magazines and newspapers), we might not have found out about a series of scams committed by our political leaders. One more example: access to knowledge has never been so wide - and it's increasing every day. After a few clicks, you can access a lecture given at Harvard University from your sofa at home in Brazil. We should remember that for a long time only very rich people, aristocrats and nobles, had access to knowledge. Today, more than half of Brazil has access to the internet - and this number is growing every year.

At the same time, the internet limits us.

In some way, we are all residents of the Library of Babel, described in a 1941 short story by Argentine writer Jorge Luis Borges. It's an infinite library whose books contain every possible sequence of letters. Therefore, on one of the infinite shelves there must be a book explaining what the library is, why it exists and how best to live within it. However, the librarians of Babel suspect that they will never be able to find this book of wisdom among so many other books that make no sense at all, made up of random sequences of letters that are nothing more than chaotic combinations of information - in other words, rubbish.

I suspect that these days we are like residents of a library of Babel. We live immersed in an ocean of information, often without fully realizing that this information may be untrue, distorted or, at the very least, insufficient to answer the big questions that are part of our lives. Sometimes unable to answer even the small questions of everyday life. This is very limiting.

What's more, the internet encourages us to adapt our lives to a certain way of living, the central value of which is to be admired. I don't mean that this is something recent. All societies have experienced this. But the massification promoted by the internet makes this process more intense than ever. As the Polish thinker Zygmunt Bauman put it, we live in a consumer society where life itself is a product, the *marketing of* which involves constructing a package that appeals to the greatest number of people.

So there is an ambivalence. Technology that liberates at the same time limits. It's up to us, as individuals and as a society, to choose the best path, taking advantage of the best - and avoiding the worst. This doesn't mean repudiating technological advances. After all, that would be a tremendous step backwards. It just means using our critical sense when using them.

CLÓVIS: In Athens, there was a guy with a reputation for being able to solve any problem, a handyman engineer, a master builder like the kind you hire to solve any problem. The queen of Crete hired him to solve a little problem: she was crazy about giving it to a bull. A bull with four legs and horns. But the bull didn't want her. The cow the bull wanted wasn't the Queen of Crete.

Our hero went to Crete in style and made a stylized cow, inside which the queen would be coupled, as if she were riding a very high-speed motorcycle, in such a way that the vulva of the supposed cow coincided with that of the queen. No problem: when he let go of the bull, he saw that VIP cow, that *prime* cow, and he put the iron to the cow with the queen inside. It was a spectacle.

The queen rejoiced, but she got pregnant. She became pregnant with a strange figure, half human and half bovine: the Minotaur. The king didn't like it. He put our hero and his assistant son inside a labyrinth from which they would never get out. Along with them, the Minotaur.

So our hero came up with a system to get out of there. He gathered sticks and, with wax wings, he and his son, Icarus, flew out of there. But the father's warning was clear: don't fly too high or too low. If you fly too high, the sun will melt your wings; too low, the humidity will weigh you down. Take it easy, in the middle of the road. The two of them flew around the islands, seeing wonderful landscapes. Icarus was enchanted and decided to take a ride up there. He climbed higher and higher, and then it happened: he lost his wings and couldn't save himself.

The moral of the story is very clear. Look at the rip-off: the guy invented the cow and so incurred the wrath of the king of Crete and ended up in the labyrinth. He invented wings and ended up seeing his son crash before his eyes. Since the days of mythology, we've known that not every technological artifact suits us. Not all technology brings us happiness. Not every invention makes our lives better.

CALABREZ: Technology today allows access. That's perhaps the key word. Access to an almost unlimited number of options.

"Options for what?"

Everything.

Apps and *shopping centers* offer menus full of clothing options, accessories, lifestyles, food, information, ideas and pleasures. But these are not small menus. Each one gives us a huge number of possibilities. Freedom like never before. Total control over who we are and who we will become.

With that, of course, must come fulfillment, satisfaction and perhaps happiness. Right?

The answer is: more or less.

In fact, deprivation of freedom (which includes a very limited number of options and possible choices in an individual's life) is associated with dissatisfaction. Not having control and diversity of options in our choices is a great recipe for producing sadness in a human being.

Prison solitary confinement is an extreme example. It takes away your freedom completely - you even lose control of your sense of time. You don't know if it's day or night, you don't know how long you've been isolated. This deprivation of liberty, when we are completely stripped of control over our lives, is psychologically destructive. Apparently, then, freedom of choice and control are associated with a better life.

As American psychologist Barry Schwartz has shown, there is a paradox. When we have too many options, in other words, too much freedom of choice, we also become distressed. In other words, a large number of options leads to dissatisfaction and, ultimately, sadness.

I'm sure you, the reader, have already experienced this. I often do. I arrive at a restaurant. I sit down at the table and open the menu. There are pages and pages of options. Dozens of them. What happens? First of all, I spend more time thinking about which option to choose. I spend half an hour choosing. What's more, I'm more likely to choose nothing or just anything because I can't think about it any longer. When I choose, here's what happens: either I'm dissatisfied because I chose something, or I'm dissatisfied because I keep imagining that I could have chosen something better - or both.

This is precisely what the studies show: a large number of options creates anguish, makes the decision-making process more difficult and increases the likelihood of dissatisfaction with the choice.

Menus with too many options are bad for restaurants. People spend more time at the table, of course. However, they are not consuming. In other words, they are occupying a table that could be used by someone who is eating.

This happens in the world of romantic relationships. The Tinder app is a great example. A menu of people with photos and a short description. The way it works is simple. You like a person. If they don't like you back, you'll never know. If they do like you back, you'll know - and you can get in touch.

Look at the genius. First of all, the app completely removes the anguish of rejection. You never know who rejected you, only who liked you. Imagine if, with every rejection, Tinder warned you: "You've been rejected", "You've been rejected"... People wouldn't put up with an app like that for a day!

What's more, Tinder offers a huge number of options. Thousands of people within reach. Sounds great. However, the paradox of choice perhaps applies here. Because it allows us so much freedom, perhaps Tinder also limits us - making the decision-making process more difficult and increasing the likelihood of dissatisfaction with our romantic relationships.

Some studies already suggest that the number of past sexual partners is associated with dissatisfaction with the current relationship. In other words, the more past partners, the greater the dissatisfaction with the current relationship. Other studies suggest that a greater number of past relationships is associated with higher divorce rates. The authors' hypothesis is simple: the more you know that there are other options, the more aware you are that there are alternatives other than the person you are with. This could make you more critical and therefore less satisfied with what you have.

Of course, you could argue that it's wrong to assume that living in a monogamous relationship is a good thing. But that's another matter. We're talking about couples who have chosen a monogamous relationship - and who therefore believed that it would bring them satisfaction.

I often call it "Netflix syndrome". If you've ever tried to choose a movie or series on Netflix, you know what I'm talking about. There are so many options that it becomes very difficult to choose. The choice takes a long time - and probably what you choose won't bring you as much satisfaction.

The problem apparently lies in the process of "maximization". The more we want a choice to be the best possible, to bring us as much satisfaction as possible, the more likely we are to be dissatisfied. As I said earlier, perfection is an illusion. When we seek perfection (maximization) in our choices, we will probably be dissatisfied. After all, once we've made a choice, we'll think that another option could have been better. Apparently, this applies to clothes, cell phones, travel, romantic partners and everything else.

Too much freedom can then be a source of anguish. Is this the karma of a consumer society?

• • • • •

Talking about karma, in fact, refers to a concept directly linked to freedom, which is very widespread these days. Many people believe that our free choices, when good, generate something positive. When bad, on the other hand, they produce negativity. Some call it energy. Others call it karma - and so on.

In a way, there is a determinism in this relationship. Good action determines good, bad action determines evil. This determinism, in a contradictory way, limits freedom. After all, if a good action always produces good things and a bad action always produces bad things, where is freedom?

You could answer: "In intentions and actions. Consequences are not free. Bad behavior always leads to bad things. Good behavior always generates good things. But our intention in acting, as well as our actions in fact - these are two things that are free and under our control!"

Perfect. But full freedom would be if a good action could cause anything (good, bad, neutral, ambiguous) and a bad action too. Full freedom, by the way, means that nothing is purely good or purely bad - everything is relative. Relativism is the freest morality, if we consider that freedom is synonymous with having as many paths as possible to choose from.

I don't mean that relativism is a good or bad view of the world. Although, in saying that, I am relativizing. But I leave the conclusions up to the reader.

CLÓVIS: Oriental thought has never been talked about as much as it is today. The impression I get is that it's much more quoted than known. In fact, this is also true of some Western classics, such as Marx and Nietzsche. Everyone talks about them, but few read them, few reflect on them.

According to Hindu philosophy, the ultimate goal of life is *moksha,* translated as enlightenment, but in fact the literal meaning of *moksha* is liberation. Now, my friend, if there is liberation, it is because there is a change, a passage from slavery to freedom. But then the question we need to answer is:

If there is liberation, what is it in relation to?

Well, to begin with, desires. Eastern sages have this obsession. Desires are the great evil. *Moksha* is overcoming desires. The enlightened and free individual knows true human nature. They reach a state in which banal distinctions, such as between being or not being, disappear. They are able to observe the world in a detached way. Transcendent, we might say. Freed from the worries of ordinary existence. For example, a Hindu sage wouldn't be like me now, worried about any traffic on the Marginal, because he has transcended these concerns. It remains to be seen whether he would always arrive on time to give his lecture.

Moksha is also liberation from *samsara,* the cycle of births and deaths. Here the perplexity increases, because the ultimate goal of life would be to free oneself from its finitude. I imagine it to be liberation from the sadness, fear and anguish that the finitude of life brings us. Of course, this deserves to be problematized. If life is good, happy and joyful, the end of it will be bad. There's no way not to regret the end of what is good. In fact, death only means nothing to those who live badly.

Hindus insist on the existence of karma and say that good deeds produce good karma, which inevitably leads to good fortune, good occurrences, joyful encounters with the world. On the other hand, bad deeds produce bad karma, which consequently leads to bad fortune, bad luck, disappointing and saddening encounters with the world.

Well, my friend, I humbly beg to differ. I disagree because I know hundreds and hundreds of cases of people, in real life and in literature, who act well, are good parents, do good, help others, but lead a life full of unfortunate encounters with the world. I disagree with the number of people who have been betrayed, humiliated in love, exploited at work and who have spent their lives doing good. Empirical experience has shown me that good deeds and good conduct can bring as much karma as you like, but that they will guarantee luck, good fortune and happy encounters with the world, oh, only if it's far away! It doesn't seem to happen around here.

3

Power

CLÓVIS: When we think of power, we can first think of the possibility that each one of us has of being able to carry out a task, accomplish an intention. For example, I have the power, the ability to write a book, to teach a class. But I don't have the power to fly or to draw a good picture.

This is not the only meaning of the word power. We understand power as a characteristic of the relationship between two or more people. When two people have a relationship and power is exercised, it is because the will of one of them determines the actions of the other. Think about it, you who work and are subordinate to a boss, that boss exercises power, since your behavior, your activities, your conduct are determined by the will of your superior. That's where the power lies: the will of one determines the conduct of the other.

The power relationship seems a little unfair at first; after all, why should someone not only define what they are going to do, but also what others are going to do? Looking at it from the point of view of those who submit, why shouldn't they be able to deliberate on their own conduct? Why can't everyone be their own boss?

We quickly realized that for life in society to happen, power relations have to be everywhere. It's simply not possible for everyone to be in charge of themselves. Power is everywhere. At university, I teach in a classroom that is clearly too small for the number of students I have, and yet it's not up to me to decide which class I teach, nor is it up to me to decide which day of the week I teach. Nor do I decide how much I earn. I am clearly subject to power relations. But it's not because I don't decide which class I teach that I'm going to pick up a gun and rebel, killing everyone I come across. On the contrary: every Thursday I go to the university, I go to the room they have assigned me and I teach during the period and at the time they have also determined. You see, I accept this power, I accept not being the holder of the prerogative to decide on these things. We can then understand that some power relations are accepted not only by those who exercise it but also by those who submit to it. In this case, we call legitimate power, the power accepted by those involved.

It's like that on the scale of society too. Laws are written by some, but obeyed by all. We could ask ourselves: why do we obey them? In other words, what is the basis of the legitimacy of the power exercised by our rulers? Why isn't there a revolution every minute? One rebellion per minute? We accept many decisions that are not made by us. That's a big question about the legitimacy of power that will be answered in the next reflection. But think about the fact that a large part of power relations, still characterized by the subordination of some and the sovereignty of others, are accepted calmly, harmoniously, without any kind of challenge. Why is it so easy for us to accept that we ourselves are not the makers of the choices that make up our lives?

•••••

It seems unbalanced, and even unfair, for someone to have to act on a decision made by someone other than themselves, which is why we could imagine a tendency to reclaim sovereignty, a certain indignation and a certain struggle to regain decision-making power over one's own life. But this is not the case.

In society, power relations sew the social fabric together, they seem indispensable, because without them society wouldn't exist. What is the basis for this exercise of power? Nature and the attributes of nature possessed by those who exercise power and those who submit to it have long legitimized and justified relationships of this kind. There is the great myth of Gilgamesh, the first recorded account. Gilgamesh, the great king who didn't want to die, exercised power over his city because of his size, an attribute of nature, the size that guaranteed the prerogative of exercising power that was understood as normal and acceptable because of the size of the ruler.

Throughout the history of thought and the history of cities, other elements of nature have guaranteed the legitimacy of the exercise of power. Probably the size of the breasts in some matriarchy, the size of the phallus in some patriarchy.

In philosophy, closer to us, nature also legitimized the exercise of political power. And the element of nature that would guarantee this legitimacy was intelligence, the use of reason. A mastery over one's own passions, over one's own body, a sovereignty over oneself, over one's own appetites in the name of the search for truth, for perfect ideas, for a transcendent world. This wise man, this philosopher, because of his intelligence, should exercise power. Bullies like Gilgamesh would now occupy a second class: those who would physically defend the city. And those who were neither very intelligent nor bullies would be left to do the rest: manual labor, servitude.

Of course, nature was not the only element that underpinned the legitimacy of power. But even today, it allows us to identify situations in which power is exercised in our relationships. Beauty, for example, clearly guarantees those who possess it prerogatives of power. So do intelligence and various other elements that nature gives us from birth. Nature has certainly lost its prerogative and monopoly on legitimizing power, but it is clear that it still guarantees an extremely privileged situation in relationships for many.

CALABREZ: There is an asymmetry in human relations. Some individuals are more socially legitimized. They become dominant. Others, on the other hand, obey the rules defined by the dominant. They are therefore dominated. It seems that there is a biological component that explains these dynamics. In other words, we have a nature that inclines us towards socially asymmetrical structures.

A few years ago, a very interesting study put monkeys in a cage where they could either look at a screen showing images, or they could choose to drink juice. One or the other, the monkey had to choose between looking at the images or drinking juice. I want you to understand this because it's very important: monkeys love juice. It can be orange, grape, it doesn't matter. If it's sugary, monkeys are crazy about juice. The straw released very little juice. In order to drink juice, the monkey had to spend a long time without looking at the screen.

What this research wanted to evaluate was precisely which images were most interesting to the monkey. After all, if the monkey chooses to stop drinking juice in order to see an image, it's because that image is really interesting to him. It's worth noting that all the monkeys in the study were male.

Guess what kind of image caught the monkeys' attention to the point where they stopped drinking juice?

Only two categories of images.

First of all, pictures of female ass. In other words, a kind of "macho" *Playboy* magazine.

Secondly, photos of the faces of the alpha males and females in the group. In other words, the faces of the most socially prominent monkeys in the society in which they lived. In other words, a sort of monkey *Face* magazine.

Remember the studies comparing the neocortexes of different primates, mentioned in the second part of the book? They were led by a guy called Robin Dunbar, an anthropologist, evolutionary psychologist and professor at Oxford University. After the comparative studies, he proposed that interest in the lives of others is a fundamental part of the evolutionary process of primates, especially great primates (of which humans are a part).

Great primates are highly social. For the members of societies of this type of animal, it is of great importance to obtain information about the other members. This information allows them to better navigate the social environment. This, in turn, allows for greater cooperation - a key factor for survival.

For many people, one of the consequences of all this is terrible: gossip. That is, the tendency that many people have to look into other people's lives, often passing on stories in a selective and extrapolated way, or in a misrepresentative and untruthful way. All of this is a kind of harmful deviation from a natural propensity that we (and most primates) have to take an interest in other people's lives, to talk about other people. Other primates don't talk, of course. Despite this, they communicate in different ways, demonstrating the same psychological and behavioral inclination. This inclination, i.e. this natural interest in the lives of others, is especially intense in relation to socially prominent people in our society.

But who are the most socially prominent people in human societies?

Socially legitimized people. In chimpanzee societies (another great primate), for example, the alpha males and females are not necessarily the strongest or biggest. They are often the members with the greatest ability to influence others, i.e. those with social skills such as conflict management and persuasion. Chimpanzee societies are highly complex.

The human species couldn't be any different. We are, after all, one big primate. However, we have a larger and more complex brain, which allows for even more complex social structures. The elements that define the "alpha" members of our group vary according to the group's culture. Among the military, the dominant ones are those with medals on their chests. Among martial arts fighters, the dominant ones are those with the darkest belt. Owning a beautiful horse was once legitimizing (in some groups, it still is). University degrees today legitimize people to work in certain dominant positions. If you traveled back in time with your Harvard degree, to a couple of thousand years before Christ, your degree would be useless.

Today, in many cultures, the dominant person is the one with the best financial conditions, represented by a nice car or a luxurious house. In the past, financial conditions were demonstrated through different material possessions. Today, among teenagers, the dominant person can be Justin Bieber or Anitta, depending on their social background. The examples are countless.

In short, in the human species, the criteria that define the legitimacy of individuals in positions of power are relative to the culture of the group we are analyzing. They are therefore multiple and constantly changing. However, it seems that we have a biological nature prone to living in - and accepting - asymmetrical social relationships. In them, a few are in charge and enjoy the benefits of power. Many others obey.

Some say that, to a certain extent, the dominated also enjoy certain benefits of obedience. They argue that many people don't want the burden of responsibility of occupying a position of power. Others say that, in fact, the ultimate desire of every dominated person is to become dominant. I'll leave that one for the reader to sort out.

4

Happiness

CLÓVIS: The Stoic thinkers were committed to thinking so that we could all live better lives. They suggested detachment from things, from people. If your joy depends on the presence of something or someone, it is obviously fragile, because things destroy themselves and people die. Before they are completely destroyed, things lose their characteristics; people change. That person who once made you happy can become a bitter person who makes you sad.

The only consolidated happiness that isn't fragile is the happiness you achieve without depending on the presence of anything or anyone. It's a happiness that you achieve with yourself. And this has a lot to do, in the case of the Stoics, with avoiding pain and suffering. If you're at peace, if you're at ease, if you're contemplating things, for them that's as good as it gets. It's not about a thousand orgasms and a life full of lust. No. It's a life of peace, a life of resignation to things as they are.

Now, stop and think: you have a boyfriend or girlfriend, at a certain moment you're kissing on the mouth, those kisses that never end, and you want that moment not to end, because it's a present that dispenses with the past and the future, a symbol of the good life. But you can't be attached. What does that mean? It means that the moment is over, the person is leaving, and you don't want them to be there at all, because that's already attachment. It's the instant for the instant. You leave, get on the bus to go home and forget what happened. Now it's the bus that's nice, even though it's crowded and has a thousand smells. Then you get home, and people ask you to tidy up your room, and you think it's really nice, you enjoy every moment, and you don't think about the kisses or the person. You'll only think about the person when they appear in front of you again. Is that so?

It's very nice to philosophize. It's very cool to believe that the instant has to exhaust its raison d'être in itself. It's very interesting to imagine that the past and the future only get in the way. But is it really possible to live as they suggest? Is it really the case that, after kissing someone a lot, you leave and can stop thinking about what has just happened? Is it really the case that, after enjoying an incredible night of love with someone, you leave and it disappears because you'll be busy with the cab that will take you to the airport?

Ah, you know, it's very nice to reflect on, almost poetry, but it has nothing to do with our experiences. At least not mine.

• • • • •

For the Stoics, philosophy is not a speech, it's not a dissertation, it's not a text, it's not an idea. But it can be all of these things, as long as it has to do with a life lived, with a happier life, with suffering less. The Stoics were concerned with actually making the good life happen. And there are a series of exercises to make life better. Many of these exercises have to do with controlling what goes on in our heads. When they say that you have to live in the present - Nietzsche's amor *fati*, Horace's *carpe diem* - and really care about the moment you're living, we're basically declaring war on the past, declaring war on all kinds of mental constructs that rehash events that have happened.

Every time you stop yourself from reconstructing events in your mind, you don't have the sensations that go with that mental production. How interesting: by declaring war on the past, you force yourself to forget. And not letting the past in means policing yourself to give the lived present such importance that there is no room for the past to come in through the window. When you police yourself against the past, you avoid a series of events in which you have suffered humiliations, disappointments, things that have hurt you and that you allow your mind to reconstruct. When you avoid this reconstruction, you avoid redoubling that dissatisfaction.

It's very interesting, because some things in life seem gigantic, catastrophic, dreadful the moment they happen. The invitation is for you to take a step back, look at things from above, know that in three months' time you won't remember it any more, that in ten years' time you'll be laughing at the situation; so you deconstruct the seriousness of a nefarious occurrence and thereby allow yourself to enter a present that is more likely to be joyful.

This is the first exercise, the constant struggle against the past. If the past was good, it will be nostalgic, and that's bad; if the past was bad, it will be full of guilt, remorse and regret, which is also bad. Therefore, there is no chance that the past, as the present production of the mind that reconstructs the lived world, is a good thing. Longing is not good, and regret is not good either.

How interesting: when Nietzsche says that a good life presupposes knowing how to forget, he is following a tradition that has its genesis long before him.

Well then, the beautiful lesson of this reflection is to fight the past by respecting the moment in which we live. This is what must accompany us, because we often give in to events that will be relived by the mind. Occurrences that have already caused us harm and could do so again. This is regrettable.

• • • • •

Things about what's going to happen cross our minds. It's only natural.

I remember a time when I was in Rio de Janeiro and I left a lecture in Niterói to give another lecture in Duque de Caxias. I left two and a half hours early for a journey that Google predicted would take 35 minutes. So I had plenty of time. But there was an accident on the Red Line and the traffic was worse than usual. My mind was flooded with images of the future.

At the start of the journey, I thought I was two and a half hours ahead of schedule and, whatever the traffic, I would arrive on time. Note that this anticipation, this projection - which we call the future - was favorable, and when that happens, we call it hope. As the traffic got worse and the time passed, another kind of image crossed my mind: that I wouldn't arrive on time. And I found myself having to apologize for the unforgivable delay. As time went by, I realized that the delay was inevitable and would be long. It was an unpleasant sensation, because what was going through my head about what was going to happen - the future - wasn't convenient for me and, since it wasn't convenient, it produced in me an affection that diminished my power and reduced my vital energy.

In the first case, there was hope of arriving on time, there was a gain in power every time the world to be lived in crossed my mind. But when I imagined being late, my power diminished and there was no hope, but fear. That's the bad feeling you get every time the future - the image you create in the present about what's going to happen - is unfavorable.

Well, someone might think that fear is a disgrace, and it is. And that includes the fear of death. But there is a nice future. It's the hopeful future. A nice future is a future in which the anticipation of what will happen brings good feelings, like arriving on time, despite the traffic.

What I want to say here, along with the Stoics, is that even when the future is nice, it's not good. Hope, although it is pleasant, although it has to do with a favorable image, is not a nice affection. Do you know why? Firstly, because when you're hopeful and think about what's going to happen, you're out of touch with what's going on, you're out of touch with the present, you're out of touch with the world as it is. You're fragile, your head in one place and your body in another.

Secondly, because this hope is a wish, it is made in ignorance of whether or not it will actually happen. Hope is an affection in ignorance and also in impotence, because when I expected to arrive on time, there was nothing I could do, nothing I could collaborate on to actually arrive on time. The traffic on the Red Line condemns me to a kind of procession with no turning back and it is also an affection without enjoyment, after all, it is always in lack, like all desire.

Anyone who expects to arrive on time hasn't arrived yet and doesn't yet feel the joy of arriving on time. Therefore, all hope is without joy, without awareness and, of course, without power. Without being able to do anything.

• • • • •

You have to remember that hope is made up of at least two things: one, what goes through your head. And what goes through your head has to do with what you would like to happen. Then there's how you feel about what's going through your head, which is sometimes good and convenient.

In addition to uncertainty, i.e. ignorance of what will happen, hope is a feeling accompanied by chastity. Do you know why? Because enjoyment is always in a relationship with the world right in front of you, enjoyment requires friction, it requires presence, it requires an encounter. Hope, on the other hand, is just a chimera, just a thought. Hope is a feeling of chastity without enjoyment, without pleasure. And finally, worst of all, hope is a feeling accompanied by impotence, and this is incredibly pertinent because, if you could make what you hope for happen, hope would become joy in the same second, it would become an encounter, a gift, pleasure, enjoyment and happiness. But since you can't make it happen, you wait.

Impotence is the hallmark of the hopeful. You expect the plane to leave on time because you're powerless to make it leave on time; you expect a woman to give you the eye because you're powerless to seduce her; you expect the bus to arrive because you're powerless to make it arrive; you expect to be promoted because you're powerless to promote yourself; you really expect your life to be happy because you're powerless to rejoice in that very second.

Ah, impotent hopeful! That's all you can do: hope. Hope that chance favors you, hope that variables you can't control make your life better because, if you really had the big bucks, you'd make it happen. And those who know make the time, don't wait for it to happen.

•••••

You'd think that this story of condemning hope would lead us to love the present, the instant. Past and future, two evils to avoid. This love for the world as it is, for things as they are, for people, for the situations that present themselves to us, in short, this reconciliation with what is real, if you think about it, is a profoundly lucid suggestion because, after all, if everything that passes through the spectacle of your perception is kind to you, seems fair and good, then of course life has every chance of being worthwhile. Whatever happens, everything will be all right. More than that: whatever happens, you'll love it. You'll always love it, always enjoy it, always smile, always love it, and then life can't be bad.

But if philosophy is willing to advise this, it's because it knows that in the world of life this doesn't happen. The truth is that many of the things that pass through our perception, right in front of our eyes, are disgusting, unacceptable, unworthy; they attack, offend and humiliate us. You can see the cowardly attack on an elderly person, lies and hypocrisy. The truth is that the world is full of scoundrels, so this story that love is for everything and no matter what happens everything is fine, we know it's not like that, it doesn't work that way, we don't tolerate everything.

So much of the world makes us happy, makes us smile, is of extraordinary beauty. And we hope it stays that way. But much of it - and I would say the vast majority - is unacceptable to us, so rather than this story that the good life simply implies a love of reality, I would rather suggest the transformation of what is bad, revolution, subversion, change. What is not good must be transformed. Transformed for us and for future generations. The mere loving contemplation of the world implies a resigned acceptance of things as they are, and you can't resign yourself to so many unacceptable behaviors, any more than you can resign yourself to a nature that trembles, generates tidal waves and kills us in droves every time it decides to get angry.

Ah, love for things as they are. It's beautiful, it's poetic, it's wise. But it has nothing to do with our lives.

•••••

Let's now put an end to the Stoics' fight with the fear of death. We can return to the *Odyssey* and Ulysses.

You remember that Ulysses was at ease in Ithaca, probably without any worries. The present moment was enough, so the past and the future were meaningless. And the fear of death was nonsense. But then Ulysses is summoned to the Trojan War. He spent ten years fighting and another ten trying to get home. In those twenty years, Ulysses was out of place, living in nostalgia; therefore, crossed by the past.

But he finally manages to return home, meets Penelope and lies down with her on the wedding bed. At that moment, the gods promote a distension of time, in other words, an instant that becomes eternity. And when an instant becomes eternity, there is no past and no future. It's just Ulysses and Penelope. It's only the present that counts, complete reconciliation with the instant, with the world. Then, of course, there's no need to fear death, because it's a thought that doesn't come. And of course, Ulysses can only love Penelope, he can only love Ithaca, he can only love the wedding bed, because all of this allows him to live a life that he enjoys and which, therefore, does not allow itself to be crossed by nostalgia for times lived, much less by the projection of times to be lived, in which death, pernicious, settles in to eat away at our lives, to embitter our existence.

The gods extend the instant. At that moment, the victory over death is consummated, the fragment of eternity is completed, and, of course, we are wise at the moment when life is good and man's intelligence has overcome his own pity, his own fear of his own condition. Finitude is just finitude. It will end, it will end. Now, thinking about it is something for people who don't have a Penelope or a wedding bed at home to make existence in a way that dispenses with this kind of cogitation.

Calabrez: I think this is the most important question. What makes us happy? Some of the world's most celebrated scientists are addressing this question today. And what are the answers? What does science have to tell us about happiness?

Talking about happiness today is somewhat paradoxical.

On the one hand, happiness is a subject that has been studied rationally since the beginning of philosophy, in a serious and profound way, as Clovis shows us from the beginning of the book. Happiness, living well, living as well as possible - this is at the root of ancient philosophical thought.

On the other hand (and here comes the paradox), there is a huge trivialization of the term. After all, you can buy happiness at McLanche. Books and more self-help books are dedicated to explaining the paths to happiness. Because of this, happiness is constantly associated with "feeling good", in other words, with what we in psychology call "positive emotions".

The happy moment, in this case, is when we are filled with positive emotions, such as joy. It's feeling good. It's the moment when we feel complete, full.

However, I prefer to understand happiness not as an "element", but as a "construct".

What does that mean?

I'll give you a parallel example. Let's think about temperature. Barometric pressure. Wind speed. Each of these things is an element. Together, these elements make up what we call "climate". In other words, temperature is not the climate. Climate is a construct - and one of the elements is temperature, another is wind speed, etc.

It's the same with happiness. It's obvious that positive emotions (i.e. feeling good, experiencing joyful moments) are an important element of happiness. But that's not all there is to happiness.

•••••

The first step to understanding happiness from a scientific perspective is to understand a disturbing discovery in psychology over the last few decades.

Studies conducted by some of the world's leading scientists are adamant: what we feel when we look in the mirror is wrong. The feeling we get when we look in the mirror is obvious: each of us feels that we are a unified being. We feel that our "I" is one. In other words, "I am Peter, and this is my life", for example.

That's a mistake.

Today we know that it's actually as if human beings had two different "selves".

We can call one of them the "experiential self", the self that *lives in the instant*. This is the self that is having the experience of reading this book right now. Studies suggest that it lasts about three seconds - in other words, it is extremely present, and therefore experiential.

We have a second self that we can call the "projective self". This is the self that *thinks about life, looking outside the now*. Looking back (to what we call the past) and forward (to what we call the future).

Realize that there is a part of us that is experiential, that lives. And another that is projective, in other words, that thinks about life. In other words, *living and thinking about life, from a psychological point of view, are two very different things*.

But one is not more important than the other. In fact, the important thing is to know how to understand the characteristics of these different "selves". After all, if they are different, it means that what makes the experiential self happy doesn't necessarily make the projective self happy. In fact, we know today that the conditions of happiness of the self that lives are fundamentally different from the conditions of happiness of the self that thinks about life.

•••••

So what makes each of our different selves happy?

The projective self, as we've seen, is the self that thinks about life. This means that it lives on stories. To look to the past is to tell a story of what once was. To look to the future is to tell a story of what you believe will come to be.

What makes these stories happy are the goals and achievements. It's looking to the past and seeing valuable achievements; looking to the future and seeing valuable goals.

Many people say: "Money doesn't bring happiness! Professional achievements don't bring happiness!". That's incorrect.

Money and professional achievements are, for many people, important, valuable goals. Many people look to the past and see value in their professional and financial achievements.

In the case of money specifically, the more it is used to buy experiences and not merely things, the greater the value perceived by the person. After all, an experience is a story, and the projective self lives on stories. That's why studies repeatedly show that traveling is a very good way to spend money - because it's spending money on an experience.

In this sense, professional and financial achievements can bring happiness - for a part of us, for that part of us that thinks about life. The problem, of course, is when someone believes that *this alone is the source of happiness*. Then we make a big mistake.

There is another important element to the happiness of the projective self, which we call "meaning". A meaningful life is a life in which you feel you belong to something bigger and more important than yourself. Many people find this in religion, spirituality and family. Some will find it at work. People who practice philanthropic activities or some kind of social activism often find these activities a great source of meaning.

It's easy to see that our society is an *expert* at promising happiness to the projective self. From birth, we are bombarded with goals to achieve. Getting into school, getting a good grade, passing the exams, getting into the best college, getting the best internship, being hired, making money, finding a great love, owning a house, getting married, having children, being professionally successful... In addition, we are surrounded by potential sources of meaning: our family, our church, our job and so on.

It doesn't matter if you were born into a simple family or in Dubai. The only thing that will change are the goals and potential achievements on offer. Obviously, the goals and achievements of the son of a billionaire will be different from those offered to the son of a slum dweller. Even so, from the moment we are born, we are offered many goals and potential achievements.

It turns out that we have another self - the experiential self. As we've seen, it's very different from the projective self. This experiential self is concerned with living, while the projective self is concerned with thinking about life.

•••••

What makes the experiential self happy in the first place is engagement. It's living as engaged as possible in your activities.

Engagement is about challenges. We know today that human beings need challenges to stay happy, to stay motivated and functioning well. When we don't face challenges or when the challenges we do face are too small for our skills, we tend to become bored and demotivated. When, on the other hand, we face a large number of simultaneous challenges or challenges that are too big for our skills, we tend to become stressed.

Engagement is the psychological state that occurs when we find a balance between the challenges we face and our competencies. In other words, when we find a challenge in line with our competencies, we face that challenge in an engaged way.

This can even lead to a psychological state known as *flow*. When we're in *flow*, we lose awareness of ourselves, we lose track of time, we immerse ourselves in the activity we're doing, we become hyper-motivated - and we only realize all this after the state of *flow* is over. You look back and think: "Wow, I was extremely engaged".

Why?

Because the experiential self lives. It's not up to it to think about life, nor to think about *flow*. It is the projective self that will perceive and think about *flow*.

• • • • •

So, as we've seen, the first thing to have a happy experiential self is engagement.

A second thing - which is also necessary for engagement to emerge - sounds simple, but it's not easy at all: it's savoring and enjoying what's happening while it's happening. It's being here with your head here. It's facing the challenges with your head in the challenges.

And there we have a huge problem.

This problem becomes clear when we look at a Harvard University study published in 2010 in the journal *Science* - one of the most important scientific publications in the world.

The researchers installed an app on the cell phones of thousands of people around the world. The app sent messages at random times to people, asking them three things.

First, "How are you feeling right now?" - and the person answered on a quantitative scale (i.e. a question directed at the experiential self). Next, "what are you doing right now?". Finally, "are you thinking about anything outside of what you're doing?".

What were the results? The study showed that 46.9% of the answers came from people who were doing one thing while thinking about another. In other words, almost half the time people are here, but their minds are elsewhere.

Here comes the most interesting result of the survey:

When people are here, but their minds are elsewhere (the researchers called it "the wandering mind"), they tend to be unhappy about the moment they are living in. The name of the article is "A wandering mind is an unhappy mind". Loosely translated, it means "a wandering mind is an unhappy mind".

To be happy, the experiential self needs us to be here, savoring and enjoying what's in front of us - and not with our heads somewhere else, wandering. Unfortunately, as we've seen, about half the time people are doing precisely what is associated with unhappiness.

•••••

We also have an aggravating factor in this situation. As I said, our society is excellent at promising happiness for the projective self: goals, achievements and meaning. But it's terrible at educating us to savor the present, to enjoy the moment, to live with our heads in what we're experiencing.

The most common thing is to wake up on Monday expecting Friday to arrive. Working or studying waiting for the vacations. Some people wake up lying down. They open their eyes and, before they even get out of bed, the first thing they think is: "How I wish I could go back to bed". These people are on the move. Always here, but with their minds elsewhere. Here, hoping to get somewhere else. You, reader, know very well: traffic is extremely stressful. In the literal sense, but also as a metaphor for life.

Before we go any further, it's important to note that these ideas have great synergy with Stoic thought.

•••••

With all this, we can understand the differences between the projective self and the experiential self.

Now we can also understand why the majority of studies that follow people through different points in their lives (from the age of 18 to the end of their lives) point out that, in terms of general satisfaction with life, human beings have a "u" curve.

What does that mean?

When we're 18, our general satisfaction with life is high. As time goes by, it decreases, decreases... Until it reaches its lowest point: on average, between the ages of 40 and 50. From then on, the curve starts to rise. The consequence is that older people are generally much more satisfied with life than people in their 30s, 40s and 50s.

What explains this curve? Why does it occur?

As I said, we are very influenced from birth to place all our bets, energy and efforts on our projective self. What's more, we've seen that this self lives on goals and achievements, looking outside the now.

At 18, we have our whole lives ahead of us. There's a lot to achieve. We're full of goals. As time goes by, we gradually achieve these goals - and adjust our lives to those we realize we won't be able to achieve.

We go to college, get a job, get our own house, find a great love, have children, achieve professional success, see our children grow up and so on... As each of these goals becomes an achievement, we adapt and move on to the next.

One example: anyone who has finished university remembers the great joy, almost euphoria, when they passed the entrance exam. A few months later, they adapted and set off for the next achievement: getting an internship. This happens with practically everything.

By the age of 40, 50, we've achieved all the things that at 18 we thought would bring fulfillment. We look ahead - and there's nothing much new to achieve. Just more of the same. Then we reach the lowest point of the curve... A kind of crisis, known as the midlife crisis. This crisis stems from the fact that, as time goes by, we achieve all the desired goals. Until we have nothing left to achieve.

"Well, why is the curve starting to rise again after this crisis?"

Because people start to appreciate what they have, what they've already achieved - what they're living, in the moment they're living it. In other words, they start living more in the present, living in the moment, savoring the things that are happening while they are there. It's as if they discovered their experiential self and began to value it.

•••••

There is only one variable that makes both the projective self and the experiential self happy. This is, in fact, the most important variable. There is nothing more important for human happiness than this: the quality of our relationships. Happy people are those who have quality relationships, who surround themselves with loved ones. One of the biggest catalysts for sadness is loneliness. As we saw earlier, attachment is a human need.

Now you know what the sciences of the mind understand as a happy life. Note, however, that none of this is very new. On the contrary, many Eastern currents of thought, such as the Vedic and Buddhist ones, and also Western currents, such as the thought of the Stoics and Spinoza, already said some of these things. The difference is that today we have the ability to confirm, using the scientific method, the importance of these ideas.

Happiness is the result of balance. It's not just about living now, nor is it about living in the past or the future. On the one hand, it's important to look to the past and see achievements, to look to the future and see goals, to look at life in general and see meaning. On the other hand, we must also appreciate, value and savor the present, being here, with our heads here, facing challenges that suit our skills. At the base of all this, it is essential to sow and cultivate quality relationships with the people we love.

We should avoid living life like a journey. On a journey, we wait all the time for our destination to arrive. We buy tickets, wait for the date, take a cab to the airport, *check in*, check luggage, get on the plane. We take off, fly, land, get off, wait for our luggage, get in a cab and only then do we arrive at our destination...

All this time, our greatest wish was that these things would end soon, so that our destination would arrive as soon as possible. Some people live like that.

An example.

The boy is a teenager. But he doesn't want to be a teenager. He wants to be an adult. He's in high school. But he doesn't want to be in high school, he wants to graduate and go to college. He goes to college. Now he doesn't want that anymore. He wants a job. He gets the job. Shortly afterwards, he no longer wants that job. You want a promotion to a better position.

This is the projective self governing life.

The idea here is to avoid living life like a journey, waiting for the destination and wanting what we're experiencing to end soon. The idea is to live life more like a walk. Every walk has a destination, of course. But the difference is that when we walk, we also enjoy and savor the journey. If the destination arrives, great. If it doesn't, at least we enjoy the road we've traveled.

So have goals. Be proud of your achievements. Appreciate, be grateful for and preserve the relationships with the important people in your life. But don't forget to savor and enjoy the moments that life gives you, to be here, with your head here, not to live all the time waiting for the goal to arrive. Instead, have the goal on the horizon, but when you lay your head on the pillow, try to find the peace of mind that today you made the most of it, savored it to the fullest and did the best you could - so that tomorrow you can get there.

NOTES AND READING RECOMMENDATIONS

Here the reader will find comments and readings that will allow them to delve deeper into the ideas discussed throughout the book.

Whenever possible, we opted for Portuguese translations. When there was no translation into our language, we kept the original titles.

We also looked for titles that were widely accessible, not difficult to understand or had excessively academic language. We followed this path with only two general exceptions. Firstly, in relation to the specific studies cited throughout the text. Secondly, we have made a point of mentioning some works which, although difficult, are very important (and worth an effort by the bravest readers).

We also recommend that readers check out the NeuroVox channel, run by Professor Pedro Calabrez on YouTube, where he publishes weekly scientific and reflective content on the relationship between mind, brain and behavior (www. youtube. com/NeuroVox).

PART I - THE REALITY

1. What is the world?

- On reality as perception in philosophy, there are two essential but difficult-to-read works: Berkeley, G., *Três dialogues entre Hylas e Philonous* (São Paulo: Ícone Editora, 2005); Ponty, M., *Fenomenologia da percepção* (São Paulo: WMF Martins Fontes, 2011).

- The world as a construction of the brain and clinical examples (synesthesia, phantom limbs and many others): Mlodinow, L., *Subliminar* (Rio de Janeiro: Zahar, 2013); Ramachandran, V. S., *O que o cérebro tem para contar* (Rio de Janeiro: Zahar, 2010); Sacks, O., O *homem que confundiu sua mulher com um chapéu* (São Paulo: Companhia das Letras, 1997).

- "The mind is what the brain does" - the phrase comes from Steven Pinker, but the idea is also very well worked out by António Damásio, neurologist and neuroscientist: Damásio, A., *O erro de Descartes: razão, emoção e o cérebro humano* (São Paulo: Companhia das Letras, 1994); Pinker, S., *Como a mente funciona* (São Paulo: Companhia das Letras, 1997).

- Blind tests: Barbosa, R., "Justiça libera-provisoriamente-anuncio com-teste cego de cervejas", February 3, 2013, at http://economia. uol. com. br/noticias/redacao/2013/02/04/justica-libera-provisoriamente-anuncio-com-teste-cego-de-cervejas. htm, accessed in January 2016.

- The "Pepsi Challenge", the preference for Pepsi in blind tests, for Coca-Cola in open tests and the neuroscientific aspects of this issue: Van Praet, D., *Unconscious Branding* (New York: Palgrave Macmillan, 2011).

- Wine study with oenology students: Brochet, F. and Morrot, G., "Influence of context on wine perception: cognitive and methodological implications", *Journal international des sciences de la vigne et du vin*, 33, 4 (1999).

- Neuroscientific study on wine flavor: Plassmann, H.; O'Doherty, J.; Shiv, B. and Rangel, A., "Marketing actions can modulate neural representations of experienced pleasantness", *Proceedings of the National Academy of Sciences*, 105, 3 (2007), pp. 1050-1054.

- Neuroscientific study on the taste of Coca-Cola and Pepsi, comparing blind test with open test: McClure, S. M.; Li, J.; Tomlin, D.; Cypert, K. S.;

Montague, L. M. and Montague, P. R., "Neural correlates of behavioral preference for culturally familiar drinks", *Neuron*, 44, 2 (2204), pp. 379-387.

- Study on pâté and dog food: Bohannon, J.; Goldstein, R. and Herschkowitsch, A., "Can people distinguish pâté from dog food?", *Chance*, 23, 2 (2013), pp. 43-46.

- On the universality of emotions, including facial expressions, one of the most cited studies is: Ekman, P. and Friesen, W. V., "Constants across cultures in the face and emotion", *Journal of Personality and Social Psychology*, 11 (1971), pp. 124-129.

- Study raising doubts about the universality of facial expressions of emotion: Crivelli, C.; Russell, J.; Jarillo, S. and Fernández-Dols, J., "The fear gasping face as a threat display in a Melanesian society", *Proceedings of the National Academy of Sciences*, 113, 33 (2016).

- For all the mentions of the brain in this book and a rigorous and comprehensive discussion of the various neuroscientific fields: Kandel, E. *et al*, *Princípios de neurociências* (Porto Alegre: Artmed, 2014).

2. The world, desires and pleasures

- Art from a philosophical perspective. The authors, philosophers, propose that art fulfills a greater purpose than transmitting values and ideas - and can help with life's big and small questions: Botton, A. and Armstrong, J., A *arte como terapia* (Rio de Janeiro: Intrínseca, 2014).

- Art, consciousness and the unconscious from a historical and neuroscientific perspective: Kandel, E., *The Age of Insight: The Quest to Understand the Unconscious in Art, Mind, and Brain* (New York: Random House, 2012).

- An essential work on desire in Plato. Accessible reading, considering philosophical texts: Plato, *The Banquet* (São Paulo: Editora 34, 2016).

- On the duality between the sensible world and the world of ideas in Plato; also the definition that distinguishes desire from will. Longer and more difficult text: Plato, *The Republic* (Bauru: Edipro, 2012).

- "Reason is, and can only be, the slave of the passions": Hume, D., *Treatise of Human Nature* (São Paulo: UNESP, 2000).

- Brain damage and deficits in planning and decision-making processes: Damásio, A., *O erro de Descartes: razão, emoção e o cérebro humano* (São Paulo: Companhia das Letras, 1994).
- Hot and cold system: Mischel, W., *The marshmallow test* (Rio de Janeiro: Objetiva, 2016).
- System 1 and system 2: Kahneman, D., *Fast and slow: two ways of thinking* (Rio de Janeiro: Objetiva, 2015).
- Money and general life satisfaction: Kahneman, D. and Deaton, A., "High income improves evaluation of life but not emotional well-being", *Proceedings of the National Academy of Sciences*, 107, 38 (2010).
- Discourses about ourselves: Barros Filho, C.; Lopes, F. and Issler, B., *Comunicação do eu: ética e solidão* (Petrópolis: Vozes, 2005).
- Cognitive consistency models: Chaxel, A. and Russo, J., "Cognitive consistency: cognitive and motivational perspectives", in Evan, A. and Reyna, V. (eds.), *Neuroeconomics, Judgement, and Decision Making* (New York: Taylor & Francis, 2015).
- "Dunning-Kruger effect", the inability to recognize one's own incompetence: Kruger, J. and Dunning, D., "Unskilled and unaware of it: how difficulties in recognizing one's own incompetence lead to inflated self-assessments", *Journal of Personality and Social Psychology*, 77, 6 (1999), p. 1121-34. Several other articles are available on Google Scholar (http:// scholar. google. com/) which expand on the original findings.
- We believe we are honest (when in fact we are not): Ariely, D., *The purest truth about dishonesty* (Rio de Janeiro: Campus Elsevier, 2012).
- We think we are more beautiful than we actually are: Epley, N. and Whitchurch, E., "Mirror, mirror on the wall: enhancement in self-recognition", *Personality and Social Psychology Bulletin*, 34, 9, (2008), p. 1159-70.
- On passion from the point of view of the brain, see the reading recommendations for Chapter 1 of Part III.
- Prefrontal cortex and its characteristics: Kandel, E. *et al*, *Principles of neuroscience* (Porto Alegre: Artmed, 2014).
- Reward, pleasure and motivation: Bloom, P., *How Pleasure Works* (New York: W. W. Norton, 2010); Reeve, J., *Understanding Motivation and*

Emotion (New Jersey: John Wiley & Sons, 2009); Schultz, W., "Neuronal Reward and Decision Signals: From Theories to Data", *Physiological Reviews*, 95, 3 (2015), pp. 853-951.

PART II - THE COSMOS AND HUMAN LIFE

- Excellent (and accessible) reading on the wisdom of myths: Ferry, L., *The Wisdom of Greek Myths* (Rio de Janeiro: Objetiva, 2009).

1. Homer's *Odyssey*

- Homer, *Odyssey* (São Paulo: Penguin Companhia, 2011).

2. Plato and the search for truth

- Plato, *The Republic* (Bauru: Edipro, 2012).

3. Hesiod's *Theogony*

- Hesiod, *Theogony* (São Paulo: Iluminuras, 2015).

4. The ship of Theseus

- The account of Theseus' ship can be found in the biography written by Plutarch. There is no Portuguese edition. We recommend the Harvard University bilingual edition, with the original and the English translation: Plutarch, *Lives I: Theseus and Romulus. Lycurgus and Numa. Solon and Publicola* (Cambridge: Harvard University Press, 1914).

5. The Aristotelian cosmos

- The question of happiness in Aristotle and the relationship between his conception of the cosmos and human conduct (ethics): Aristotle, *Nicomachean Ethics* (Porto Alegre: Artmed, 2009).

- Alexandre Koyré's analysis of the cosmos from ancient Greece to Newtonian perspectives: Koyré, A., *Du Monde Clos a l'Univers Infini* (Paris: Gallimard, 1988).

- There are no complete Portuguese editions of Aristotle's *Physics*. We recommend the Harvard bilingual edition: Aristotle, *The Physics: Books*

I-IV (Cambridge: Harvard University Press, 1957); Aristotle, *The Physics: Books V-VIII* (Cambridge: Harvard University Press (1934).

• Aristotle's main cosmological treatise: Aristotle, *Of Heaven* (Bauru: Edipro, 2014).

6. Stoicism

7. Our role in the cosmos

• General and accessible introduction to Stoicism: Ferry, L., *Aprender a viver: filosofia para os novos tempos* (Rio de Janeiro: Objetiva, 2006).

• *A* dense and more complete text on Stoicism: Inwood, B. (org.), *Os estoicos* (São Paulo: Odysseus, 2006).

• Accessible text by Marco Túlio Cícero: Cícero, M. T., *Saber envelhecer e a amizade* (São Paulo: L&PM, 1997).

• Epictetus' complete works in a bilingual collection, with the original and the English translation (the manual is known as the *Encheiridion*): Epictetus, *Discourses - Books 1-2* (Cambridge: Harvard University Press, 1925); Epictetus, *Discourses - Books 3-4, The Encheiridion* (Cambridge: Harvard University Press, 1928).

• The complete works of Marcus *Aurelius* in a bilingual edition, with the original and the English translation: *Marcus Aurelius, Marcus Aurelius* (Cambridge: Harvard University Press, 1916).

8. The transition between Antiquity and the Middle Ages

• Analysis of the transition from a historical-philosophical perspective (and a good introduction to philosophy): Ferry, L., *Aprender a viver: filosofia para os novos tempos* (Rio de Janeiro: Objetiva, 2006).

• Introduction to pre-Socratic thought: Marcondes, D., *Uma iniciação à filosofia: os pré-socráticos* (Rio de Janeiro: Zahar, 2016).

9. The Copernican revolution

• Detailed analysis of the Copernican revolution, as well as the structure of scientific revolutions: Kuhn, T., *A revolução copernicana* (Portugal: Edições 70, 1990); Kuhn, T., *A estrutura das revoluções científicas* (São Paulo:

Perspectiva, 2009). See also: Koyré, A., *Du Monde Clos a l'Univers Infini* (Paris: Gallimard, 1988).

10. The (un)ordered cosmos: Renaissance, Modernity and Humanism

- Historical-philosophical analysis of the Renaissance, Modernity and the Enlightenment: Ferry, L., *Aprender a viver: filosofia para os novos tempos* (Rio de Janeiro: Objetiva, 2006).
- Rousseau and perfectibility: Rousseau, J., *Discourse on the origin and foundations of inequality between men* (São Paulo: L&PM, 2008).
- Sartre, J. P., *Existentialism is a humanism*. Petrópolis: Vozes de Bolso, 2012).
- The clean slate: Locke, J., *Essay on human understanding (Books I and II)* (Portugal: Calouste Gulbenkian, 2014).

11. The deconstruction of Humanism

- Introduction to Nietzsche's thought: Ferry, L., *Aprender a viver: filosofia para os novos tempos* (Rio de Janeiro: Objetiva, 2006).
- Nietzsche's work is dense and complex. Most appropriate for those who have not yet had contact with it: Nietzsche, F., *Twilight of the Idols* (São Paulo: Companhia das Letras, 2006).
- Work by Charles Darwin that revolutionized the natural sciences: Darwin, C., *The Origin of Species* (São Paulo: Martin Claret, 2014).
- "Darwin's dangerous idea" is an allusion to the title of this work: Dennett, D., *Darwin's Dangerous Idea* (London: Penguin UK, 1995).
- Analysis of the impact and current relevance of Charles Darwin's central idea (that all living beings derive from the same common ancestor, evolving through the process of natural selection): Coyne, J., *Why Evolution is True* (New York: Penguin, 2009).
- Freud is a rare thinker, whose reading is accessible and generally enjoyable. We recommend two texts for those who don't know his work - "The malaise in civilization" and "The self and the id", found in: Freud, S., *Freud vol. 16 (1923-1925): The self and the id, autobiography and other texts* (São Paulo: Companhia das Letras, 2010); Freud, S., *Freud*

vol. 18 (1930-1936): The malaise in civilization, new introductory lectures and other texts (São Paulo: Companhia das Letras, 2010).

12. Stoic philosophy vs. contemporary philosophy

- Differences between ancient and contemporary philosophy: Ferry, L., *Aprender a viver: filosofia para os novos tempos* (Rio de Janeiro: Objetiva, 2006).

13. Poetic naturalism

14. Laplace's demon

15. The direction of time

16. The cosmos tends towards disorder

17. A pale blue dot

- For the cosmological vision presented in these chapters: Carroll, S., *The Big Picture* (New York: Penguin, 2016).
- Interesting discussion between a naturalistic and a non-naturalistic view of the cosmos: Chopra, D. and Mlodinow, L., *War of Worldviews: Where Science and Spirituality Meet - and not* (New York: Random House, 2011).
- The idea that black holes will evaporate was proposed by astrophysicist Stephen Hawking. We recommend the original article (difficult to read) and a book by the author (more accessible): Hawking, S. (1973), "Black hole explosions?", *Nature,* 248 (1973), pp. 30-31; Hawking, S., *Black holes* (Rio de Janeiro: Intrínseca, 2016).
- Recommended works by the authors mentioned at the end of Chapter 13: deGrasse Tyson, N., *Origens* (São Paulo: Planeta, 2016); Einstein, A., *Como vejo o mundo* (Rio de Janeiro: Nova Fronteira, 2015); Hawking, S., *O universo numa casca* de *noz* (Rio de Janeiro: Intrínseca, 2015); Kaku, M., *Mundos paralelos* (São Paulo: Rocco (2016); Kaku, M., *O futuro da mente* (São Paulo: Rocco, 2015); Krauss, L., *Um universo que veio do nada* (São Paulo: Paz e Terra, 2013); Mlodinow, L., *De primatas a astronautas* (Rio de Janeiro: Zahar, 2015); Sagan, C., *O mundo assombrado pelos demônios*

(São Paulo: Companhia de Bolso, 2006); Sagan, C., *Pálido ponto azul* (São Paulo: Companhia das Letras 1996).

- The allegory of the island of knowledge: Gleiser, M., *The island of knowledge: the limits of science and the search for meaning* (São Paulo: Record, 2014).
- The allegory of the cosmic calendar was taken from the original *Cosmos* series, presented by Carl Sagan. It was reinserted in the most recent version of the series and continues to be used by a number of authors today.

18. Brain: a cosmos within the cosmos

- A comprehensive and sufficiently in-depth introduction to neuroscience: Kandel, E. *et al*, *Principles of neuroscience* (Porto Alegre: Artmed, 2014).
- An excellent introductory book on how the brain works, which inspired this and other chapters: Eagleman, D., *The Brain: the Story of you* (New York: Pantheon, 2016).
- On the number of neurons in the brain: Azevedo, F. A. C.; Carvalho, L. R. B.; Grinberg, L. T.; Farfel, J. M.; Ferretti, R. E. L.; Leite, R. E. P. and Herculano-Houzel, S., "Equal numbers of neuronal and nonneuronal cells make the human brain an isometrically scaled-up primate brain", *The Journal of Comparative Neurology*, 513, 5 (2009), pp. 532-541; Herculano-Houzel, S. (2016), *The Human Advantage: A New Understanding of How our Brains Became Remarkable* (New York: MIT Press, 2016).

19. Being born and growing up

- The pianist's metaphor to describe the relationship between biology and the environment: Pinel, J., *Biopsychologia* (Porto Alegre: Artmed, 2005).
- The biological nature of the mind and the behavior of human beings: Pinker, S., *Tábula rasa: a negação contemporânea da* natureza *humana* (São Paulo: Companhia das Letras, 2005).
- Hierarchy of needs: Maslow, A. H., "A theory of human motivation", *Psychological Review*, 50, 4 (1943), pp. 370-396.

- The social nature of human beings (and criticism of Abraham Maslow): Lieberman, M., *Social: Why Our Brains Are Wired to Connect* (New York: Broadway Books, 2014).

- Comparative studies between the neocortexes of different primates and the evolution of the brain: Dunbar, R., *Grooming, Gossip and the Evolution of Language* (Cambridge: Harvard University Press, 1998).

- Birth policies in Romania: Gail Kligman, *The Politics of Duplicity. Controlling Reproduction in Ceausescu's Romania* (Berkeley: University of California Press, 1998).

- Reports on Romania's orphanages: Eagleman, D., *The Brain: The Story of You* (New York: Pantheon, 2016).

- *Attachment* theory: Mooney, C. G., *Theories of Attachment: An Introduction to Bowlby, Ainsworth, Gerber, Brazelton, Kennell, and Klaus* (St. Paul: Red Leaf Press, 2009).

- Hunger winter in the Netherlands and its consequences for the health of individuals conceived during this period: Hart, Nicky, "Famine, maternal nutrition and infant mortality: a re-examination of the Dutch hunger winter", *Population Studies*, 47 (1993), pp. 27-46; Roseboom, T. J.; Painter, R. C.; van Abeelen, A. F. M.; Veenendaal, M. V. E. and de Rooij, S. R., "Hungry in the womb: what are the consequences? Lessons from the Dutch famine", *The European Menopause Journal*, 70, 2 (2011), pp. 141-145.

- The intrauterine period and child and adult development (including accounts of the "winter of hunger"): Paul, A. M., *Origins: How the Nine Months Before Birth Shape the Rest of our Lives* (New York: Free Press, 2011).

- Stress, depression and anxiety during pregnancy and increased risk of problems in the neurobehavioral development of the fetus: Kinsella, M. T. and Monk, C., "Impact of maternal stress, depression & anxiety on fetal neurobehavioral development", *Clinical Obstetrics and Gynecology*, 52, 3 (2014), pp. 425-440.

- The term "Facebook depression" (with quotation marks) returned 686 results on Google Scholar (http://scholar. google. com) in January 2017.

- Obesity and overweight in childhood and adulthood: Ng, M. *et al*, "Global, regional, and national prevalence of overweight and obesity in children and adults during 1980-2013: a systematic analysis for the Global Burden of Disease Study 2013", *The Lancet*, 384, 9945 (2014), pp. 766-781.

- World Health Organization report on hypertension, highlighting the problem of salt consumption by children, as well as sugar and fat consumption by the general population: "A global brief on hypertension: silent killer, global public health crisis" (2013), at http://www. who. int/ cardiovascular_diseases/publications/global_brief_hypertension/en/, accessed in January 2017.
- Pornography and the human brain: Kühn, S. and Gallinat, J., "Brain structure and functional connectivity associated with pornography consumption: the brain on porn", *JAMA Psychiatry*, 71, 7 (2014), pp. 827-834.
- Impact of pornography on the mental health of adolescents: Owens, E. W.; Behun, R. J.; Manning, J. C. and Reid, R. C., "The impact of internet pornography on adolescents: a review of the research", *Sexual Addiction & Compulsivity*, 19 (2012), pp. 99-122.

20. Maturing

- The importance of emotional processes for the formation of memories and learning: Immordino-Yang, M. H., *Emotions, Learning and the Brain* (New York: W. W. Norton & Company, 2015).
- The fall in couples' satisfaction with marriage after the birth of children: Twenge, J. M.; Campbell, W. K. and Foster, C. A., "Parenthood and Marital Satisfaction: a Meta-Analytic Review", *Journal of Marriage and Family*, 65, 3 (2003), pp. 574-583; Walker, C., "Some variations in marital satisfaction", in R. Chester and J. Peel, *Equalities and inequalities in family life* (London: Academic Press, 1977).
- The development of the adolescent brain, its self-consciousness and the accentuated perception of the *self* (psychological self): Sommerville, L. H.; Jones, R. M.; Ruberry, E. J.; Dyke, J. P.; Glover, G. and Casey, B. J., "The medial prefrontal cortex and the emergence of self-conscious emotion in adolescence", *Psychological Science*, 24, 8 (2013), pp. 1554-1562; Bjork, J. M.; Knutson, B.; Fong, G. W.; Caggiano, D. M.; Bennett, S. M. and Hommer, D. W., "Incentive-elicited brain activation in adolescents: similarities and differences from young adults", *The Journal of Neuroscience*,

24, 8 (2004), pp. 1793-1802; Spear, L. P., "The adolescent brain and age-related behavioral manifestations", *Neuroscience and Biobehavioral Reviews,* 24, 4 (2000), pp. 417-463; Heatherton, T. F., "Neuroscience of self and self-regulation", *Annual Review of Psychology,* 62, (2011) pp. 363-390.

- An interesting philosophical reflection on the idea that we are never "ready": Cortella, M. S., *Não nascemos prontos!* (Petrópolis: Vozes, 2009).

- Study on the hippocampus of taxi drivers in London: Maguire, E. A.; Woollett, K. and Spiers, H. J., "London taxi drivers and bus drivers: a structural MRI and neuropsychological analysis", *Hippocampus,* 16, 12 (2006), pp. 1091-1101.

- The decline in metabolic activity that accompanies ageing and the increase in fat accumulation: Bouchard, C.; Despres, J. P. and Mauriege, P. (1993), "Genetic and nongenetic determinants of regional fat distribution", *Endocrinology Review,* 14 (1993), pp. 72-93; Chumlea, W. C.; Rhyne, R. L.; Garry, P. G. and Hunt, W. C., "Changes in anthropometric indices of body composition with age in a healthy elderly population", *American Journal of Human Biology,* 1 (1989), pp. 457-462; National Cholesterol Education Program (US), "Expert Panel on Detection Evaluation and Treatment of High Blood Cholesterol in Adults". Third report of the National Cholesterol Education Program (NCEP) Expert Panel on Detection, Evaluation, and Treatment of High Blood Cholesterol in Adults (adult treatment panel III): final report. The Program, Washington, D.C., 2002.

- Data on the prevalence of dementias by country: Alzheimer's Disease International, "World Alzheimer Report 2015: an analysis of prevalence, incidence, cost and trends", at: https://www. alz. co. uk/research/ WorldAlzheimerReport2015. pdf, accessed in January 2017.

- Being bilingual delays the onset of symptoms of Alzheimer's disease: Craik, F. I. M.; Bialystok, E. and Freedman, M., "Delaying the onset of Alzheimer's disease: bilingualism as a form of cognitive reserve", *Neurology,* 75, 19 (2010), pp. 1726-1729; Woumans, E.; Santens, P.; Stieben, A.; Versijpt, J.; Stevens, M. and Duyck, W., "Bilingualism delays clinical manifestation of Alzheimer's disease", *Bilingualism: Language and Cognition,* 18, 3 (2014), pp. 568-574.

• Physical activity, diet and other protective factors against Alzheimer's disease: Scheltens, P.; Blennow, K.; Breteler, M. M. B.; de Strooper, B.; Frisoni, G. B.; Salloway, S. and Van der Flier, W. M., "Alzheimer's disease", *The Lancet*, 388, 10043 (2016), pp. 505-517; Winblad, B.; Amouyel, P.; Andrieu, S.; Ballard, C.; Brayne, C.; Brodaty, H.; Cedazo-Minguez, A.; Dubois, B.; Edvardsson, D.; Feldman, H.; Fratiglioni, L.; Frisoni, G. B.; Gauthier, S.; Georges, J.; Graff, C.; Iqbal, K.; Jessen, F.; Johansson, G.; Jönsson, L.; Kivipelto, M.; Knapp, M.; Mangialasche, F.; Melis, R.; Nordberg, A.; Rikkert, M. O.; Qiu, C.; Sakmar, T. P.; Scheltens, P.; Schneider, L. S.; Sperling, R.; Tjernberg, L. O.; Waldemar, G.; Wimo, A. and Zetterberg, H., "Defeating Alzheimer's disease and other dementias: a priority for European science and society", *Lancet Neurology*, 15, 5 (2016), pp. 455-532.

• With regard to the importance of sleep for cardiovascular health, it's important to note that, in general, every cardiovascular benefit inherently has a cerebral benefit. Neurological and psychiatric disorders generally have vascular and inflammatory aspects (for example, Alzheimer's disease and depression): Cappuccio, F. P.; Cooper, D.; D'Elia, L.; Strazzullo, P. and Miller, M. A., "Sleep duration predicts cardiovascular outcomes: a systematic review and meta-analysis of prospective studies", *European Heart Journal*, 32 12 (2011), pp. 1484-1492.

21. Death

• Lucretius' poem in a bilingual version, with the original and English translation: Lucretius, *On the Nature of Things* (Cambridge: Harvard University Press, 1975).

• In the *Georgics*, Virgil attributes to Lucretius the idea that the fear of death is the root of the illusion of the immortal soul: Virgil, *Bucólicas, Geórgicas e Eneida* (Portugal: Temas e Debates, 2012).

• Seneca's ideas on death: Seneca, *Sobre a brevidade da vida* (São Paulo: L&PM Pocket, 2006).

• For the Stoic view, see recommendations in Chapter 6, Part II.

• The text quoted from Hannah Arendt is in: Arendt, H., *Between the past and the future* (Rio de Janeiro: Perspectiva, 2014).

22. God

- Pascal's "bet" and other ideas from the great mathematician and thinker: Pascal, *Pensées* (Paris: Folio France, 2004).
- The illusion of immortality
- The ideas in this chapter are very much inspired by Stoic philosophy. See recommendations in Chapter 6, Part II.

PART III - LIVING AND SOCIALIZING

1. Love and passion

- An excellent book on love seen from different philosophical perspectives: Comte-Sponville, A., *O Amor* (São Paulo: WMF Martins Fontes, 2006).
- Love in Spinoza is defined in this important (and difficult) book: Spinoza, B., *Ética* (Rio de Janeiro: Autêntica, 2010).
- For Lucretius, see recommendations in Chapter 21, Part II.
- Scientific view of love in two phases: Fischer, H., *Why We Love: The Nature and Chemistry of Romantic Love* (New York: Henry Holt, 2004).
- The neurobiology of love: de Boer, A.; van Buel, E. M. and Ter Host, G. J., "Love is more than just a kiss: a neurobiological perspective on love and affection", *Neuroscience*, 201 (2012), pp. 114-124.
- On motivation and pleasure, see recommendations in Chapter 2, Part I.
- The mention of Vinicius de Moraes refers to his "Soneto de fidelidade".
- On the brain processing physical and emotional pain in a similar way: Lieberman, M., *Social: Why Our Brains Are Wired to Connect* (New York: Broadway Books, 2014).
- The observation that the quality of relationships is the main element of a happy life is present in dozens of studies. One of the most important is a longitudinal study by Harvard University that has been following participants for over seventy years (and is already studying the children and grandchildren of the original sample). A compilation of the results of the study and its implications can be found in: Valliant, G. E., *Triumphs of experience: The Men of the Harvard Grant Study*, (Massachusetts: Belknap Press, 2015).

2. Freedom

- The concept of bad faith: Sartre, J. P., *O existencialismo é um humanismo* (Petrópolis: Vozes de Bolso, 2012).

- The trial of Socrates: Plato, *Apology of Socrates* (São Paulo: L&PM, 2008).

- Bauby's book, written while he was suffering from incarceration syndrome: Bauby, J., *O escafandro e a borboleta* (São Paulo: WMF Martins Fontes, 2014).

- On Descartes' error and a critique of dualism: Damásio, A., *O erro de Descartes: razão, emoção e o cérebro humano* (São Paulo: Companhia das Letras, 1994).

- Two current reviews on the brains of psychopaths: Cummings, M. A., "The neurobiology of psychopathy: recent developments and new directions in research and treatment", *CNS Spectrums*, 20, 3 (2015), pp. 200-206; Del Casale, A.; Kotzalidis, G. D.; Rapinesi, C.; Di Pietro, S.; Alessi M. C.; Di Cesare, G.; Criscuolo, S.; De Rossi, P.; Tatarelli, R.; Girardi, P. and Ferracuti, S., "Functional neuroimaging in psychopathy", *Neuropsychobiology*, 72 (2015), pp. 97-117.

- Association between dementia and benzodiazepines (such as clonazepam/Rivotril): Billioti de Gage, S.; Bégaud, B.; Bazin, F.; Verdoux, H.; Dartigues, J. F.; Pérès, K.; Kurth e T.; Pariente, A., "Benzodiazepine use and risk of dementia: prospective population based study", *BMJ*, 345, e6231 (2012).

- Two works on the concept of the unconscious from a current scientific perspective (unrelated to the Freudian unconscious), the first difficult, dense and profound, the second easy and accessible: Hassin, R. R.; Uleman, J. S. and Bargh, J. A., *The New Unconscious* (New York: Oxford University Press, 2011); Mlodinow, L., *Subliminar* (Rio de Janeiro: Zahar, 2013).

- Study on wine purchases: North, A. C.; Hargreaves, D. J. and McKendrick, J., "In-store music affects product choice", *Nature*, 390 (1997), p. 132.

- Study on cold/hot coffee: Williams, L. and Bargh, J. A., "Experiencing physical warmth promotes interpersonal warmth", *Science*, 322, 5901 (2008), pp. 606-607.

• Study on disgust and harsher judgments: Schnall, S.; Haidt, J.; Clore, G. L. and Jordan, A. H., "Disgust as embodied moral judgment", *Personality and Social Psychology Bulletin*, 34, 8 (2008), pp. 1096-1109.

• Study on political views with and without the hand sanitizer gel pot: Helzer, E. G. and Pizarro, D. A., "Dirty liberals! Reminders of physical cleanliness influence moral and political attitudes", *Psychological Science*, 22, 4 (2011), pp. 517-522.

• Study on tips given to *strippers*: Miller, G.; Tybur, J. M. and Jordan, B. D., "Ovulatory cycle effects on tip earnings by lap dancers: economic evidence for human estrus?", *Evolution and Human Behavior*, 28 (2007), pp. 375-381.

• The brain decides before the decisions are conscious: Soon, C. S.; Brass, M.; Heinze, H. and Haynes, J., "Unconscious determinants of free decisions in the human brain", *Nature Neuroscience*, 11 (2008), pp. 543-545.

• Philosophical critique of the concept of free *will* supported by neuroscientific studies: Harris, S., *Free will* (New York: Free Press, 2012).

• Looking in the mirror and feeling good as an important contributing factor to well-being: Hamermesh, D. S. and Abrevaya, "Beauty is the promise of happiness?", *European Economic Review*, 64 (2013), pp. 351-368.

• More than half of Brazil has access to the Internet: Gomes, H. S., "Internet arrives for the first time in more than 50% of homes in Brazil, IBGE shows", April 6, 2016, at: http://g1. globo. com/tecnologia/noticia/2016/04/internet-chega-pela-1-vez-mais-de-50-das-cas-no-brasil-mostra-ibge. html, accessed in January 2017.

• "The Library of Babel": Borges, J. L., *Ficções* (São Paulo: Companhia das Letras, 2007).

• Life as a product for consumption: Bauman, Z., *Vida para consumo* (Rio de Janeiro: Zahar, 2008).

• *The* "paradox of choice": Schwartz, B., *The paradox of choice* (New York: HarperCollins, 2016).

• Study suggesting an association between a greater number of past sexual partners and greater dissatisfaction with the current relationship: Rhoades, G. K and Stanley, S. M., "Before 'I do': what do premarital experiences have to do with marital quality among today's young adults?", *The National Marriage Project* (Charlottesville: University of Virginia, 2014).

• Study suggesting that a higher number of past relationships is associated with higher divorce rates: Teachman, J., "Premarital sex, premarital cohabitation, and the risk of subsequent marital dissolution among women", *Journal of Marriage and Family*, 65, 2 (2011), pp. 444-455.

3. Power

• Study of monkeys choosing between drinking juice and looking at pictures: Deaner, R. O.; Khera, A. V. and Platt, M. L., "Monkeys pay per view: adaptive valuation of social images by rhesus macaques", *Current Biology*, 15, 6 (2005), pp. 543-548.

• Interest in the lives of others is a fundamental part of the primate evolutionary process: Dunbar, R., *Grooming, Gossip and the Evolution of Language* (Cambridge: Harvard University Press, 1998).

4. Happiness

• The elements that make up happiness (positive emotions, engagement, meaning, quality relationships and achievements): Seligman, M., *Florescer* (Rio de Janeiro: Objetiva, 2011).

• The state of "*flow*": Csikszentmihalyi, M., *Flow* (New York: HarperCollins, 2004).

• Harvard study on the wandering mind: Kilingsworth, M. and Gilbert, D., "A wandering mind is an unhappy mind", *Science*, 330, 6006 (2010), p. 932.

• The u-shaped curve of general life satisfaction: Blanchflower, D. and Oswald, A., "Is well-being u-shaped over the life cycle?", *Social Science and Medicine*, 66 (2008), pp. 1733-1749; Stone, A.; Schwartz, J.; Brodericka, J. and Deatonc, A., "A snapshot of the age distribution of psychological well-being in the United States", *PNAS*, 107, 22 (2010).

• The idea of the projective *self* and the experiential self comes from psychologist Daniel Kahneman, who uses the term *remembering* self to define the projective self. We chose the term "projective" because we believe it better represents the psychological phenomenon. See: Kahneman, D., *Fast and Slow: Two Ways of Thinking* (Rio de Janeiro: Objetiva, 2013). See also Kahneman's TED talk (www. ted. com).

- Quality of relationships as the main element of happiness: Valliant, G. E., *Triumphs of Experience: The Men of the Harvard Grant Study* (Massachusetts: Belknap Press, 2015).

BOOKS TO CHANGE THE WORLD. YOUR WORLD.

To find out about our upcoming releases
and available titles, visit:

www.**citadel**.com.br

/citadeleditora

@citadeleditora

@citadeleditora

Citadel – Grupo Editorial

For more information or questions about the work,
please contact us by email: